The JOY of COLLECTING
Antiques and Collectables
in Ireland

Sale in progress. Mealy's (of Castlecomer) auction marquee at Fenagh, Co. Carlow.

For James, Janice and Stephen

Mezzotint by R. S. Clouster after Reynolds.

The JOY of COLLECTING
Antiques and Collectables
in Ireland

Helen Coburn

WOLFHOUND PRESS

First published 1992 by
WOLFHOUND PRESS,
68 Mountjoy Square,
Dublin 1

Cataloguing in Publication Data available from the British Library.

ISBN 0–86327–330–0

Cover and book design: Jan de Fouw.
Cover photograph courtesy of George Mealy & Sons, Castlecomer
Typesetting: Wolfhound Press
Colour separations: Pentacolour. Cover separations: Graphic Reproduction
Printed in the Republic of Ireland by Colour Books

Photograph acknowledgements

For colour photographs, and for most of the black and white photographs, we acknowledge the generous assistance of Mealy's of Castlecomer.
Additional photographs were supplied by Adams, Dublin (pages 16 top, 22 bottom, 171, 173, 174); Glendinings, London (pages 12 bottom left, 175-179, 180); Hamilton Osborne King, Dublin (pages 24 bottom, 28, 38 bottom, 61, 64, 84, 86); Blackstaff Press, Belfast (page 102 left and bottom, 105).

Acknowledgements

Thanks are due to the many people who have helped me in the writing of this book. Special mention should be made of Bridget Kenny, at the auctioneering firm of George Mealy and Sons, Castlecomer, Co. Kilkenny, who performed Trojan work in the assembling of large numbers of photographs. Thanks are also due to George and Phonsie Mealy for their ever-helpful advice and assistance during the past few years. Sara Kenny of Hamilton Osborne King also obtained for me some very fine photographs.

I am grateful to Mairéad Dunlevy of the National Museum for the trouble she took in guiding me around the ESB's Georgian house at Merrion Square, Dublin, while she gave me the benefit of her extensive knowledge of eighteenth-century artefacts. I would also like to thank Dr Patrick Duffy of St Patrick's College, Maynooth, for allowing me to read his unpublished essay on Irish topographical paintings, and to express my gratitude to the staff at the library of the same college, where I was able to do background reading as well as examine a number of antiquarian books that do not often appear on the market.

Finally, my appreciation is due to Mary Large, who patiently typed a not always well organised script, and to my editor at Wolfhound, Josephine O'Donovan, who made a number of useful suggestions.

CONTENTS

Preface

Although there are a good many books available on general antiques, few, if any, deal with the Irish antiques market and the needs of the Irish buyer. It was this gap that encouraged me to write this book. Almost all the objects mentioned have appeared for sale in Ireland, and the prices, with very few exceptions, are drawn from Irish auctions.

In recent years, television and the popular press have regularly carried stories of people who buy something old at a knock-down price only to find that it is worth hundreds, or even thousands, of pounds. Less is heard about those who spend a considerable amount of money on an old piece that turns out to be worth a good deal less than was paid for it, or even perhaps worth nothing at all.

It is the aim of this book to help the collector avoid the second occurrence, though it cannot guarantee that the first will ever happen. I hope that by reading the book the new collector may succeed in bypassing the expensive mistakes that can discourage people from continuing to pursue an interest in antiques. If it can show the collector how to buy quality objects at a reasonable price it will have succeeded in its purpose.

I have concentrated primarily on buying at auction. To a large extent this has been a matter of personal preference, even indulgence, on my part, for I find auction-going a hugely enjoyable pastime, and I do most of my own buying there. Nothing teaches the collector more about antiques than seeing and handling them at auction views, and indeed, this helps one to buy more confidently from a dealer whenever this is found to be quicker or more convenient.

The antiques and collectables discussed in this book are, for the most part, drawn from the low to medium price range and include a number of inexpensive but interesting areas that may appeal to the new collector. Inevitably some subjects have had to be left out, for a perennial risk in a book of this sort is that of spreading oneself so thinly that what one says is too lacking in detail to be really useful. However, the most important areas of interest to buyers in Ireland have been included, and there is material on some subjects which, although they attract significant numbers of collectors, are seldom mentioned in the fine arts columns of the newspapers and journals. Among these are books, prints, coins, and militaria.

The book includes price bands for virtually all items that commonly appear for sale in Ireland. The *value* of an object, however, is something else, and it ought always to be remembered that a thing is worth what someone is prepared to pay. Desire determines worth far more than rarity does. Provenance, too, is important to some buyers, and great sales at important country houses or dispersals of the collections put together by distinguished connoisseurs always tend to yield the highest prices. This has been most conspicuously so in recent times with the antiquarian books market, where sales of collections like the Bradley Martin library, the Garden collection and the books of Richard Manney have seen prices paid that were many times higher than those that would have been reached at an ordinary sale in Dublin. The value remaining from such provenance after a book has subsequently spent a number of years in the library of an unknown collector is another matter.

Despite the fact that this book is, to a certain extent, 'market driven', I would be disappointed if the reader were to form the conclusion that antique collecting is all about money. Collecting should, above all, be about enjoying what you have, learning as much about it as you can, and using it to forge a link with the traditions of the past. In an ideal world antique collecting would be seen as a branch of social history rather than as a commercial activity. I hope that readers will use not just this book but the reading list included at the end to increase their knowledge of what they own and buy beyond mere questions of what things are worth.

Chapter One

BUYING ANTIQUES — WHY BOTHER?

 hy indeed? After all, most good department stores stock a perfectly good range of household goods. This stock will generally be sold to you with certain guarantees. It will be of merchantable quality. If there is a defect it will be replaced. The price will be predictable. The object will be what it is supposed to be. If you buy what you assume is, say, top-quality porcelain, you are unlikely to discover, when you get home with it, that it is just kitchen-grade crockery. If you buy a dining-chair, close examination after purchase is most unlikely to reveal the unpleasant fact that the upholstery is rotting and that underneath, where you hadn't had the wit to look before, is a labyrinth of busy woodworm activity. If you buy a nice mahogany desk at a good retail shop, the chances of your subsequently finding that it was nailed together from the leavings of an old dressing-table and a down-at-heel chest of drawers are fairly slight.

Yet every day people go blithely out to auctions or to antique dealers about whom they know nothing and, in their desire to furnish their homes with what is old, expose themselves to the risk of such appalling and expensive mistakes. So why do people do it? One could put forward some rational reasons for such behaviour: that antiques are a good investment; that they are better quality than modern things; that the ownership of antiques confers status; that they are part of our national heritage. No doubt such considerations do weigh with many buyers. Certainly the investment value of many antiques has been most satisfactory over the years, although a quick comparison between the price of antiques and the general rise in inflation over the last twenty years or so will reveal that the returns are by no means as great as in some other investments. As for quality, the truth is that if you are willing to pay a fair price, the modern craft worker is just as capable of turning out a fine piece as his eighteenth or nineteenth-century counterpart. And the people in the nineteenth century were just as efficient at the manufacture and accumulation of junk as we are.

No, I don't think we're likely to find the driving force of the keen antique collector in the realm of rational consideration. The truth is that antique collecting is, as someone once said about love of horses, a disease from which, once it is contracted, there is no recovery. That's the bad news. The good news is that there could scarcely be a more pleasant disease from which to suffer. The person who dabbles his or her feet at the edges of the

Enjoyment

antique world has hours, days, years of unalloyed pleasure ahead. Every town visited will hold the prospect of an antique or junk shop to browse in. The purchase of the weekend newspapers will carry a never-failing thrill as he or she turns eagerly to the antiques page to find out what price everything made last week and what auction sales are in the offing in the coming days. Long, absorbing hours will be spent at auction views handling antiques, turning them upside down and inside out, drinking in the texture and appearance of old materials and their characteristic smells, and always learning, learning.

And then sale day! The thrill of the chase, the banter of the auctioneer, the press of dealers with their dishevelled hair, casual smiles, and knowing eyes. The disappointment, the tension when the last bid has come from you and the hammer is raised - 'Just have one more, lads, tomorrow will be too late,' urges the auctioneer — and you don't know whether to fear or to hope that someone will outbid you for an item that is costing about twice what you thought you'd have to pay. The quiet triumph when an item is knocked down to you, especially if the contest was between you and an experienced dealer, and you feel — at least until you count the cost — that you have not merely outbid him but outwitted him as well.

Nor does the pleasure end there. The collector will find a subtle change creeping into the nature of his leisure reading. Nothing can substitute for what the trendy managers call 'hands-on experience' when it comes to antiques; but books about antiques, like books about books, make for hugely enjoyable reading. Visits to art galleries, museums and stately homes, too, assume a new dimension when you become a collector. Unless you are wealthy you will not be buying the sort of objects you find in these places but there is a lot you can learn about design and period detail by looking at pieces that are of the highest quality and that you know are genuine.

All this sounds, I suspect, as if most of the enjoyment to be derived from antiques arises from pursuing them rather than owning them. In fact, I think that for many collectors this is the case. I know of a number of collectors who buy pieces, keep them for a little while, and then sell them on, hopefully at a profit, and buy something different. This constantly changing household landscape must have an extremely unsettling effect upon the family of the collector but is, of course, essential for hopelessly addicted antique hunters who, if they are to find room for all their purchases, must sell as often as they buy. However, I find that there tends to be method in the madness of many such collectors, in that they are generally moving steadily up the antiques ladder, as it were, by replacing previous purchases with better items and all the time increasing their knowledge and refining their taste. Many of them end up by becoming dealers, thus turning their knowledge into profit and enabling them to indulge their buying instinct without having to worry about constraints of space!

The Occasional Buyer

Most of us, of course, will remain occasional buyers, acquiring relatively modest antiques in order to give our homes just a touch of something different. And that, for me, is one answer to the question why one should bother with antiques. There can be a dreadful sameness about modern furniture, especially in the middle to lower price range. There is certainly some well-designed modern furniture, but it is often expensive. The person with less than, say, £1,000 with which to furnish a dining room will tend to find that they might as well buy their pieces in the first shop they walk into as the last. Everywhere they go they will find that such furniture is dominated by plum-coloured, heavily polished mahogany veneer on fibre or chipboard, with tables and chairs in pseudo-Georgian style and wall units with sliding glass doors. If you have limited funds and like occasional furniture, your main problem will be the narrow range of such pieces available. All too often the selection seems limited to coffee tables, nests of tables and round tripod wine tables. If you want a canterbury, a revolving bookcase, a music cabinet, a work-table or a games table, the chances are that you will find yourself turning to the antique shop or auction room. You will find that such pieces are relatively expensive, reflecting, perhaps, a demand for a variety of small furniture pieces that modern manufacturers are not sufficiently meeting. Even so you will find that at most saleroom auctions or large house clearances there will be a reasonable selection of small pieces under £500.

However, it is with regard to the larger pieces that the new collector will make the possibly surprising discovery that not everything that is termed antique is expensive. With £1,000 or even less to spend on your dining-room furnishings, what old pieces could you buy that would make sure that your room did not look exactly like that of the people next door? Your cheapest alternative to the modern wall unit would be a 1930s oak sideboard. I have seen these sold at auction for as little as £30 — although the best ones may fetch a couple of hundred. Or perhaps you might prefer an Edwardian mirror-backed sideboard in mahogany or oak, for which you would probably pay about £400 at a saleroom — with luck, you might even manage to get one for less. If you were prepared to settle for just four dining-chairs, you could probably pick up a set of oak ones to complement your sideboard for less than £200. Sets of six Edwardian dining-chairs, which are often made in walnut, are regularly sold at auction for sums between £300 and £500. If you decided to simply build up a collection of six single chairs, you could hope to purchase odd Victorian and Edwardian ones for less than £40 apiece.

The dining-table could present a greater challenge to your ingenuity, for it has to be admitted that good-quality tables do not come cheap. You might have to spend quite some time prowling about the auction rooms before you got what you wanted. However, I think you would be unlucky if you did not eventually secure a Victorian drop-leaf table for around £400 or a nineteenth or early twentieth-century Georgian-style table, capable of seating six people, for about the same figure. An early twentieth-century oak table could be bought for significantly less than that. Some 1930s examples were made from plywood veneers; they are in general of poor quality and are best avoided, but attractive solid oak ones were made and can often be bought at salerooms for under £150. Thus within this budget you could furnish your dining room for a figure anywhere between £400 and £1,300. Even were you to choose the humbler oak pieces you would be getting solid timber; spending the higher figure you would be buying pieces of considerably better quality than those you would get for the same money if you bought modern furniture. In addition you would have the satisfaction of possessing pieces that were not identical to those in the homes of your friends.

Dining-Room

Of course, like most things in life, all this is not quite so simple as it seems. The first point to be noted is that the price of old furniture is rising all the time - and although the antiques trade is bound to suffer, as all businesses do, from periodic recession, the underlying price trend during the last twenty or so years has been inexorably upwards. Every article, every book about antiques that is published serves to draw the attention of more and more people towards the advantages of buying old pieces, and this naturally increases demand and therefore prices. The second point is that buying antiques wisely demands both time and knowledge. Trying to furnish your room cheaply but with some quality, you would in all likelihood have had to attend half a dozen or so auctions before getting what you wanted at the price you could afford.

Dealers and Shop Owners

Some of this difficulty, at least with regard to time, can be surmounted by the use of a reliable dealer. Most dealers and shop owners, if they do not have what you want in stock, will be happy to get it for you. Of course you will pay for this service, and, in general, goods bought in a shop or through a dealer will cost more than if you had bought them at auction yourself. This is not always true, though. Auction prices, especially at large and well-advertised house clearances, can rise to dizzying heights that bear little relation to the scarcity or desirability of an item, and here the experienced dealer is less likely to get carried away than the private buyer. Moreover, a dealer, if a piece is slow to move or if he has a number of similar pieces in stock, may be quite happy to let something go at a relatively modest profit. Cash flow is always a problem in the antiques trade, and the buyer who complains of the profit margin the dealer may allow himself should bear in mind that the dealer may have thousands of pounds wrapped up in stock that may be on his hands for a much as a year and more.

You also need knowledge if you are to buy successfully at auction, and it must be said that this knowledge is often painfully and expensively acquired. This is because the novice collector will inevitably make mistakes by buying things that were not what they appeared to be or by paying far too much for them. You will have to be fairly philosophical about this, remembering that the person who makes no mistakes learns nothing. Every mistake you make will have something to teach you, and as time goes by they will become fewer and fewer. The paradox is, though, that as your knowledge grows and your errors become rarer, you will also become increasingly conscious of how little you know. But never mind! One of the chief reasons for buying antiques is, after all, that the buying never ceases to be an adventure. However, you don't want this adventure to be fraught with *too* many unexpected twists, particularly of the kind referred to at the beginning of this chapter. So, what is the best way to set about buying?

Chapter Two

ENTERING THE MARKET

here are three main ways in which a private buyer can purchase antiques: in an antique shop, through a dealer who does not himself own a shop but who buys goods both for shops and for private customers, and at auction.

Buying Through a Dealer

The dealer who buys (on commission, of course) for private customers is probably most useful to the knowledgeable collector who has money and some expertise but little time to attend all the sales that might be necessary to find what he or she wants. There is a large band of dealers in Ireland who spend their entire lives at auctions, travelling long distances to attend promising-looking sales, and they can usually come up with any particular sort of piece relatively quickly. Many of these men and women have been in the trade a long time and are extremely knowledgeable. The best approach to this method of buying is to check the auction results carefully for a while in your newspapers or magazines to establish the current price band for the kind of piece you want. It will also be useful to consult a reliable price guide, such as *Miller's*. When you are ready to buy, approach your chosen dealer, describing the sort of piece you want and the approximate price you wish to pay. And how does one choose a reputable dealer? Word of mouth is undoubtedly the best way, but if you know very few people in the antiques trade it might be a good idea to have a chat with someone you trust in an auction house and ask him or her for one or two recommendations.

I have to say that I personally would find this a rather dull way to buy antiques, in that it would deprive me of the entertainment of the auction and the pleasure of browsing around for myself. However, I have been told by a discerning collector that it is by far the most satisfactory way to buy, resulting in a great saving in leg work and, he claims, significantly less expense, especially at the beginning of a collecting career, by reducing the number of mistakes that would otherwise be made through inexperience.

Antique Shops

It is often through looking in the windows of antique shops that the new collector is first drawn to the world of antiques, and it is often, I imagine, in these shops that he or she makes the first small purchases. Most antique shops are run by one or two dedicated enthusiasts who will be happy to discuss

Cast-iron money box, early 20th century.

TOP LEFT: George III secretaire cabinet with ebony stringing to the drop front writing compartment. TOP RIGHT: Expert evaluation. ABOVE LEFT: Large Mason's dinner service. ABOVE: At auction. LEFT: A very valuable Macedonian silver tetradrach of the mid 4th century BC; this coin raised £27,000 at auction in London in 1986.

their stock with you. Use such chat to sound out their reliability and expertise. Try not to waste their time, though, if you have no real intention of buying anything then or in the future; many shop owners claim that too many people look on antique shops as handy places to pass the time in while they wait for the next bus!

Although it seems to be slowing down now, the late 1980s saw something of a proliferation of antique shops that opened for just a short time before going out of business. Very often such shops offered a low level of expertise and an unjustifiably high level of prices. It would be all too easy to say, on the basis of this, that you should confine your attentions to the long-established businesses in the larger towns, but in fact this would be most unfair to the many small recently opened shops that offer an excellent service to their customers. The advice must be that you examine the stock in the shop, critically and carefully, taking note of quality and prices and engaging the proprietor in as much conversation as he is prepared to give you. If you are a novice buyer it pays to shop around to see the prices of the items you like elsewhere before you part with your money.

The received wisdom is that buying in an antique shop is always more expensive than buying at auction. As I have suggested before, this may not always be the case. To cite a few examples: I recently went into a large shop in Dublin that sells a wide variety of old furniture, from high-quality Regency sideboards and tables to purely secondhand kitchen chairs and cupboards. I saw there a number of fine Victorian pieces, the prices of which were no more than I had seen fetched at house clearances for similar items. I found a very nice Edwardian chest of drawers for £185, which was £100 less than I had seen an almost identical piece make at auction about two weeks before. The owner of this shop buys many of his fine pieces in the north of the country and from private vendors, by whom he is sometimes asked to clear a whole house. In this situation both he and the seller can avoid auctioneers' fees, and he is able to offer his customers pieces at somewhat less than he could if he bought exclusively at auction. In another shop I visited lately I was told that the profit margin was worked out on each piece as it went into stock and it didn't generally change, regardless of whether auction prices for that kind of piece went up or down.

In contrast, at an auction I attended in Co. Wicklow I saw a small apprentice's chest sold for £110. A few weeks later I caught sight of it at a Dublin antiques fair, on the stand of an upmarket shop. With interest I lifted up the price tag and saw that it read £600! A friend to whom I related this incident immediately asked me how much that little chest was really worth. In asking that question she cut to the heart of one of the most difficult areas of the antique trade: that of valuation. The truth is that antiques, like all works of art, are to a large extent worth what somebody is prepared to pay for them. There is the country auction price, the prestigious saleroom price, the Grafton Street price. There is the Bond Street price, the Fifth Avenue price, and the price two determined bidders are prepared to pay to get what they want and vanquish each other. The best you can do is to keep an eye on what antique dealers call the 'price band' for the object you want; but in the end, the decision about what you should pay will depend on what the piece is worth to you. Of course it is against this background that the notion

A word of caution: people have rather a habit of assuming that there is a greater chance of finding something of value for half nothing in a shop that has a junk-like display and that looks as if it hasn't been gone through in years. But beware: that fine print in its dusty frame or that set of chairs that has caught your eye may be the best bit of stock the proprietor has had in months and he may well be seeking the very best price for it. Worse, you may have stumbled into the premises of a dealer with very little knowledge of the antiques market, who may quote high prices that bear no relation to the value of the piece you wish to buy.

One advantage of buying in an antique shop is that if you are dissatisfied with your purchase, if you find that it was not what it was said to be or that there was extensive damage or restoration that was not obvious to you in the shop and that the proprietor failed to point out to you, you have some form of redress. A reputable antiques business will generally go to considerable trouble to ensure that you go away happy. To protect yourself, whenever you buy antiques in a shop you should make sure that you always receive a receipt plus a docket, signed and dated by the dealer, briefly describing your purchase, its condition, its age, and its price.

Shops

of buying antiques as an 'investment' becomes problematic. If you buy some shares today in the hope of making a secure long-term investment, or if you buy a house for the same reason, and you find, by some mischance, that you must sell again soon afterwards, you would be very unlucky not to get at least as much as you paid for them a short time before. This is not so with antiques. If you buy an expensive item in a shop and need to sell again fairly quickly at auction, or even to another dealer, it's very unlikely that you would get what you paid for it unless the dealer from whom you bought it agreed, as a favour, to take it off your hands. Of course it is possible that you might get more at auction, especially if the piece were put into a sale that also included a house clearance or if it were included in a particularly high-class saleroom auction. It might happen - and again it might not. And that's when you realise that the financial side of antique buying is really more speculation than investment. Pieces should be bought primarily because you like them rather than because you imagine that you're going to make a great financial killing from a rapid rise in value.

When you have seen something that you like in a shop, don't be afraid to attempt to bargain a little. Some shop owners hate customers who do this, of course, and many of them will have set prices that they have no intention of altering. Others, especially those away from the more exclusive thoroughfares, are a bit more flexible. A little friendly conversation will quickly establish which kind you are dealing with. But do remember when you are assessing prices that a shop owner's overheads are considerable and

Collection of advertising signs.

stock often slow-moving, and the expertise he offers has often been dearly and painfully bought through the expensive mistakes of the past. In general, profit margins in the British antique trade are judged to be between 10% and somewhat over 100%, and there is no reason to suppose that Irish margins should be very different. The tendency is for items that sell rapidly to carry profit margins at the lower end of the range, while pieces for which a good deal has been paid but that tend to sit in a shop for months need to show a higher profit.

Auctions

The kind of protection you have when buying from a reputable dealer does not generally apply when you buy at auction. In general, auctioneers accept no responsibility for the correct description, genuineness or authenticity of any lot and, in the words of the most commonly seen conditions of sale, 'make no warranty whatsoever.' However, you may occasionally come across a clause in the conditions of sale known as a recission. This declares that where a buyer can prove that a lot that he purchased was a forgery, the auctioneers will set aside the sale and refund the buyer the cost of the item. Christie's, for example, are willing to entertain such claims for up to five years from the date of the auction, subject to certain conditions. Such recission clauses have begun to appear in Irish catalogues too, and at the time of writing I am aware of four auction houses that have adopted this practice, although the time allowed for submission of a claim is only as generous as Christie's in one case. I hope the scope of recission clauses will be expanded in the near future and indeed that all auction houses will include them in their conditions of sale.

It must be understood, of course, that this practice only applies to forgeries and not to instances where a buyer finds that he has made a mistake in his understanding of the catalogue description, or that the item was damaged or restored, or worth less than he paid for it. The protection offered to the buyer at auction is negligible, and you must be aware of that fact. It may very well be that there is a case for the law being amended so as to afford you more protection, but until that day dawns, you must always read carefully the conditions of sale printed on your catalogue and make sure that you understand them and are prepared to live with them.

In spite of this, many collectors find auctions the best and most interesting way of buying antiques. Despite their hazards, despite the heavy commitment in time required to attend them frequently, auctions remain the best way to learn about antiques. The great thing is that at the viewing you can handle everything, and it is through the handling that you learn. The learning does not come easily, and early buys will often be cause for later regret. Years into your collecting career some items will remain stubbornly difficult to date; fine late nineteenth-century copies of Adam-style furniture, for example, will continue to baffle and infuriate, while the Chinese habit of marking porcelain with the reign marks of earlier emperors frequently confuses even the very knowledgeable. But don't despair; every piece you look at, whether it is a fine Sheraton-period side-table or a rickety plywood sideboard, is a lesson, and eventually you will

Georgian mahogany dumb waiter.

Victorian boulle
card table.

develop an eye for the patination and workmanship, for the subtle differences in style that mark out the different periods and the good-quality piece from the bad.

Some experts will tell you that the good collector's eye is born and not made. Don't believe it; and don't allow those more experienced than you in the antiques trade to convince you that there is any special mystique or arcane knowledge about old pieces that can't be taught. It can; but it will take time, and you will probably find as you go along that you will develop a strong interest in a few specialist areas, gradually becoming more knowledgeable about those than about others. This is inevitable. The field of fine arts and antiques is enormously wide, and no one life would be long enough to learn about all the great paintings, all the great porcelain works, all the great silversmiths. In any case, you will probably find that some antiques 'do more' for you than others.

For example, although I know that late eighteenth-century furniture is beautifully styled and made and is certainly very fashionable right now and the best pieces are extremely expensive, the fact is that I prefer Victorian furniture. I love round wooden handles, the comfortable solidity of a balloon-back chair, the heavy turned leg of a sturdy mahogany table of the highest quality. I prefer late nineteenth-century pedestal desks to slender George III writing tables, and chiffonniers to slim long-legged sideboards, and I have no desire to own a Chippendale carved mask table — even if I could afford it. I have also found that I prefer porcelain to silver and would rather buy coloured glass than crystal, and that I love old books best of all. You will find that you spend more time looking at and reading about the things you like than those you don't and that you will end up being more knowledgeable about what especially attracts you. Eventually, you may discover to your surprise that in your own specialist area you have become even more expert than many general dealers who are forced to spread their interests very widely.

One of the biggest dangers attending the novice auction-goer is that of getting too excited about what is seen. Some item catches the eye and you feel you just must have it; the thrill of it all is such that no thoughtful examination of the piece is made and if faults are half-noticed they are brushed aside as being of no matter. The inevitable result is that you are sold a pup, and it is your own fault. It is important that you view what is on offer with a certain detachment so that you can make a calm appraisal of what you see.

In general, auction views are held the day before the sale. This applies both to house clearances and saleroom auctions. Ring up the auctioneer in advance and find out how many lots there will be; and if you can manage to get a catalogue before view day so much the better. Always allow plenty of time for viewing. I find that at the typical house clearance I can get through four hundred lots in about two hours, but of course this varies according to the proportion of antique lots as against household goods and the degree of interest I have in some of the items.

The sale catalogue is an indispensable aid to viewing. It is a false economy not to buy one – though the price of catalogues supplied by some auction houses has increased enormously in recent years – and in any case the majority of auctioneers won't admit you to the viewing without one.

Regency style bow fronted chest.

You will find early on that catalogues vary greatly in quality, from the detailed and fully illustrated ones provided by the prestigious fine art houses to the few sheets of stapled typescript supplied by the small establishments that only handle such sales a couple of times a year. The level of expertise that goes into the cataloguing varies too, so keep alert, and if you are in any doubt about the accuracy of a description, ask the auctioneer to help you.

If you are attending a house sale, especially one being held at a large country house where items are likely to command higher prices because of the anxiety of private buyers to acquire something, however small, from a famous mansion, and where even dealers may give a little more for a piece which may have some historical interest for their future customers, pay special attention to the wording at the front of your catalogue. Sometimes, auctioneers accept individual items, or even small collections, from other clients and 'drop' them into a house sale where they may be expected to fetch a higher price than if they were offered at a saleroom. Such items may not always be easily identifiable to buyers, so if you are one of those who occasionally feels disposed to pay a little extra for a piece from a house which interests you, do make sure that you end up with what you are paying for. Most auctioneers will indicate at the front of the catalogue if outside items have been included. Phrases like 'with the part contents of another residence', 'with some items from the collection of a lady' or 'with some additional lots' will alert you. However, a few auctioneers can be a little coy about the matter in a way which may fail to warn the novice buyer. You may, for example, come across catalogues in which the auctioneers declare that they are offering the entire contents of Such-and-Such House 'and the contents of the dining room'. This should be taken to mean that the 'contents of the dining room' have been introduced from elsewhere. If you are in any doubt, check with the auctioneer, and make a note of the numbers of any outside lots.

One of a pair of Windsor chairs. *See also next page.*

Probably the next thing in the catalogue that catches your eye will be the conditions of sale. Read them! Make sure you understand the terms and abbreviations used by the auctioneer in the descriptions of the various lots (many of the most commonly found are included in the glossary at the end

Windsor chair.

of this book). Note the level of auctioneers' fees that you will pay on purchase, and remember that the Government now charges VAT on auctioneers' fees at a rate of of 21%. The auctioneers' fees range from 7% to 10% of the purchase price, with the most frequently met figure being 10%. One would expect that the variations in these figures would be accounted for by the differing levels of expertise on offer, but it isn't so. I have come across auctioneers who rarely deal with antiques charging 10%, whereas one of the best auction houses in the country is charging the more modest 8%. It is sensible to take account of these charges when you are deciding your final bidding prices; in practice I find that very few people do!

Take note also of the times that purchases are to be collected. This can usually be done for the couple of hours following the sale and for the whole of the following day. Most auctioneers state that purchases cannot be paid for and taken away during the sale, and some are very strict about this. Some don't mean it, however. Keep a sharp look-out towards the end of the sale for people appearing with purchases under their arms. If you have finished buying, you can save yourself time spent queuing by paying for your goods and taking them before the rush starts.

Auction Views

The best way to view a sale is simply to start with lot 1 and work your way systematically to the end. When you see an item that interests you, stop and take things very slowly. Read the catalogue description, and decide whether the piece you see matches this, at least in a general way. Then put your catalogue down and examine the piece thoroughly. If it is a chest or table, look at the top. What timber is it? Is it solid or veneer? Are there any cracks or repairs? Does the top match the rest of the piece? You may find that the top of a piece that has been placed under a window for a long time has become paler than the rest; but is the timber the same, with the same kind of grain and feel? Has the piece been polished, waxed, or varnished?

Bend down and look beneath the top. If the piece is a chest, does the top sit comfortably on it or are there any strange spaces in there that suggest that the top may not be original? Does the top look wide enough for the piece, and does it go all the way to the back, or do the edges of the top seem to extend too far over the sides of the chest, suggesting that it might have come from a larger piece? If you're looking at a table, crawl underneath. Are there any fresh nails or new pieces of wood in there that might lead you to suspect that the top and undersection are rather too recent acquaintances? Look at the legs. Are there any unusual joinings at the top that might be the result of new legs being added? Do the legs all match one another? With drop-leaf tables, do the leaves fit? Have the hinges been replaced? If the leaves are not up, put them up. Do they come into place smoothly, without stiffness? Is the timber on the leaves the same as that at the centre? Are they twisted or warped?

With chests and desks you must remove all the drawers. Go down through each in turn. Open the drawer. Look at the inside of the front. Can you see the back of the handles? If you can, they are probably replacements, and if they are bright and shiny they are recent replacements. Are there any holes where handles used to be? Do those holes show on the outside? If they don't, this piece has a later veneer. Now look at the dovetail joint at the front of the drawer. Is there a gauge-line, that is, a faint incision, running along the dovetails? If there is, the joint is hand-cut, not machine-cut: a good sign of age. Are the pins and the fans of the dovetail joint the same width? If they are, you are probably looking at a recently made drawer. Look at the sides, or linings of the drawer. These should all match and be of the same colour, the unpolished wood of a dull hue and fairly smooth. If the wood looks very fresh or if it is rough to the touch, then it is probably new. If it looks rather black, it may have been stained to disguise the fact that it is new. Pull out the drawer completely. Turn it upside down. A lead pencil mark on the base can often give the game away if it is a replacement. When the drawer is out, look inside the carcase. Do any shiny nails or fresh timber indicate the presence of recent work? Replace the drawer and stand back a little. Does it fit well into the space allocated to it or does it look too small or too large, indicating that it does not truly belong to the chest?

Some repairs to drawers are acceptable, particularly the replacement of drawer handles and runners - the wood along which the drawer runs in and out. In daily use, too, people are inclined to overfill drawers, leading to straining, cracking, and breaking, especially of the base and back. In these circumstances it may have been necessary to repair or replace these sections on some of the drawers. But I would not be very happy if, on an expensive chest, *all* the backs and bases were clearly new; I would be even less happy if the sides of the drawers seemed recent replacements. Over all, if you get the uneasy feeling that the drawers were not originally made for the piece you are looking at, it is best not to buy.

Finally check the back and feet of the chest, again for fresh timber. A replacement back, well made and fitted to a chest (or wardrobe) may not

Auction Views

A dealer gives the goods a close inspection at a house contents view.

disturb some buyers, but it should be considered when it comes to price. Replacement feet may be a more serious matter, especially if the piece is an expensive Georgian or late nineteenth-century one. Victorian bun feet can often be neatly enough replaced (sometimes they were made from deal, which is prone to woodworm), but I would not accept it on a more valuable piece. In any case, the replacement of Georgian bracket or ogee feet is a tricky job, and when seen, which it occasionally is, it has all too often been botched.

Everything in which you are interested must be subjected to the same kind of examination if nasty post-purchase surprises are to be avoided. The objective is to avoid seriously damaged pieces and things that are in fact 'marriages', that is, made up of parts from different pieces. This is frequently encountered in bureau or cabinet bookcases, where the top and bottom may be quite unrelated. It is usually detected fairly easily when the bookcase is a Victorian one with carved ornament. If the carving or decoration on top doesn't match that on the bottom, then the two halves did not start life together. With plainer, Georgian pieces, things may be a bit trickier. Check the back. Are the two halves made of the same timber? If they are noticeably different, this may clinch the matter straight away, but, unfortunately, if they are similar they could still be unrelated. If you have discovered that despite fitting neatly enough at the front the top portion of the piece overhangs at the back, then these two are not true mates. Stand back from the front, asking yourself if the top looks too wide or too narrow for the base. Look at the slope of the bureau if the base is one of these. The slope of a bureau made for a bookcase is generally steeper than that on a bureau alone. If there are drawers at the base of the upper portion, check them against the little drawers inside the bureau to see that they match. Look at the small frieze or moulding that covers the point at which the bureau and shelves join. In general this frieze should be on the bureau part, with the top fitting neatly in. If it doesn't fit, the piece is a mismatch. See if you can get your fingers between the two halves — sometimes you may be able to persuade the top to move a bit. If you find raw wood in there, and you've already decided the two halves match, then this is a very good sign. In general, only bureaux that were designed to stand alone were polished or veneered the whole way back.

Edwardian oak and silver mounted tantalus.

Mason's Ironstone tureen.

However, this was not always the case, and sometimes the bureau top was fully treated.

In judging these pieces it tends to be the accumulation of a reasonable number rather than *all* points of matching that will decide the buyer. If the piece looks well proportioned, you may decide to buy despite some doubts about its authenticity. But you must make sure that the doubts are reflected in the price. And sometimes, even when it is known for certain that the two pieces are a 'marriage' (sometimes described as 'bureau with associated bookcase' in your catalogue), the piece may be a perfectly acceptable and useful purchase, although in no way as valuable as a complete piece.

Ceramics, silver, glass and all other collectables should be looked at in the same way, and with sets, such as porcelain dinner services, do take the time to go through each piece, checking for damage. You may, of course, decide that you like a damaged piece enough to want to buy. That is up to you; but make sure you adjust your price accordingly. With regard to 'marriages', the fact is that they are, all too often valueless, at least in the sense that no discerning collector or dealer is likely to want to buy such a thing from you should you ever wish to sell . There are some circumstances where this may not be so. As has been said, composite bookcases may have some value if there is a reasonable similarity between the parts. There may be instances where a top has been added to a fine sideboard or chest without damaging the piece. The top could be removed and the more valuable object restored to its original condition. But to the run-of-the-mill Victorian and Edwardian pieces that the modest buyer may bid for at auction, this does not usually apply. When it comes to price, it is far better to pay a sum over the odds for a good-quality item than to pay even a small price for something that is not what it is supposed to be. The quality piece will appreciate in value and, with luck, time will eventually wipe out your mistake. The 'marriage' will always remain worthless and stand in your home as a constant reproach to your carelessness.

The Auction Sale

And so to sale day. I always like to arrive early to get a last-minute look at the lots I am really interested in. Occasionally, the fresh light of morning will reveal to you a serious flaw that escaped your eye the day before. When you have viewed all you can, try to find yourself a place where the auctioneer will see you properly. As you enter the sale you may be asked for your name and address and issued with an object rather like a table tennis bat, which carries a number. This is known as a paddle, and when a lot is sold to you, you just hold it up and the auctioneer makes a note of the number.

There are some phrases the auctioneer may use that it is helpful for you to know. He may say that he is 'selling from the catalogue'; this generally means that items will not be displayed to the buyers and they will have to rely on their memory of the view. Sensible buyers will have made descriptive notes in their catalogues against the items that interest them! He may mention that he has a 'commission bid'; this is where a buyer who cannot attend the sale authorises the auctioneer to state bids on his behalf. When the auctioneer says 'it's in the room' it means that the commission bidder has been beaten;

A word about estimates. These are intended as a guide only and, rather like rules, seem often made to be broken. They only become vexatious when unknown to the buyer, a piece has a reserve that is higher than the estimate - a practice that has become rather too common in recent times and that, I hope, will soon be abandoned. If a piece is of high quality and you like it, you must decide what it is worth to you, even if that figure is over the estimate. On the other hand, don't ignore something you fancy merely because it seems likely to fetch a price in excess of what you would be able to pay. You never know. There may be less interest in it than you think, and you may get in on the bidding after all. It is very frustrating to have to let something you like pass you by because you didn't have the foresight to look at it properly the day before.

That brings me to another of my own rules about auctions. I suppose there are experienced dealers and collectors who can assess a piece from the floor even as the auctioneer's assistant holds it up to the room on sale day. But my own experience is that to buy an object that you haven't examined at the view is an almost certain way to buy yourself a nasty surprise. I have succumbed to this impulse a couple of times, and on each occasion lived to regret it!

Georgian mahogany
bedside cupboard.

when it's 'against you all' it means that the absent buyer has been successful. If, after bidding has ceased, the auctioneer says "We'll have to pass it", he means that the pice has not reached its reserve and will not be sold at the price offered by the last bidder. A reserve is the price below which the seller — called the vendor by auctioneers — is not prepared to let an item go.

Bidding, oddly enough, seems largely a matter of temperament. One experienced dealer I know rushes up and down examining the lots as they are held up, while bidding amid a stream of witticisms. There is another who merely winks his right eye to indicate a bid. The main thing is to make sure the auctioneer sees and understands you. You can start the bidding, or you can wait until everyone else seems to have finished before joining battle. If there is something you are determined to have and you know you can afford to bid well up to the estimate, it may be a good idea to start the bidding and to keep bidding fast and confidently. This sometimes has the effect of intimidating other bidders, with the result that they may drop out a little earlier than they intended and you end up getting the piece for somewhat less than you had expected! If it happens that the auctioneer fails to notice your bid and you see the item you want just about to be sold to someone else, call out politely to him. If there is any dispute about whose was the final bid, the auctioneer will almost invariably put the lot up for sale again. However, if you hesitate and he moves on to the next lot, it is too late. Disputing the bid is something you have to do at once.

If, when an item you wish to buy is held up, you have a sudden surge of doubt about it, don't be afraid to go up and have another look. You will notice that the dealing fraternity do it quite often, and it's better to do that than bring home a pup. When a lot is finally knocked down to you, you immediately hold up your paddle so that the number can be seen, or you call out your name to the auctioneer. You need to remember that, at most auction houses, the moment an item is sold to you, you are entirely responsible for it. For this reason it is always better, if you can, to take away your purchases straight after the sale ends. If you intend to buy porcelain and glass, bring newspapers and cardboard boxes with you. Auctioneers tend not to provide these necessities, and you don't want your precious buys tumbling all over the back of your car.

If you are lucky you will find auction-going a source of entertainment as well as learning. Auctioneers tend to have lively personalities, and many of them are superb wits. The ones that irritate are those that move at a snail's pace; the average speed of sale is about 80 lots an hour, with specialist sales averaging about 120 per hour. Don't forget to note in your catalogue the price made by every piece. You will find past catalogues an invaluable source of reference if you do, supplying you with your own instant price guide. And remember to record the condition of the lots as well, together with any other comments you might find useful later.

19th century French bonheur du jour.

Chapter Three

SILVER

Solid or Plated?

ne of the things that may puzzle the collector who begins to take an interest in old silver is the problem of telling 'solid' silver from plated ware. The good news is that, in this regard, the buyer of antique silver is protected by one of the oldest forms of consumer protection: the hallmarking system. Each silver piece carries its special set of symbols, which not only tells the buyer that it is genuine but gives a little of its origin and history as well. These marks are quite different from those stamped on plated ware, and only a very little experience is necessary before one can tell one from the other. This is not to say that plated objects are in any sense to be despised by the collector. Far from it. Fine quality pieces in both Sheffield plate and electroplate are sought after and can fetch prices that rival those of silver.

The metal that is sometimes described as 'solid' silver by collectors is not, in fact, solid at all. Silver, like gold, is much too soft to stand up to daily use or to hold its decoration, and so an alloy is added to the basic metal to make it hard enough for shaping and working and for practical use. Silver is normally alloyed with copper, in the proportions of 92.5% pure silver to 7.5% copper. This is known as the sterling standard, and goes back all the way to 1238, when King Henry III of England laid down that these proportions were to be the standard for all English coinage. However, silversmiths complained that foreign craftsmen were sending into England pieces of low-quality wrought silver and that this constituted unfair competition. In 1300 King Edward I responded by requiring that all manufactured silverware be of the 'esterling allay or better' and that English silverware be tested or 'assayed' in London and stamped with the mark of the leopard's head. This was the first hallmark; and later, marks denoting the maker's name and the year of manufacture were added. In 1544 a heraldic mark, depicting a lion 'passant' or walking, was punched to denote that the silver was of the legal standard; and between 1784 and 1890 a mark in the form of the sovereign's head was included to show that appropriate duty had been paid.

Assay offices were later established in other cities, including Dublin, Chester, Birmingham, and Sheffield. The symbol for Chester before 1777 was three demi-lions passant and one-and-a-half wheat sheaves; after that year an upright sword between three wheat sheaves was stamped on. The mark of the Birmingham assay office, set up in 1773, was an anchor while

Hallmarks

RIGHT: *Left to right*: George III
Irish bright cut cream jug;
English 18th century sparrow
beak cream jug; 18th century
Irish cream pail; late Victorian
helmet shaped cream jug in
rococo style; Irish George IV
cream jug. BELOW: *Left to right*:
London Victorian engraved
silver tea and coffee set with
plated kettle and burner en suite.

that of Sheffield, which began assaying in the same year, was a crown. In Dublin a crown, harp and, from 1730, a figure of Hibernia were used.

It is essential that you are familiar with these hallmarks if you intend to spend money on silver. In addition, you will need to be able to read the various date letters that indicate the year of manufacture of a piece. This can be quite tricky, as the letters of the alphabet are used in rotation with the type of script, changing as the end of the alphabet is reached. Many collectors find that the best solution is to take to sale views a book that includes a full table of hallmarks. One to be recommended is Elizabeth de Castre's *Observer's Book of Silver,* which contains not only a table of marks but a text that is an invaluable reference for novice and expert alike. Best of all, it's small enough to slip into a handbag or pocket.

The Growth in Domestic Silverware

Before the sixteenth century there was not a great deal of domestic silver in the private home. It was the opening up of the Americas and the exploitation of the silver resources there that took silver beyond the royal courts and onto the tables of the gentry and affluent middle class. Spoons, ewers, basins and, above all, the elaborate standing salts sometimes reaching two feet in height began to mark the status of the squire or comfortable merchant. Unfortunately, much of this silverware, both in England and Ireland, was melted down to meet the expenses of the English Civil and Cromwellian Wars. The restoration of King Charles II in 1660, however, ushered in a period of rich and flamboyant taste, which affected all the decorative arts, including the manufacture of silver. The late seventeenth century saw an influx of Huguenot silversmiths into Britain and Ireland, bringing with them a high level of sophistication in the casting and decoration of silver. They were particularly associated with the introduction of what is known as cut-card work, a technique whereby thin layers of sheet silver were soldered onto a piece and then formed into decorative motifs without weakening the structure of the vessel by hammering out the decoration from the back.

By the end of the seventeenth century the invention of the rolling mill meant that silver could be rolled out into thinner sheets, making silver wares significantly cheaper than before. Naturally, demand rose — to the point, in fact, where the government became concerned at the quantity of raw silver being taken out of general circulation to be made into domestic pieces. In 1697 it was decided to recall all silver coinage for reminting and to offer a large payment to those who yielded up their wrought silver. At the same time, to discourage people from putting their money into domestic silver a new, higher standard was set for such pieces, raising the proportion of silver from 92.5% to 95.8%; the idea was to make wrought wares more expensive. This was known as the Britannia standard, and was marked by a seated figure of Britannia and a depiction of a lion's head with a torn neck, called in heraldry a lion's head 'erased'.

In England the Britannia standard lasted until 1720, when there was a general return to sterling, although individual silversmiths could continue with the higher standard if they wished. The change of marks between 1697 and 1720 makes English silver of this period particularly easy to identify, although it must be said that little of it will come within reach of the modest

Hallmarks

collector. A Queen Anne coffee pot by a maker such as John Rand or Richard Raine would cost at least £5,000, while a pair of cast candlesticks by a smith like Henry Lyon might be bought at auction for perhaps double that. It's interesting to note, by the way, that many of the coffee pots and, even more frequently, chocolate pots were made with their spouts to the side of the handle rather than opposite it, leaving the modern collector wondering how the hot liquids were poured out without scalding!

Irish Silver

The 1697 legislation did not apply to Irish silver; its standard remained unchanged. The collector will not see many Irish pieces from this period coming up for auction, but the National Museum houses a good collection, which is well worth seeing if you can. Styles, as with English smiths of the time, tended to be plain, with the emphasis on shape and lustre rather than elaborate decoration. The style can best be seen in the work of Thomas Bolton, a smith of truly remarkable skill, several of whose pieces can be viewed at the National Museum, including a superb chocolate pot made in 1696, featuring the typical side spout. Two-handled cups were extremely popular with the Dublin smiths; one by Joseph Walker was sold in London for around £300 some years ago, and it would surely make considerably more now. A somewhat damaged salver made by Walker in 1704 was sold at a Co. Kildare house clearance for £720, and, despite the damage to its veloute feet, this was quite a modest price for a rather grand piece. Irish tankards of the period may occasionally turn up in the saleroom. A Queen Anne tankard by Philip Tough was sold in London recently for around £4,000, and Christie's has sold a fine covered tankard by Walker for over £2,200. The oldest existing piece of Irish hallmarked silver, incidentally, is not for sale; this is a flagon in the collection of Trinity College, Dublin, and carries the Dublin hallmark for 1638.

Georgian and Victorian Silver

The end of the 1720s saw a move away from plain styles towards what is called the rococo taste, which called for extraordinarily elaborate forms of decoration. During this period the silversmith as artist came into his own, and some of the finest craftsmen ever to work in silver flourished: Paul de Lamerie, Nicholas Sprimont, Paul Crespin, James Shruder, and in Ireland, Robert Calderwood, John Wilme, and Thomas Walker. By the end of the 1770s the rococo had, through sheer extravagance, burnt itself out, and there was quite an abrupt move back to simpler, even rather severe, styles of neo-classicism that echoed the fashions introduced by the Adams brothers in furniture and architecture.

By the early years of the nineteenth century the slim classical shapes had begun to be overlaid by heavy ornament, strongly reminiscent of the old rococo styles. This trend was continued into the Victorian period, sometimes indeed with an attempt to 'improve' Queen Anne and neo-classical pieces by adding opulent decoration in keeping with the new fashions. As far as the collector is concerned, such additions generally reduce the value of a piece. It is important when you are examining early or late eighteenth-century pieces that you give consideration to the decoration to ensure that it looks right for its period and has not been added later.

Styles in Irish silver generally reflected English fashions, although they tended to arrive on these shores a little later. The rococo taste, for example, was probably introduced to Ireland by means of a dinner service commissioned by the Earl of Kildare in 1745 from the London maker George Wickes — although there is a strong hint of rococo in the sweep of the scrolled rim of a sauceboat made by Robert Calderwood in Dublin in 1740 and now in the possession of the National Museum. To the rococo period belongs that apparently uniquely Irish example of the silversmith's craft, the dish ring. These are often wrongly described as 'potato rings'; they had nothing whatever to do with potatoes but were used to keep hot plates from the surface of dining-table and serving-boards. They occasionally turn up for sale; one recently was sold at a Co. Dublin house clearance for £3,800. This was made in Dublin in 1772 and, stylistically, was similar to one made by the Dublin smith Charles Townsend in 1771 and which is owned by the National Museum.

During the second half of the eighteenth century the output of Irish wrought silver increased enormously, and by the 1780s around 80,000 ounces of silver was being assayed at Dublin every year. The Act of Union facilitated the import of a good deal of English silver and this hit the native smiths, but the arrival of new mining techniques began, in the early years of the nineteenth century, to make silver less expensive, thus creating demand from new customers among the gentry and middle classes, and staving off, for a time, the period of decline.

Buying Silver

As a modest collector you may imagine that Georgian silver must be well beyond your means, but in fact much Georgian silver, especially small pieces and part sets, is surprisingly inexpensive. In general, Irish silver is more expensive at auction in Ireland than are English pieces, except, of course, in the case of outstanding smiths such as Storr, Crespin, Lamerie, and others, whose work commands high prices wherever it is sold. Nevertheless, the work of many excellent Irish smiths is quite within the reach of the ordinary buyer. For example, an oval sugar basket with swing handle by William Bond of Dublin, made in 1802, was sold in Dublin recently for £140, while a sugar bowl with two handles made at around the same time by Dublin maker Joseph Johnson made £220. A George III oval cream jug made by Byrne of Dublin in 1807 sold at auction for just £90; and a very ornate George IV sugar basin and milk jug decorated in early nineteenth-century rococo style by Edward Twycross of Dublin was sold for £280.

Of course, these were all part sets; full tea services of the late eighteenth and nineteenth century generally consisted of at least three pieces: teapot, milk jug, and sugar bowl. Often a coffee pot was added, and occasionally there was a fifth piece in the form of a kettle and stand. Such sets are considerably more expensive than making up a service by collecting single items, and good-quality tea services even of the Victorian period and the early twentieth century do not come cheap. With Victorian sets, it tends to be the richness of decoration that sends up the price; at a Dublin saleroom lately a Victorian melon-shaped four-piece service made in Dublin in 1852 was bought for £1,200; but at the same sale a set decorated with repoussé

Early 20th century plated wine bottle holder.

Entree dish by the great London maker Paul Storr. Dated 1801.

and chased scrollwork, dated Dublin 1888, took £3,000, although the weight of the set, at 92 ounces, was only three ounces more than the cheaper one. Good Edwardian sets are expensive, too, but large numbers of simple but attractive services in the late Georgian style were made during the early years of this century, and such sets can be got at auction from around £200 for three pieces.

Beginning

The collection of silver cutlery is an ideal way for the beginner to make the acquaintance of the very best smiths; it can be bought gradually, and good pieces can be got at surprisingly low prices. Even sets and part sets need not break the bank: twelve George III dinner forks can cost as little as £250 - indeed I recently saw a good set of Scottish forks of that period sold for just £180. Fiddle-pattern spoons are most popular and usually easily obtainable: expect to pay £50 to £80 for sets of six teaspoons and from £140 for dessertspoons. Georgian knives do not often come up at auction — the most popular style in the middle years of the eighteenth century was the 'pistol grip' - and most collectors have to be content with nineteenth-century knives, silver or bone-handled, to go with their Georgian forks. Bone-handled knives are very inexpensive; you could buy a dozen steel-bladed ones for under £20, while half a dozen silver-handled Victorian dinner knives shouldn't set you back more than £60 or so.

There are a number of other areas of small silver collectables open to the modest buyer; as with cutlery, they can be a way of acquiring the work of fine makers at little cost. One interesting field is the collection of travelling silver. In the eighteenth and nineteenth centuries, when coach journeys were long, travellers often carried a range of personal belongings made in silver for use at the inns along the way or when they were guests at the homes of their friends. During the eighteenth century especially, complete travelling sets were made, which included items such as a travelling mug, a knife, fork, and spoon, a nutmeg or spice grater, a corkscrew, some toilet articles, and perhaps a marrow scoop and a pair of scissors. These generally came in a wooden or shagreen fitted case.

Over the years, of course, most of these sets became broken up, and, though occasionally seen, such a set would be very expensive. But collecting individual small pieces can be a fascinating hobby, and prices can start at just a few pounds. It is possible to buy a Georgian marrow scoop at auction at around £50; for one by a good Dublin maker you could pay up to £80. Silver-mounted Georgian and Victorian miniature toilet bottles cost from about £10 individually; they're usually offered at auction in multiple lots of

Selection of Irish and English Georgian cutlery.

three or so. Travelling cups start at around £50; the nicest ones are those that fold up in the manner of a telescope, and for these, prices start at around £100 for well-made and decorated examples. Silver spice boxes are pricy, and good ones start at around £500, but simple nutmeg graters can be found for £100 or a little less. Few great ladies of old cared to travel without a vinaigrette, a small perforated box containing a sponge soaked in aromatic vinegar or smelling salts. These would sustain her should she meet with an unpleasant incident on her journey and succumb to an attack of the vapours. Though tiny, many of these boxes display beautiful workmanship and, at auction, can be bought for between £80 and £400, depending on style and quality. The ones most popular with collectors tend to be those made in the shape of little bags or portmanteau. Travelling sets often contained needle cases for emergency repairs; for these, prices begin at around £50, rising to about £500 for the finest eighteenth century examples. Victorian gentlemen liked to travel with a nip of brandy close to hand, and small spirit flasks sell at auction from around £130 or so.

Smoking and drinking, of course, took up a good deal of the time of the Georgian and Victorian gentleman, and there are lots of small silver pieces connected with these activities to interest the modest collector. Smoking accessories, no doubt because of the fall-off in the numbers of people smoking, are now much cheaper than they used to be. Silver cigarette cases can now be found at auction for as little as £20, and for, say, £100, a really well-decorated one could be bought. Cigarette boxes for the table cost from around £50, and table lighters come in the £100 to £250 range. Vesta cases were widely used during the nineteenth century to carry small quantities of matches in the pocket. They form a very popular collecting area nowadays, and the best of them, sometimes in gold or silver gilt, can make surprisingly

Smoking Accessories

Buying Silver

Wine Accessories

Irish Silversmiths

One of a pair of
Edwardian candlesticks.

high prices for such tiny items. Still, the buyer on a budget should find plenty of opportunity to buy good examples at between £20 and £40. Specialist silver sales and good salerooms that include silver sections at their auctions generally offer a wide selection and are the best and cheapest places to buy.

Antiques relating to wine are another specialist area in which many of the items are made in silver. The collection of decanter labels has long been popular, and examples can be quite expensive, especially if they come in matched sets of three or more. A good set of three early nineteenth century Dublin or London ones could cost anything from £500 to £2,000, but single, later examples can be got from about £50. Wine coasters are almost always expensive, even for pairs; fours are even more desirable. Fairly recently, at a Dublin house clearance, a pair of George III Sheffield coasters with scalloped rims on wooden bases was sold for £1,400, and at the same sale a set of four William IV coasters, made in Sheffield in 1834, with vine leaf borders, fetched £5,500. Wine funnels are an interesting curiosity accessible to the small collector. One by the famous Cork smith Carden Terry was sold in Dublin lately for just £120. This was something of a bargain, for in London similar objects, no better made, have been selling for between £250 and £300.

Some silver collectors like to collect by maker rather than by type of object or by period. In Ireland this tends to mean Irish makers; and provincial smiths who worked outside Dublin, especially in Limerick or Cork, have a particular following. This needn't mean that if you become interested in an eminent maker you won't be able to afford anything by him. Carden Terry of Cork, for example, made extremely fine pieces in the neo-classical style, and his smaller items are well within the reach of the ordinary buyer. Apart from the wine funnel mentioned above, I've seen a set of three matching teaspoons by him make £60, and a fine soup ladle with scallop bowl and fluted handle fetch £260. Working at a period when neo-classical styles were giving way to more ornate styles was a fine Dublin maker named James Fray. Much of his best work is expensive, but not all. A matching teapot and sugar bowl, very ornate in style, with floral decorated bodies, was sold at a specialist sale in Dublin for £800; however, at the same sale a pumpkin-shaped sugar bowl by Fray, with a reeded body and in the neo-classical manner, was sold for £200. Another fine Dublin smith working in the early nineteenth century rococo mode was Edward Twycross. Prices for his pieces would be similar to those paid for work by Fray; recently, the richly chased sugar and milk jug set, mentioned earlier, which sold at auction for £280 was a fine example of his work on smaller pieces.

One interesting collecting idea would be to concentrate on the work of women silversmiths, of whom there were a surprising number. Many of them were the daughters and wives of silversmiths but it is not to be supposed that all of them merely inherited a shop and that the pieces made under their names were made by others. A list of 142 female apprentices registered at the London Goldsmiths' Hall indicates that many actually worked at the craft; others who did not serve their time but entered their marks after the death of a husband or father certainly made pieces with their own hands. One of the most gifted was Ann Tanqueray, who carried on the business of her late husband, David, after 1720. She had been trained to the craft by her father, the London smith David Willaume the elder. Her work has come up

Selection of good quality plated ware.

for auction in London but it is very expensive. A measure of her skill can be gleaned from the fact that she was commissioned to make two pairs of superb silver gilt water jugs to be part of a service for the Empress Catherine of Russia in 1726; today these are in the Hermitage Museum at Leningrad. More affordable is the work of Hester Bateman of London, who worked under own mark from the 1760s, later taking into partnership her sons Peter and William. A silver teapot by Hester herself would probably cost between £500 and £600, a pair of wine labels around £150, and a small table item such as a mustard pot around £300. Cutlery by Hester Bateman comes up for auction quite often; a pair of monogrammed tablespoons with decorated bowls sold in Dublin lately for a modest £50 and, also in Dublin, a bright-cut helmet-shaped milk jug was recently sold for £110.

Ireland had its female silversmiths, too, of whom Catherine Fox and Jane Williams are probably the best known. Fox worked in Dublin during the late eighteenth century; there is an attractive salver by her in the National Museum collection. Jane Williams was the daughter of Carden Terry of Cork, and after the death of her husband, who was also a smith, her father took her into partnership in 1807. For the modest buyer, cutlery will again be the most easily obtained, with single dessertspoons and tablespoons costing £40 to £80, and teaspoons somewhat less. Jane's work generally appears under the mark of Carden Terry & Jane Williams. Other Irish women smiths include Esther Forbers and Jane Dancell from the earlier part of the eighteenth century, and, from the Victorian period, Ann Cummins.

Although a number of fine smiths were working during the early decades of the nineteenth century, the truth was that the Irish silver industry was badly affected by the Act of Union and the disappearance of protective tariffs. It seems that by the middle of the century there were no smiths left in Limerick and Cork, and in Dublin far fewer than there had been fifty years

Irish Women Smiths

Edwardian George III style plated salver.

earlier. Nevertheless, the reputation for quality Irish silver continued to be maintained by a number of Dublin firms throughout the Victorian period. Among these were Thomas Bennett and James West & Sons, both of whom sent examples of Irish work to the Great Exhibition of 1851, as did the firm of G. & S. Waterhouse which also imported silver into Ireland. These firms regularly commissioned pieces from local craftsmen.

Rococo revival was the predominant style, as it was in England; but during the last decades of the century the rise of the national independence movement led to a revival of interest in old Celtic patterns in silvermaking. There is a splendid tea-set in the National Museum collection made in 1870-74 by John Smith from the firm of James West. Consisting of teapot, hot-water jug, sugar bowl and milk jug, it is beautifully decorated with panels of Celtic-style interlacing. The Ardagh Chalice was discovered in 1868 and provided inspiration for a large number of silver pieces. Individual cups and jugs in this pattern can be found from £100 or so; but a complete tea service in the Ardagh style made in Dublin in 1926 was sold at auction lately for £1,450. With the Sheraton revival of the early twentieth century, the Irish firms started to produce objects in a neo-Georgian style, and small table items such as jugs and mustard pots can be bought at auction from £60 upwards.

Because a good deal less silverware was made in Ireland during the Victorian period than during the Georgian, it is not as often seen at auction and is consequently quite expensive. In general, as a collector of Victorian rococo silver you will find yourself buying mainly English pieces, of which there is no scarcity at sales and which start at around £50 for small bowls and condiment items. Even with Victorian silver cutlery you will find Irish pieces to be somewhat more expensive than those made in England. A matched set of ten London 1845 and 1852 fiddle-pattern table forks sold at auction lately for just over £200, while at house clearance a composite set of twelve fiddle-pattern dessert forks which included six made by Peter Walsh of Dublin in 1840, was sold for £400.

Things to Beware of

Fakes

It may come as a surprise to some collectors to learn that silver objects can be faked. Clearly this is not really a problem at the lower end of the market, as it is hardly economic to meddle with pieces that are only going to fetch small sums. Nevertheless it is as well to be aware of the kind of deception that may be practised, if only because most collectors who start by buying small items eventually hope to buy something of more importance as their experience increases.

One form of dishonesty is the stamping of false hallmarks. That is why, if you plan to invest large sums in silver, you must become familiar with the design techniques and workmanship of the periods that interest you, so that you can decide when the appearance of a piece does not seem appropriate for the date on the hallmark or to the silversmith whose mark the piece bears. It is important to ask yourself if the hallmarks look odd or misaligned in any way. For example, the hallmarks on a Georgian mug or coffee pot should appear in a cluster rather than in a straight line. You must also ask yourself if the wear on the hallmarks coincides with the level of handling you would have expected at that particular place on the object.

Another type of fake is the one where a hallmarked section of an inexpensive piece is inserted or 'let in' to a more costly item. For example, the base of an Edwardian eighteenth century style coffee pot could be removed and the base of a modest Georgian tankard or jug slipped in, thus greatly increasing the value of the coffee pot. Objects with bases made as separate discs are vulnerable to this practice, but it is also possible to 'let in' a portion of a Georgian spoon, say, into a heavily decorated item of Victoriana. Again, knowledge of the decorative styles of the hallmarked date must be your guide, and you must note whether marks are in the places you would expect them to be. There may be some difficulty in that often, during the eighteenth century, Dublin silver was not date-marked at all. Your knowledge of the styles of the time and some research into the marks punched by the makers will help.

Also met with are 'marriages' or conversions by which part of one piece is merged with part of another, or where a less saleable object such as a tankard has been converted into a more desirable item like a jug by the addition of a spout and handle. Look for fresh solder in unexpected places, and when a piece is made of two parts, check that the marks on both sections match. If knives have silver handles and blades, make sure that both sets of marks are the same. See that lidded items have matching marks on lid and base, remembering that lids do not always carry a full set of marks but often, with English silver, merely the lion passant and the date letter. When buying sets of cutlery, check that the same marks appear on each piece, and that the number of pieces stated in your sale catalogue is actually present. If the set is a composite one, made up of similar pieces from different sources, your catalogue should say so, and the price you pay should reflect the fact.

Sheffield Plate

Of course, it is not just sterling silver that interests the collector. In recent years good-quality plated silver, especially that known as Sheffield or 'fused' plate, has been making increasingly high prices. The technique for the making of Sheffield plate was devised around 1743 by a Sheffield cutler named Thomas Boulsover, who discovered that a sheet of silver could be fused with a sheet of copper through heating, and when rolled out the copper and silver would expand at the same rate. Before long the great eighteenth century entrepreneur Matthew Boulton had seized on the technique, and his silver works at Soho in Birmingham was soon producing all kinds of tableware in the new plate. It was virtually mass production; and by the 1780s a piece of Sheffield plate could be had for about a third of the price of a similar item made in sterling silver. This did not mean that there was anything shoddy about fused plate; on the contrary, the makers of Sheffield plate went to great lengths to ensure that the style, decoration and durability matched anything the silversmiths could produce. Indeed they were so successful that it was not long before the wealthy were ordering candelabra, tureens and huge table and sideboard pieces to be made in plate rather than sterling silver.

The marks on Sheffield plate present some problems for the collector. During the middle of the eighteenth century some of the plate makers punched marks onto their products in such a way as to cause considerable confusion between their marks and those of sterling silver. It may be that

Sheffield Plate

this was their intention! As a result, between 1773 and 1784 it became illegal to mark Sheffield plate at all. In 1784 the plate makers were once again permitted to stamp their goods with a symbolic device and with the maker's name. Some of these devices include an open umbrella used by Tonks & Co., a globe and cross by Hawksworth, Eyre & Co., and a bishop's mitre by Younge & Co. However, many companies continued not to mark their products at all, and very often all that can be seen are the marks made by a journeyman to show which employee of the factory made the piece. The works of the famous Boulton factory, however, were usually marked at this period. The mark resembles a sunburst consisting of a circle surrounded by a starry halo.

Electroplate

It is not surprising, then, that the identification of Sheffield plate can cause difficulty to the novice collector, whose most frequent mistake is to confuse it with later electroplate. One helpful feature is that because fused plate could not be cast, each separate piece - for example the spout, the handle, the feet and the lid of a teapot - had to be individually die-stamped. This means that objects made from Sheffield plate invariably have seams indicating where the die-stamped pieces were fitted together. These seams tend to have a yellowish stain. Examine plated pieces to see what the base metal appears to be; if it is copper this is likely to suggest Sheffield plate, but not always. Copper was sometimes used for electroplating too, although this tends to show through as a rather rustier-looking brown than those of fused plate. If a close examination of a clearly plated piece leads you to the suspicion that the mounts or, perhaps, a let-in shield appear to be of sterling silver, then you are probably looking at a fused piece. One way of recognising these sterling silver additions is the fact that they will usually be less tarnished than the main plated body, a helpful guide that is usually, unfortunately, obliterated by the tendency of auctioneers and dealers to polish silver objects before putting them on view. These let-in shields became popular, incidentally, because many buyers of fused plate wanted engraved sections included on their pieces, and engraving fused plate presented the problem of exposing the base metal when the silver coating was cut through.

Left: George III Irish bowl chased in rococo style. *Right*: George III tureen cover and stand by Edward Power, Dublin, c.1818.

Ultimately, of course, the best way of learning to distinguish Sheffield plate is to handle and examine thoroughly every piece you see described as Sheffield in your sales catalogues. A reasonable amount of fused plate comes up for sale in Ireland, and it often seems as though most of it is in the form of candelabra. There is generally good demand for these, and the prices are quite high, with good pairs starting at around £500. A single candelabrum should be obtainable at around £150. Candlesticks are also popular, with pairs starting from about £150. Two-handled trays were a common item of fused plate, and they cost from £200 or a little less at auction, depending on size and quality. You would probably pay around £150 for a good dish and cover, with pairs and fours being more expensive, and prices going up according to size. Early Sheffield teapots cost from £60 to £100; a complete tea service would cost from £500 upwards.

One word of warning: much Sheffield plate is seen in very poor condition, bent and damaged and with much 'bleeding', that is, with very large areas of copper exposed. Certainly a little bleeding is no harm - indeed the purist will find it desirable - but it is questionable whether very badly bleeding pieces are worth buying. As a new collector you may find, of course, that even from such badly damaged wares you can learn a good deal about the techniques, the decoration and the makers of fused plate. If that is so, then there can be no harm in it — but don't pay too much, for them and don't expect them to appreciate in value!

'Bleeding'

The Arrival of Electroplate

Despite the fact that the development of Sheffield plate had considerably reduced the price of high-quality sideboard and table ware, it could not be said that it had yet arrived within the reach of the ordinary working person. It was the invention of electroplating around 1840 that was eventually to put silverware on the tables of almost everyone. The patent for this was first taken out by the firm of Elkington, and differed from Sheffield plate in that the object to be plated was first cast and decorated in an alloy of nickel, copper, and zinc, before being placed in a plating vat to be coated with silver

Left: Celtic Revival cup made in Dublin 1919. *Right*: Heavily chased Monteith cup by Charles Lamb, Dublin c.1905.

by means of an electric current. Electroplating had the advantage not only of cheapness but of the fact that the plated metal was close to the colour of silver and so the problem of the silver layer wearing away to expose the copper beneath was eliminated. In addition, because electroplated silver could be cast, a greater variety of styles and decorations was possible for the maker than had been possible with the fused plate. By the time of the Great Exhibition in 1851, at which a large quantity of electroplate was displayed, it was clear that the new process was here to stay. In a remarkably short time it had almost totally replaced Sheffield plate.

On the collectors' market, although Sheffield plate generally makes higher prices than even nineteenth century electroplate, the latter is still worth buying. In recent years plated cutlery has been much in demand, but consideration should be given to any well-designed nineteenth century item. Many of these are still relatively inexpensive. The main caution is to avoid confusing electroplated pieces, especially wares made in the last quarter of the nineteenth century and the early twentieth century, with older Sheffield plate, because it can be seen that the metal beneath the plating is copper — and thus being led to pay too much for them. A good deal can be learnt by, as always, examining any marks on the piece. Descriptions such as 'Britannia Trade Mark' or, strangely, 'Sheffield Plated' indicate that the object is electroplated. Most electroplate makers punched a special factory mark alongside the initials of the firm: *J.D. & S.* indicated J. Dixon & Sons, while Elkington & Co. used the device of *E. & Co.* with a crown over it. Later twentieth century pieces will, of course, carry the letters *EP* or *EPNS*.

Electroplate Prices

Prices for electroplate pieces vary enormously; starting at just a few pounds, they go up according to age, quality, and condition. A full Victorian tea service made by firms like Elkington's would set you back at least £500. Full sets and canteens of Victorian plated cutlery are much in demand. Cased sets of twelve pearl or bone-handled fishknives with matching forks make from £200, and fruit knives and forks, often very decoratively made, fall into the same price range. The tall claret jug was a very fashionable item on the Victorian table; expect to pay at least £80 for a glass one with good-quality electroplated lid and mounts. Silver-plated tantalus stands and cruet stands with tall cut-glass bottles were also much used, and prices for these, complete with bottles, start at around £100. Good pairs of nineteenth century electroplated candlesticks, while not as expensive as Sheffield plate ones, are still popular, and prices tend to fall between £60 and £100.

Entrée dishes and covers and large platter or meat covers don't appear to be very popular at present. Many tend to be damaged or to have large areas of the silver plate worn off, but undamaged ones are, I think, well worth buying and can make your table look spectacular. I saw a fine oval entrée dish and cover with gadroon edging and a detachable cover sell at a Dublin saleroom not long ago for £50, and at another sale an even better one fetched just £30. I have seen a good pair of rectangular vegetable dishes and covers sell for only £50 and a huge, undamaged high-domed dish cover bought for £35. Matched sets of such covers, especially when marked by a desirable firm such as West's of Dublin, are pricier. A set of four covers, in graduating sizes, retailed or commissioned by West's was recently sold for £420 – but that was still scarcely expensive for some really quite magnificent items.

Single table items such as good-quality teapots, jugs, bowls and biscuit baskets tend to come in the £30 to £50 range, though they are often sold as job lots, in which you must just take pot luck. Cased condiment sets, always useful as wedding presents, start at around £30. Victorian electroplated salvers were often very high-quality pieces with fine engraving or chasing. The larger ones are ideal for use as drinks trays. Prices start at about £15 for very small ones - these would have been used originally by the housemaid or butler for carring visiting cards to the master or mistress - to about £100 for more usefully sized, well-engraved examples. Of course, it is also possible to buy nineteenth-century electroplated trays; good ones tend to hover around the £200 mark. Small Victorian plated items like small dishes, odd candlesticks, muffin dishes, salt cellars and so on seem always to be sold in job lots at auction, and prices for such things generally work out at about £5 or so each, and sometimes less. Names that indicate good-quality work in electroplate are, in addition to Dixon and Elkington, Martin Hall & Co., Mappin & Webb, and Walker & Hall.

Top: William IV machine turned snuff box; Cowrie shell snuff box; coin case. *Middle*: Victorian pocket flask flanked by engraved cigarette cases. *Bottom*: 9 carat gold two compartment sovereign case.

RIGHT: Collection of
Mason's Ironstone jugs.
BELOW: *Left*; Late 19th
century Meissen shepherd
and shepherdess. *Centre*;
One of a pair of Vienna urn
shaped vases. *Right*; One of
a pair of late 19th century
sweetmeat dishes.

Chapter Four

CERAMICS

 he field of ceramics – pottery and porcelain – is extremely wide and complex, perhaps even more so than silver or furniture. Unlike most other antiques, ceramic ware develops no particular signs of aging, and many pieces that were made in the eighteenth and nineteenth centuries still look much the same as they did when they left the factory. The collector is left to rely on markings, the quality and nature of the painting, if any, and the general design of the object in order to decide both its age and the place of manufacture.

Ceramics and the Collector

Factory markings do not present the same guide to buyers of porcelain and pottery as do the hallmarks on silverware. To begin with, many important pieces, especially those from China, carry no markings at all, and in other instances the marks have been faked. During the nineteenth century, for example, many perfectly reputable makers of English ceramics, including Derby and Minton, made pieces in the Meissen style and placed them on the market, complete with spurious Meissen marks! Towards the end of the eighteenth century, at a time when the famous Sèvres porcelain works was coming out of a period of decline, its new management decided to do a clean sweep of undecorated reject ware by putting it on the international market. These undecorated wares continued to be sold off by Sèvres until about 1840. They were bought up by manufacturers in England and elsewhere and subsequently decorated by their own workers. Such objects can be quite difficult for the collector to tell from genuine Sèvres ware. And then there was M. Samson, who made his living by copying everything! His Paris factory, set up in 1845, produced copies of Sèvres, Meissen, Ming, Kakiemon, Bow and almost every other kind of ceramic the market demanded. By and large these were not deliberate forgeries, and very often the linked *SS* symbol of Samson appears beside the false Meissen, Sèvres or other mark. The trouble is that it was, and still is, all too easy to gently sand away Samson's mark, leaving the spurious one behind.

The twentieth century has as many forgers at work in the field of ceramics as did the nineteenth. With valuable pieces the straight fake is, of course, relatively common, and early Wedgwood, Chelsea, Lowestoft and Chinese Tang and Ming ware have all been targeted by the faker. False marks can easily be inscribed on unmarked pieces, and this is a particular danger

Markings

with Chinese ware. Another trick is to erase the painted pattern from an old piece of a rather less desirable design and overpaint it with one that is more marketable. In recent years new techniques of ceramic repair have meant that it is possible to mend even extensively damaged pieces so that the repair is not visible to the naked eye. It is always important to hold ceramics up to a light source when you are examining them. Some repairs are only visible under laboratory examination; but since such repairs are extremely expensive they are generally only applied to the most valuable of pieces and are unlikely to concern the average collector.

It's no wonder, then, that you could spend your life in the study of ceramics and still not know all there is to know. It also means, though, that pottery and porcelain can be among the most fascinating areas of collecting. There is plenty of genuine ware about, and you can start a collection on almost any budget, working your way up the scale as you acquire experience. Irish people in the past do not seem to have purchased very much porcelain. I have noticed, going to house clearance sales, that in many older homes there is just one major porcelain or earthenware service, with Mason's ironstone and Spode and Copeland china being particularly popular, but apart from that there is often surprisingly little to whet the appetite of the ceramics collector. This is undoubtedly changing, and in recent years one comes across good porcelain in houses where pieces have been collected by business or professional people. The modest collector, however, may find that this kind of ware, put together by the newly wealthy, tends to be expensive. For those on limited budgets, saleroom auctions may provide richer pickings, and holidays in Britain can also provide the opportunity to browse through the plentiful selections of ceramics that are on offer there both in shops and in the auction rooms.

In Ireland, too, antique shops can supply a happy hunting ground for the ceramics collector. Take care, though. There are many excellent shops where good dinner and tea services and other decorative pieces can be purchased with confidence, but it has to be said that there are some antique shops where very run-of-the-mill ceramics are sold by dealers with scant knowledge of the field and at grossly inflated prices. The area of ceramics is one, I think, where 'book learning' can be of rather more help to the collector than in some other areas of antique buying. Try to find out as much as possible about the objects that interest you before you start parting with substantial sums of money. Become familiar with the markings on ceramics, if necessary taking a little book on such marks to sale viewings. For British wares a little volume entitled *The Pocket Book of British Ceramic Marks*, (Faber & Faber) is cheap and useful. Also worth having is of Chaffer's *Handbook of Marks on Pottery and Porcelain*, which covers international ceramics.

Irish Ceramics

Just as it would appear that the Irish did not buy very much high-quality ceramic ware, so they did not make very much either, at least before the middle of the nineteenth century. Everyday pottery — earthenware — was manufactured, and excavations at Trim Castle and other sites have confirmed

that much local pottery was in use during the late middle ages and beyond. However, such excavations have also revealed that medieval Ireland was heavily dependent on imported pottery, particularly of the kind known as Ham Green ware, which seems to have been traded through the English port of Bristol. It is clear that French earthenwares were also widely used. Irish pottery seems to have been fairly basic in style but not unattractive: local ware excavated at Trim was found to be very heavy, with brownish-yellow and black-brown glazes.

The number of Irish potteries seems to have expanded during the eighteenth century, but we do not know as much as we would like to about these establishments. It seems likely that the greater number of them were located in the north of Ireland, notably at Ballymacarret near Belfast. The National Museum possesses a ceramic shoe inscribed *MH★R 1724 Belfast*, which appears to have been made at the Leathes factory, established around 1688. Some delftware was made in Dublin during the eighteenth century at a workshop called the Pot House on the North Strand, but this appears to have ceased trading around 1770. In 1752 it had been taken over by a Captain Henry Delamain, and during his ownership the range of wares increased considerably. At one point it seems that enough pieces were being produced to support quite a respectable export business. However, after his death in 1757 sales and production began to falter, and although the house was taken over by James Roche & Co. in 1769, their best efforts could not save the works.

As late as the 1850s such potteries as there were continued to be, in the main, in the north of the country. Not surprisingly, few of the pieces made by the early Irish potteries are likely to find their way into the hands of the private collector, but a number of very interesting pieces are in the collection of the National Museum and are worth looking at. Occasionally pieces by the Delamain factory do turn up at auction. Towards the end of

In autumn 1992, a similar dish, definitely attributed to Delamain, sold for £1,500.

1991 a pair of plates was offered for sale in London and made over £4,000, and some weeks before that an early Irish blue-and-white octagonal dish that could conceivably have come from the Delamain works was sold at a Kilkenny house clearance for £650.

During the eighteenth century a number of shops opened in Dublin for the sale of fine ceramics from abroad. Among these was one owned by the famous Josiah Wedgwood, who also for a time maintained a small workshop in Dublin where special painting and decoration could be carried out on pieces ordered by customers in the city. Another important shop was that of James Donovan of George's Quay. He had his name painted on a number of the pieces he sold, but there is no evidence that he actually made ceramics himself.

Belleek

The famous factory at Belleek, Co. Fermanagh, was not opened until about 1857, and full production seems to have begun around 1863. The factory was set up to manufacture porcelain, made out of local feldspar and kaolin but the porcelain body was not perfected until the middle of the 1860s. Until that time, earthenware was produced, and, contrary to popular belief, earthenware and not porcelain was the mainstay of the factory for much of its existence, not ceasing to be made until 1947. In 1863 William Bromley, who worked with the Stoke-on-Trent firm of W. H. Goss, arrived in Ireland with at least twelve experienced craftsmen to begin the manufacture of the porcelain for which Belleek was to become world-famous.

Not surprisingly, the style of early Belleek was influenced by the wares of the Stoke factory. The characteristic glaze of Belleek porcelain was, and still is, what is termed nacreous, which means that it is iridescent, reflecting the colours of the light. The finest products of the Belleek factory are generally held to be the woven porcelain baskets with their applied flowers, all of which are hand-made. Even more rare - partly, no doubt, because of their extreme fragility - are fine cake plates that take the form of a spider's web. At auction, prices for these objects start at around £2,000. Rare and highly sought after are Belleek figures and busts, generally made in a white Parian material. A fine Parian bust of the 'Queen of the Hops' has been sold for well over £1,000, and a first-period figure of a woman holding a basket on her head, sold with another damaged figure, took £1,500 at a recent sale.

Belleek Marks

The collector will generally find Belleek pieces described in sales catalogues as being of a particular period. The most highly priced are wares of the 'first period', which lasted from 1863 to 1891. Marks include *Belleek Co. Fermanagh, Fermanagh Pottery* and a crowned harp device. Later wares include the words *Ireland* and *Co. Fermanagh* and show the device of the hound, tower and harp with the word *Belleek* beneath.

Not all Belleek ware makes very high prices and there is plenty around for the modest collector. Undamaged early or first-period pieces can be expensive, especially if they are the desirable figures and baskets, but many small pieces are quite reasonable. Items such as single candlesticks, small jugs and saucers can be got for under £50. Vases are more expensive, with prices starting at several hundred pounds, and you could expect to pay about £400 for a first-period teapot. Quite rare and very attractive are the Belleek beehive-shaped honeypots: £400 to £500 for the first-period examples. Belleek early earthenware may also be found; prices start at around £50 for single items such as plates and dishes. Second-period pieces, again aside from rarities, will in general be affordable by the modest collector. Vases start at between £100 and £200 and teapots at about £60. The very attractive pink-and-white glazed teapots may cost a little more, with prices at around £80. For a shell-pattern teaset, comprising teapot, jug, and sugar bowl you could pay about £300 to £450. Small dishes can be got from £50.

Slightly damaged pieces of first and second-period Belleek can be got more cheaply, and if they are still functional and attractive and you like them, there is no reason why you shouldn't buy. But don't pay too much, and bear in mind that such pieces are really for your own enjoyment and cannot be seen as an investment. This may not always apply to truly rare pieces; some examples are so highly sought after that even some damage does not prevent high prices being reached. But in general, if you want your purchases to increase in value, you will have to seek out perfection, and pay for it.

Oriental Porcelain

Because of the limited amount of Irish pottery and porcelain on the market, it is inevitable that most of the ceramic ware the Irish collector is concerned with will have been made in England, continental Europe, or the Far East. Early English delft and pottery is not often seen in Ireland, and Dutch delft too is relatively uncommon. As a modest collector you will find that most of what you can afford will be nineteenth-century English and Continental ware and, from China, the type of popular export pieces made towards the end of the nineteenth century that are generally described as Cantonese. The Japanese ware known as Imari (not because this was the name of its manufacturer but because it was exported through the port of that name) also embraces a large selection of reasonably priced ceramics.

Chinese
Porcelain

Porcelain was invented by the Chinese in the ninth century, and by the eighteenth century more than a million people were employed in its manufacture. It was during the sixteenth century that Europe began to import large quantities of porcelain from China, and during the following century a seemingly inexhaustible craze for blue-and-white ware fed demand. It was not until the eighteenth century that coloured, or polychrome, wares began to be imported into Europe in large numbers, and some of the finest pieces on the European market date from this period.

The nineteenth century marked a serious decline in the quality of export ware. The designs became rather uninventive, and were often poorly executed copies of earlier patterns. Many are quite attractive, though, and for the modest and even, given recent price trends, the not-so-modest buyer they offer a wide range of collectable porcelain at a variety of prices.

When you first become interested in Chinese porcelain you may be puzzled by some of the terms used to describe the pieces: famille verte, famille rose, wucai, ducai, and so forth. These simply refer to the colour range, or palette, employed in the decoration of the piece. The most common is famille rose, which may include blue, yellow and green but is always partly coloured in rose-pink enamel. Famille verte is a little older, having been devised during the seventeenth century, and includes iron-red, yellow,

SOME EXAMPLES OF CHINA MARKS

BELLEEK
1857 onwards

BLOOR DERBY
1815 1840

SEVRES

blue

COPELAND
1847

1847

COPELAND & GARRETT
1833

1847-1891

NEW
FAYENCE
1833-1847

SPODE
1770

1770-1797

impressed
1784

SPODE & COPELAND
1813

SPODE SON
& COPELAND

SPODE & COPELAND
1813-1833

DAVENPORT
1793-1882

VIENNA
1719 1864

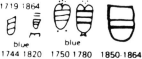

blue   blue
1744 1820   1750 1780   1850-1864   modern

DOULTON
1815

pre 1836   1872

WEDGWOOD
1730 1795

Wedgwood

W. & B.

Wedgwood
& Bentley

WEDGWOOD

modern

MASONS
1795-1854

WORCESTER

Dr Wall 1751-1783

Flight 1783-1793

Flight&Barr 1793-1807

MEISSON
1713

1713-1724

1725-1750

modern

BFB
1807 1829

1850

1851

MINTON
1793 onwards

1800-1836

1851

1860-1880

ROCKINGHAM

blue-purple and always a strong, brilliant green. Famille jaune has a dominant yellow ground, while famille noir has a black background, sometimes unglazed. The ducai palette comprises blue, red, yellow, green, and a dull purple. And if, having read this, you despair of ever being able to remember the different combinations, then don't worry. It won't really interfere with your enjoyment of Chinese porcelain, and in any case even the Chinese did not always apply the palettes wholly consistently. Another term you will frequently come across in relation to Chinese porcelain is 'armorial' ware. These pieces, which are much in demand at auction today, were originally made to order for wealthy families in Europe and included the family coat of arms in the design.

On international markets, Chinese pottery and porcelain of the earlier dynastic periods, such as the Tang (618-907), during which porcelain was developed, and the Sung (960-1279,) are extremely important. The Tang period is particularly associated with the production of beautifully modelled pottery horses, and for these, prices can easily reach as much as £20,000. During the Song dynasty celadon ware was developed, a thickly potted ceramic with a characteristic greenish glaze that, though rather pale in shade, still has an extraordinary depth of colour. The use of this kind of glaze continued to be popular during the succeeding centuries, partly, it seems, because it was widely believed that celadon could reveal the presence of poisoned food. Customers both in China and in the west remained anxious to get their hands on this salutary product, and versions of such wares are still made today. A good Sung dynasty celadon dish could cost £10,000, but nineteenth century celadon dishes and plates should be available from around £100 upwards, with small, undamaged vases being somewhat more.

During the Ming dynasty (1368-1644) the art of painting porcelain in a palette of different-coloured enamels was developed, and it was also from this time that the production of Chinese porcelain expanded with an extraordinary rapidity. It seems to have been the Dutch East India Company that first brought large quantities to Europe, at first mainly blue-and-white wares and then later the whole range of brilliantly coloured palettes. Under the Ching or Manchu dynasty, which ruled from 1644 to 1911 the porcelain industry, though it continued to produce and export many fine pieces, saw a gradual drift towards mass production and a certain rigidity in design.

Prices for Chinese porcelain range from just a few pounds to hundreds of thousands, with Ming porcelain being the 'bread and butter' of the serious side of the international trade. The top end of the market is subject to unexpected fluctuations, triggered by such things as the state of the dollar or uncertainty in the business world of Hong Kong, where most of the important sales of oriental ceramics are held. Luckily the small buyer does not have to worry about such things, and at present you should be able to find such items as small Cantonese tea trays and teapots at between £50 and £75, ginger-jars from £60 to £80 and 'Nanking' (Nanjing) blue-and-white dishes from about £120 a pair. Good Cantonese famille rose plates work out at around £100, and they regularly come in sets, often of six and sometimes of eight. The price rises if the quality of enamelling or the interest of the scenes depicted is unusual. Well-decorated small Cantonese dishes can cost up to £200 or so; an attractive bowl could be twice as expensive.

Chinese Porcelain

Prices

Chinese blue and white baluster jar and cover with dog finial to cover.

Tall Cantonese baluster vases are probably the most popular items of Chinese porcelain among Irish collectors, and they are most desirable in pairs. A simple late nineteenth-century baluster vase of, say, eighteen inches in height and without a cover or attractively moulded handles would cost perhaps £300 at auction. As the quality of painting and the richness of the enamels increases so do prices, and pairs of high vases with handles, reaching thirty or so inches in height, cost between £2,000 and £4,000. The presence of original covers on baluster vases increases the price, and cracking or other damage can reduce the value of a piece considerably.

The prices paid for the better pieces of Chinese porcelain, however, shouldn't deter you from developing your interests. For the slender of pocket, multiple lots of small pieces are well worth looking out for, and useful and decorative wares can often be bought surprisingly cheaply, particularly on occasions when fairly large amounts of Chinese porcelain are being offered for auction. At a large country house sale held recently I saw a selection of six Chinese cups of varying patterns sold for just £50 the lot; two Cantonese teapots made £65, and a pair of blue-and-white jars and covers was sold along with a Nanking sauce tureen and cover for £200. You will occasionally come across rather high, deep bowls, usually painted in strong background enamels, such as famille jaune, and weighing rather heavily. Very often these will be described in your catalogue as jardinieres, or potted plant containers. In China, however, many bowls of this sort were used as goldfish bowls, and if you peer inside you will sometimes spy scattered paintings of fishes. Prices for these range from several hundred pounds each to several thousand for well-decorated and undamaged pairs.

Japanese ceramics don't display such a colourful variety of palettes as the Chinese wares, and they do not seem to be as popular in Ireland with collectors, although high prices are paid for really fine pieces. The popular market tends to be dominated by Imari and Satsuma ware. Imari porcelain was made at the town of Arita, and the palette tends to be characterised by blue, orange-red, and some gilding. It was rarely if ever marked, and none of it dates from before the seventeenth century, when the Japanese porcelain industry was founded by an immigrant Korean potter. Prices for all but the best Imari are generally fairly modest at auction. A richly decorated charger, a large plate usually hung on a wall or shown as a centrepiece on a cabinet, could cost £600 or so, but small vases and covers can be got for about £50, with more for pairs, and nineteenth-century cylindrical vases cost much the same. Be careful of paying too much for modern copies, which are very often seen.

Satsuma ware is not porcelain but earthenware with a warm cream background and enamelling in red, blue, and gold. Much nineteenth-century Satsuma is painted in floral designs in which the flowers are not unlike those of the millefiore paperweights of France. Prices start at around £50 for

Japanese
Ceramics

The vase second from left is Japanese, the remainder Chinese. At each end is one of a pair of typical but good quality Cantonese vases, one with some damage to the rim.

modest bowls and jars, but several thousand pounds could be paid for a good-sized vase depicting an interesting scene or object.

Noritake

At house clearances you may come across a type of Japanese porcelain marked *Noritake*. This was a factory set up at the end of the nineteenth century to supply mass produced porcelain to the European market. Very often the pieces were made to western designs, and they tend to be rather despised by collectors for their predictable flower patterns and unsubtly painted borders. However, not all the products of the factory are as dreadful as all that, and early examples may be worth looking out for. I own a small Noritake ashtray quite attractively painted with a typically Japanese seascape; and some of the Noritake tea services are very pleasantly decorated. They are not expensive to buy - you could pick up a tea set for as little as £25 - so keep an eye open for the better-painted wares. Early ones carry a mark rather like a very skinny crab or scorpion, and many have *Noritake* printed on them. Pieces from later in the century may carry *Made in Japan* and they are still being manufactured today.

European Porcelain

It took Europe almost a thousand years to crack the secret of porcelain making, and it is not surprising that in a continent with a mania for all things Chinese, the early European makers strove to make their wares look as oriental as possible. During the eighteenth and nineteenth centuries many European factories turned out an endless stream of copies of Chinese and Japanese ceramics. It seems the secret of porcelain making was discovered in Europe, after many fruitless efforts, virtually by accident. In 1701 the Elector Augustus of Saxony employed a young chemist called Johann Bottger to try to produce gold artificially. Needless to say the experiment was not a success, and it was decided to attempt the production of synthetic gemstones instead. By about 1707 Bottger had come up with a hard substance made from red clay, which he displayed and polished as if it were a jewel. Perhaps he hoped that the world and, more importantly, his patron would take this material for a real gemstone. In this he was destined to be disappointed, but during the following months, by means of experiments in which he employed white instead of red clay, the young chemist found himself the inventor of the first hard-paste porcelain to be produced in Europe. The substance was manufactured from the same ingredients that the Chinese had used and guarded so well: kaolin, the fine white clay to mould the pot, and feldspar, the stone of the same material, which produced the glaze. One of the great advantages of the new material was that it could be hardened and glazed in one firing.

Neither Bottger nor Augustus was slow to appreciate the importance of what had been found, and by 1710 the Elector had set up the factory at Meissen, which soon began to produce fine porcelain pieces in the oriental style. The porcelain figures for which, perhaps, Meissen is most famous began to be made very soon afterwards, one of the first being, not inappropriately, a small figure of the Elector Augustus himself. The manufacture of porcelain at Meissen continued to be veiled in secrecy for a time, with workmen frequently living in forced isolation and with severe punishment meted out to those who tried to escape. All was in vain; within a few years porcelain factories had begun to mushroom all over Germany, France, and England, quickly gaining confidence in the new product and turning out wares not only in the oriental style but in new, native patterns as well.

It's unlikely that the modest collector can aspire to ownership of pieces of the earliest Meissen, but you should be familiar with the name of J. J. Kändler, probably the most talented modeller in porcelain who ever lived. He is best known for his figures, yet it was probably as a result of his work on the vast 'Swan' service made for Saxony's chief minister, Count Bruhl, that he first came to the attention of many of the wealthy patrons of Europe. This service contained over two thousand individual pieces, of which the great beauty lay not in the painting which was in fact sparing, but in the superb quality of the moulded decoration that embellished the various bowls, dishes, tureens, candlesticks, platters and cups that made up the set. The service was completed in 1741, and by the following year Kändler was working on a series of vases for King Louis XV of France. In 1742 he had made a statuette of the Russian empress, Elizabeth II, seated on horseback; she must have been pleased with the work, for two years later she ordered a set of large vases, mainly modelled in the white, to be made by Kändler.

The most popular of Kändler's works are probably what are known as the 'crinoline' groups, which centred on women in colourful, billowing skirts. These models are usually vividly painted, as are the series of figures that many collectors feel to be his finest: his theatrical models from the Italian Comedy, which include all the well-loved characters such as Harlequin, Columbine, and Scaramouche. Also connected with Kändler is the famous 'Monkey Orchestra', made in 1747, possibly as a joke at the expense of the orchestra maintained by Bruhl. The full set consisted of twenty-five monkeys, seven being the work of Kändler and eighteen by Peter Reinicke.

They are extraordinarily skilfully modelled, with each monkey face having an amusing character all its own. I have seen some of these for sale in Ireland, but they are, not surprisingly, very expensive, and naturally the more that are gathered into one collection the more expensive they become. Individual figures from Kändler's Italian Comedy on the international market sell for £5,000 upwards; Harlequin seems to be the most desirable, and some of Kändler's originals sell for between £30,000 and £50,000. Fine crinoline groups can make just as much.

This kind of figure was copied by other porcelain factories - notably Fulda, Vienna, Ludwigsburg, and Fürstenburg - but figures from these factories would scarcely be less expensive than the original Meissen. The Monkey Orchestra was copied by the English Chelsea factory in 1756, but sets of these too would be a great rarity.

These prices, of course, only apply to the very best products of the eighteenth-century porcelain factories. Many of them also sold scaled-down or less elaborately decorated versions of these pieces, and some of these may be affordable by the smaller collector today. A few years ago many such pieces would have been sold at auction for a couple of hundred pounds, but that situation has changed in recent times with many even of the simpler Meissen figures of the middle and late eighteenth century selling at around £2,500 or so. Even nineteenth-century copies of Kändler's 'Cries of Paris' are now making around £600 apiece. If you can afford such objects, do be careful to examine them thoroughly at views for repaired cracks, later decoration, and hidden restoration. At these prices it begins to become worth while to apply a little skilful workmanship to damaged pieces.

Staffordshire figures.

During the nineteenth century, many versions of the eighteenth century figures were made not just by Meissen itself but by most of the German factories. The best are not cheap, but lots of them are both attractive and reasonably priced. Good Meissen figures tend to start around £500, with well-decorated plates and dishes obtainable from about £200 each. Vienna wares are very much liked by Irish collectors, and a seventeen piece tea set recently made £1,000 at auction, and a pair of Vienna comports with matching urn made £620. Irish buyers also like nineteenth-century Meissen basket-style dishes, with £520 being paid lately for a matched pair. Single cups and saucers are an ideal way to begin a collection of nineteenth-century porcelain. A Vienna or Meissen matched cup and saucer would probably cost just over £100, with Sèvres pieces fetching similar amounts. Incidentally, you could probably buy an English cup and saucer from, say, the Worcester or the Derby factory for about half the price of the Continental example, and it would often be just as attractive.

English Ceramics

In England many factories during the eighteenth century used what is called a soft-paste porcelain, a mixture of white clay and ground glass, rather than the hard-paste variety made from the kaolin clay and stone. This did not mean an inferior product, however; indeed, the softer, more subtle appearance of the decoration of soft-paste is preferred by many collectors. At the end of the eighteenth century it was discovered that the soft-paste formula was improved by the addition of calcinated animal bones, and so bone china, the staple of the British porcelain industry, was born. Bone china is generally agreed to have been first made by the Spode factory. By the early 1820s it was being widely manufactured, with the chief advantage being that it could be made fairly cheaply and with fewer losses during firing than with soft-paste porcelain.

Good eighteenth-century English porcelain is really very seldom found at Irish sales. A strongly painted Derby service dating from between 1800 and 1848, the end of what is known as the Bloor Derby period, would probably cost between £2,000 and £5,000, depending on the number of pieces in the suite, the quality of the painting, and the number of major items, such as tureens, dishes and covers, comports, and so on. An eighteenth-century Derby teapot on its own could cost over £500, again depending on quality and decoration. Some Derby porcelain was produced with rather insipid floral painting; these wares are not so well liked, at least by the Irish collector. For example, an early nineteenth-century Derby dinner service painted with a scattering of small flowers on a white background was recently sold for just £750. As the suite comprised forty-six pieces, and included a large tureen and stand, various large dishes and bowls, and half a dozen meat platters of useful size, as well as the usual soup and dinner plates, I would say that this represented very good value.

Worcester

For many people English porcelain means Worcester wares, and it is true that many of the most attractive examples of soft-paste and bone china were produced there. Spectacularly coloured wares were produced at Worcester from the middle of the eighteenth century, the most striking being those that included a strong blue ground, and they are highly sought after by today's collectors. Care has to be taken if buying these, for it appears that there are a good many fakes and later copies, and the Samson factory copied them in large numbers. The buyer of large services needs to be most wary, of course, but you will find that you can take your chances when buying single items like cups and saucers, which can be purchased from about £50 for odd examples. Plates are generally more expensive, as they can be decoratively displayed more easily; nevertheless, I recently saw two Worcester plates, one with strong blue and gilt ground and painted with an exotic bird, selling at a Dublin sale for just £90. Pieces of all kinds from the Flight and Barr period at Worcester (in its various partnerships, dating from 1783 to 1840) are in very strong demand at present, but even so it's still possible to buy a cup, saucer and plate for about £120 at auction, while richly decorated plates can be got for around £100 for odd ones. Dinner services from the Flight and Barr period are expensive, and several thousand pounds could be spent on even a part set of plates and dishes; and for pairs of urns and vases prices start close to the £4,000 mark.

The Chamberlain factory at Worcester was set up as a breakaway from the Flight factory in 1783, and its best wares were produced during the period 1810-1830. The rarest Chamberlain porcelain is expensive, but for their more ordinary products, prices at auctions are often rather less than those for Flight and Barr, so they can make a very good buy for the small collector. In general the painting on Chamberlain ware is more restrained than that on Flight and Barr, but for some modern collectors this may be all the more pleasing. Pairs of plates may be purchased from about £120 a pair, odd jugs from about £300 or so depending on design (particularly interesting is a range of wares by Chamberlain showing views of Worcester), and teapots for around the same sum. More luxurious, heavily painted pieces are more expensive. A large sucrier (tureen-style sugar bowl) could make up to £1,000, and a large pot and cover would probably make more.

Grainger's factory at Worcester was yet another breakaway establishment, this time from Chamberlain's, where Thomas Grainger, a sales manager, defected around 1806. The main object of the new factory seems to have been the less affluent mass market, and many of their routine wares were unmarked. The better-quality, marked pieces can be expensive for the collector. A good mug or tankard could cost £1,000, and recently that sum was paid for a twelve-piece rococo-style Grainger's dessert service painted in a variety of flowers.

The products of the nineteenth-century factories of Spode, Wedgwood, Davenport, Ridgeway and many of the smaller works offer collecting possibilities to buyers of all means. In addition, many products, especially of the Staffordshire firms, were unmarked, but to the modest buyer keeping a lookout for quality they can mean good buys at fairly small cost. Wedgwood is seen often in Ireland, although the collector may be forgiven for imagining that Irish buyers of the past had a particular passion for that factory's green leaf-shaped dishes. Spode will be encountered from time to time at house clearances, usually in the form of substantial dinner services. These are popular with private buyers and can be expensive. A very good feldspar Spode tea and coffee service sold at a recent house sale for £1,800. Ridgeway wares are less often seen, but they are worth looking out for, because they were a very important firm that employed several outstandingly

Part of a Flight Barr and Barr dinner service.

talented ceramic painters, notably George Hancock and Joseph Bancroft. The Ridgeway factory began in 1808 and continued under the Ridgeway name until 1855, when it was taken over by Bates, Brown-Westhead, and Moore. Many of the early wares were, alas, unmarked, although they may carry pattern marks. The firm made some superb dinner services, working to royal and aristocratic commissions, but odd pieces can be purchased fairly modestly; a very fine Ridgeway tureen cover and stand decorated with flowers and wide peach-coloured bands was sold lately at a Dublin sale for £420.

Mason's Ironstone

Not a porcelain but important in the enthusiasm it arouses in modern collectors is Mason's Ironstone. Indeed, it may even be that these ceramics are slightly more expensive here in Ireland than in Britain, such is the demand for them at sales. I am going to risk uttering a heresy here, because it has long been my opinion, that considering the quantity of Mason's that was originally made and still exists, and given the similarity of so many of the wares and the fact that it is still being made today, Mason's Ironstone is rather overpriced in today's market. Dinner and part dinner services seem to make as much money at house sales as do porcelain suites, and often more, yet the porcelain wares are usually better potted, better moulded and better painted than the Mason's wares, which were, by the way, not originally intended to be a luxury product at all, in the way that porcelain was. Indeed it was originally conceived of as a product aimed at those who could not afford porcelain and the firm advertised as one of ironstone's advantages the fact that it could stand up to the heat of ovens and to other hazards of the kitchen

Part of a Chamberlain Worcester Imari style tea and coffee service.

and the servants' hall. Some finer luxury wares were produced, in the form of vases, urns, and decorative plaques for the drawing–room, yet one suspects that many of the large services that wealthy buyers are now so eager to acquire were originally purchased for use below rather than above stairs! Even single items of Mason's, such as the ubiquitous octagonal jugs, and single plates and bowls, now regularly make more than English porcelain equivalents from the same period. It's my view that such porcelain offers the collector better value for money, but I am aware that, at the moment, I am in a minority!

Mason's Ironstone

The patent for Mason's Ironstone was taken out by Charles James Mason in 1813, although it's generally agreed that it was his father, Miles Mason, who invented the process. Ironstone was a strong earthenware, made from clay with the addition of a glassy slag-based substance that came from the local ironworks. In 1815 the firm of Mason's moved to the Fenton Stone Works, where a vast array of products was made: full services, jug sets, toilet sets, hip baths, and even bedposts. Fireplaces too were made, generally with a white background and colourful leaf and flower patterns. Much of the inspiration for the designs was taken from oriental porcelain, but Mason's colours were stronger, tending sometimes to the garish, with warm orange and deep blue being especially favoured.

Despite the popular success of his ironstone, Charles James went bankrupt in 1848, and both his mansion and the pottery works were sold. A few years later he re-started his business at a new location but was unable to make it financially viable and was finally forced to give up the attempt in 1853, three years before his death. This was not the end of Mason's Ironstone, however, for the factory of Geoffrey Ashworth came into possession of Mason's drawings and moulds towards the end of the 1850s and began to make pieces according to Charles James's designs. The Ashworth company continued to mark the wares as Mason's, using the name over a crown with the words *Patent Ironstone China* set into a banner below. The word *England* was added in 1891, and makes a useful aid to dating. From 1957 there was a new mark: the name *Mason's* over a tree and, beneath, *Patent Ironstone, Made in England*.

Sets of Mason's are, as I have said, expensive, although, as often with sets and services, the prices for the individual items bought this way can average out at a fairly modest sum. For example, a dinner service of around a hundred pieces should be obtainable for £3,000 to £5,000, that is, between £30 and £50 per piece. Toilet sets of between six and twelve pieces tend to sell for around £500, especially if they include their chamber pot. I may say that on a day when I saw a Mason's set sell for precisely that amount at a house sale, I noticed that a very attractive Minton majolica toilet set, which included a slop pail and cover and a large jug and basin, along with a number of smaller items, was picked up by another buyer for just £150. This was painted with a yellow ground and birds perched on branches, and I would have preferred it to the Mason's!

The octagonal jugs, usually printed in a quasi-oriental design with vibrant colours, tend to sell for around £110 each. Buying them in groups of three and four doesn't seem to affect the price much; I've seen three sold for £320 and, at the same sale, four for £400. Occasionally the larger jugs can rise to £250 to £300. In the more usual floral designs, single Mason's meat dishes make £150 or so, but there are some rarer patterns that make more. These would generally include the landscape paintings, which for really scarce ones, like the Durham Ox, could make up to £1,000.

Wemyss Ware

This lovely pottery is Scottish, and it has a small but dedicated following in Britain, where prices can be quite high. There is not a great deal of it in Ireland, but when it does turn up at auction it tends to attract a lot of interest, although prices are usually not quite so high as they are in Britain. So it could represent a good long-term buy for the Irish collector. It is an exceptionally fragile ware, fired at low kiln temperatures, and this partly accounts for the rarity of good undamaged pieces. Typical Wemyss (pronounced 'weemz') ware went into production around 1881 when an artist named Karel Nikola was employed at the Fife Pottery to teach native artists the techniques of ceramic decoration. The wares became known for their bold, rich design, especially the use of large pink and deep-red cabbage roses. Model animals were made in some quantity, the most common and the most popular being rather tall cats and rather fat pigs. Pieces are generally marked. The Fife Pottery lasted until 1930, although an English firm, Bovey Tracy, took over some of the designs and continued a limited production until 1952.

Highest prices for Wemyss ware are given for the pigs and cats. Prices for very simple examples start at around £250, with really rare ones making several thousand. Of the pigs, the very simplest make around £200, rising to a couple of thousand for the largest and best. The most desirable ones are those painted with cabbage roses; a fairly modest one, six inches long, sold at a recent sale for £360. Inkstands are occasionally seen, and they make around £250. Many of the single dishes, pots, candlesticks, ring stands and

Shelley Art Nouveau black glazed vase.

jugs are actually the surviving members of the toilet or washstand sets that Wemyss made in quite large numbers and that became very fashionable for a period in the late nineteenth century. Full sets are very rarely seen, even in Britain, and curiously enough, the last one I saw come up for auction was at a saleroom in Ireland. There were ten pieces, presumably from an original twelve, for there were no jugs, and normally in good Victorian sets there were two. Nevertheless it did include a large baisin, a chamber pot, two large tin trays, and two candlesticks, along with the smaller items. The final bid was £1,300, so it represented good value to the buyer, especially as it was in the desirable cabbage rose pattern.

Beginning to Collect

Many collectors of pottery and porcelain buy in what might be called a thematic way, in that they confine themselves to the products of one factory, or one period, or perhaps they just collect figurines or animals, teapots or plates. This reflects the sheer breadth and complexity of the whole field, for if you want to spend your money wisely you must be fairly knowledgeable, and you cannot be an expert on everything. During your initial reading, your interest is bound to be aroused by some kinds of ceramics more than by others, and it is great fun to go out to auction views to see if you can find any examples of what you have been reading about. Unfortunately as a modest buyer you are going to find that much about which you have learnt is out of your financial reach, especially at first. Single pieces of Worcester, Meissen or Berlin may be all that can be managed, but you shouldn't overlook the many colourful and attractive wares from the nineteenth and early twentieth century that, although they do not bear the marks of the great factories, can be very collectable and useful all the same. The products of the Stanley or the Jones factories, of the Adderley or the David Chapman works, offer you the chance to buy very attractive pieces and even whole services at a cost far less than that of modern china. Also reasonable are many of the Doulton speciality items and 19th-century Staffordshire figures, which are a surprisingly absorbing collecting area where prices start around £30.

In Ireland several ceramics factories have produced some very attractive wares, which the collector with an eye to the future might now think of buying. Among these would be the special decorative plates made by the Arklow pottery, which range from special editions with Celtic designs to older pieces featuring ladies and gentlemen in period dress. Early Royal Tara pieces might be of interest too, but look for the best designs. Some interesting Art Deco objects were made by the Carrigaline pottery during the late 1920s and 1930s and would, I think, be a very good buy now. Good art and studio pottery is worth considering, too, and of the most recent potteries I suspect that the products of the Moss factory in Co. Kilkenny, might please your children or your grandchildren. They are based on the designs painted on a very old type of earthenware called spongeware, and are extremely decorative.

It need not always be a mistake to buy damaged items, provided that you have observed the damage beforehand and are allowing for it in the price you pay. Sometimes it can be a way for you to actually get your hands on a real piece of Meissen, Sèvres, or early Derby. If the damage is not too visible

Staffordshire Figures

Little Red Riding Hood and the Wolf

Toby Jug.

Red Riding Hood

ABOVE: *Left to right*: 19th century Chinese Imari style plate; one of 25 French painted Meissen dessert plates; Chinese blue and white plate. BELOW: *Left to right*; Belleek tulip vase; early Belleek scallop shaped plate; first period Belleek wall plaque; second period Belleek plate; second period Belleek tree stump vase.
Centre: Second period Belleek jardiniere.
Bottom: First period Belleek basket.

such pieces can be perfectly functional, and you can learn a great deal from handling them. One problem you may come across if you buy cracked pieces is that dirt has lodged in the crack, making the piece rather ugly to use. You could try soaking it for a couple of hours in a solution of detergent and cool water at a strength of about one dessertspoonful to a pint. This is unlikely to clear the grime entirely but it should improve matters. For pieces you have bought in one or more broken segments, modern epoxy resin is extremely effective and doesn't stain like the older animal glues. Choose a glue that is formulated for china, use it sparingly, and wind around a little adhesive tape to hold things together while the glue sets. It should go without saying that you must leave the repair of all valuable ceramics to a professional.

Chapter Five

GLASS

t the time of writing, the antique glass market is rather intriguing. After years in which old glass, apart from Waterford and other antique crystal items, seemed to arouse little interest and modest prices, it lately seems as if something is stirring. Between 1988 and 1990 there was a pronounced increase in the demand for all quality antique glass and prices seemed to be shooting up. By 1991 the downturn in the antiques trade seemed to have dampened matters somewhat, and at a major Dublin house clearance that included a large glass section, prices were staying within and even a little below estimate. Compared with the international market, old glass seems to be rather undervalued in Ireland, and it is likely that as soon as the trade recovers, glass prices will continue to go up. So it may be a good time to buy!

The History of Glass

Glassmaking has a very ancient history, and it seems that glass beads were first made about five thousand years ago in the middle east. Almost two thousand years were to pass before craftworkers discovered how to make glass vessels, and it was not until the Romans invented the blowpipe around 50 BC that glass became available to any but the wealthiest individuals. The arrival of glass blowing is associated with the development of colourless glass; before that, most glass objects were coloured, because of the difficulty of eliminating impurities from the materials used. Until the eighteenth century glass remained expensive. For one thing, the process of manufacture was still unreliable, resulting in much reject ware. As well as that, the early glassmakers had great difficulty in obtaining consistent and sufficient supplies of fuel for their furnaces. It has to be remembered that glassmakers need to heat their furnaces to temperatures of more than 1,000 degrees Celsius - no easy matter before the age of cheap coal arrived in the nineteenth century.

The chief ingredient of glass is sand or, formerly, flints. To this is added a substance that lowers the melting-point of the sand to around 1,000 degrees, usually potash or sodium carbonate. The combination of sand and sodium produces what was known as soda glass, and it was this sort of glass that comprised most of the everyday ware of the eighteenth and nineteenth centuries. Lime was also added to the metal, as the glassmakers called it, to make it more stable.

Lead crystal, so closely associated with the Irish glass industry, was not developed until the seventeenth century. It was first patented in England, | Lead Crystal

Lead Crystal

where in 1674 George Ravenscroft, a London merchant, displayed his method of making glass to which was added a proportion of lead oxide, resulting in a product that resembled 'rock crystal'. It was clearer and more durable than conventional glass, and more suitable for engraving and deep cutting. Early attempts to make Ravenscroft's glass resulted in 'crizzling', a process where the surface of the glass breaks down, but within a few years this problem had been overcome. During the eighteenth century the proportion of lead used in such crystal could be as high as 36%; nowadays full lead crystal, such as Waterford, contains 30% lead. Continental crystal, from quite an early date, contained as little as 20%, making it relatively easy to tell, simply by weight, the Continental from the Irish or English product.

Irish Glass

Not long after Ravenscroft perfected his technique, the first lead crystal to be manufactured in Ireland appeared. This was produced at a glassworks called the Round Glass House, which was founded around 1700 by Captain Roche and Christopher and Richard Fitzsimons at a site near St Mary's Lane, Dublin. However, after the early years of its existence the Round Glass House seems to have contented itself with marketing imported ware, as did another establishment in Fleet Street, also set up – in 1734 – for the manufacture of table glass. One of the great problems for the Irish glass houses was that, as the glassmaking materials were imported from England, it was very difficult to produce Irish-made glass at competitive prices.

A more successful enterprise was the Charles Mulvaney Glass House, established in 1785 at Potter's Alley, Dublin, and offering a full range of tableware 'from first process to finishing'. Mulvaney seems to have marked some of his pieces with the inscription *C.M. and Co.,* and two dishes survive that bear this mark. However, as we know that the glass house produced 'glasses, decanters, goblets for the sideboard, epergnes, bowles' and other objects, it seems likely that other pieces by the company exist but, like so much eighteenth and nineteenth-century glass, were unmarked. Mulvaney's successor at the glass house was his partner Edward Irwin, whose family managed the business until 1863, when it was taken over by the famous Pugh family. The Pughs manufactured both crystal and a wide range of coloured ware, much of it exported, and they employed several skilled engravers. Many personalised pieces were made to order, some inscribed with the owner's name and many carrying popular mottoes such as *Erin go Bragh*. The National Museum houses a good collection of Pugh glass, and for those anxious to acquire more knowledge of these wares and, indeed, other Irish glass, the museum has published some very useful material.

Although much everyday glass made by Pugh must appear unnoticed on the antiques market, the Irish Revival style of glass made by them or in their manner is both distinctive and popular. Engraved motifs include round towers, wolfhounds, harps, shamrocks, and sprays of fern. The most attractive pieces decorated in this style were their tapering or baluster water and claret jugs, although these engravings occur on goblets and tumblers as well. Prices for these pieces – and they do not appear at auction all that often – would be from about £180 for the jugs and a little less for goblets.

Cork Glass

A glassworks whose products are highly sought after by collectors was the Cork Glass House, founded in 1782. A wide range of objects was offered by this company: lustres, lamps, rummers or stemmed drinking-glasses, wine coolers, pickle glasses, and much more. The firm did mark some of its pieces on the base — but beware: there are fakes about, particularly decanters. Like virtually all Irish glass houses, the Cork company sold many unmarked objects, and these are ideal candidates for the inscribing of false marks attributing them to a house that is in demand by collectors. As in most fields of collecting, marked pieces carry a higher premium than unmarked ones. An Irish glass dish with moderately elaborate cutting, dating from, say, 1800 would probably fetch about £200; with the mark of the Cork Glass Co. on its base it could make several times that.

Another famous Cork glass house, the Waterloo Glass Company, was founded by Daniel Foley in 1810 and six years later was extensive enough to be employing over a hundred workers. Nevertheless its life was a short one, and it ceased trading around 1834. The Cork Glass House had shut its doors in 1818. Some of the pieces from the Waterloo House were marked, but again it is necessary to look out for false inscriptions.

Dudley Westropp, the authority on Irish glass, suggested that Cork glass may be distinguished from Waterford by its slightly darker tint, although he cautioned against overconfidence in making attributions. I have often, in my own mind, attributed glass with rather little cutting and in a neo-classical style to the Cork houses — but I could be wrong! In sales catalogues you will often find glass referred to as 'possibly Cork'; essentially you will have to make your own judgement. Recent auction prices for 'possibly Cork' items include £320 for a punch bowl simply cut in the Adams style with a band of swags suspended from stars; a boat-shaped bowl, sparingly cut and very attractive but with its foot replaced, for £220; a cut claret jug at £200,

Left to right: Old cutglass celery vase; early 19th century urns and covers (pair); late 18th century cutglass Irish bowl on square foot; small late 18th century Irish urn and cover; 19th century cutglass fruit bowl.

and a pair of shallow oval dishes also at £200. With regard to more definitely ascribed or marked pieces, a beautiful navette-shaped bowl with diamond cutting on moulded knob stem and fluted base recently made £2,800, being purchased by a museum.

Waterford Glass

It comes as a surprise to many people to whom Waterford glass is synonymous with Irish glass to learn that the old Waterford glass factory was only in production for sixty-eight years, before closing its doors in 1851. For a century after that, until the modern Waterford glassworks was established, there was virtually a complete break in the city's glassmaking tradition. The original factory was set up in 1783 by George and William Penrose. They introduced about seventy English glassworkers from Stourbridge and other centres into the factory. Not surprisingly, the style of Waterford glass owed much to English fashion, as indeed did much of the glass made in Ireland. Some years later the firm passed into the hands of the Gatchell family, who remained closely associated with the factory until its closure.

In his book on Irish glass, Dudley Westropp wrote that 'if all the alleged Waterford glass in existence today were genuine, despite the output of the factory and the vast amount that has been broken, it would probably have taken two or three glasshouses to produce it'. He stressed the difficulty of establishing, in all but a few cases, 'the exact place of manufacture of any old glass'. The truth is that much Waterford and other Irish glass was unmarked, that the makers used patterns similar to those used in England, and that much of the glassware used in Ireland during the eighteenth and nineteenth centuries was imported, mainly from England. Consequently, a good deal of the antique glass the collector sees on the Irish market is of English, not Irish, origin, and it would appear that much of the glass made in England and at other Irish glass houses is often rather too readily passed off as Waterford.

It is true that there are surviving patterns for old Waterford (many of which have gone into production at the modern factory), and some of these can be examined in Westropp's book. There is also some information about patterns used at the Cork Glass Company. However, because the Irish factories seem to have borrowed one another's designs, and glassworkers often came from England and sometimes no doubt brought their own patterns with them, such information is not quite so useful as it seems. In addition, it also appears that glass blanks were imported into Ireland to be cut here. Reference to the old Waterford patterns and the careful study of old glass at salerooms and in museum collections can be of enormous help in identifying Waterford pieces. But with regard to unmarked pieces, certainty remains elusive.

Collecting Old Irish Glass

As you may have already guessed, the buyer of old Waterford and other Irish cut glass is faced with a few problems. To begin with there are some fakes, especially at the upper end of the market; it seems that these started to appear in England in the years after the First World War, and it is probable that over

Rare Irish cut double flask, possibly Waterford, early 19th century.

time a certain number of these have found their way across the Irish Sea. The situation is further complicated by the fact that during this century honest copies of old glass have continued to be made, and as they acquire the cast of age they can become quite difficult to tell from the pre-1850 article. Nothing can take the place of handling and looking at the real thing, and even when you don't intend to buy, you should make constant use of the opportunity to handle glass at auction viewings. You will also find it useful to examine some modern Irish crystal. Getting a feel for what is new can often help in the detection of what is old. It will be noticed, for example, that the cutting of old ware is less even than that of a modern piece, and that sometimes the thickness at the side of an old piece can vary. The tint of old glass may be a little darker than that of the new, and in general will shine with less brilliance.

'Pontil Mark'

You will often read of the existence of a 'pontil mark' as a means of authenticating old glass. The pontil is a long rod that was attached, while the glass was still hot, to the base of a goblet to steady it while the shaping of the rim was completed or, as with jugs, for the handle to be added and the spout shaped. The pontil rod was then broken away from the base, leaving a distinctive rough mark at the centre. This, it is often said, is a sure way to distinguish old glass. Unfortunately the situation is not quite so simple as that. To begin with, the pontil mark was often ground away; this was especially so from the late eighteenth century. Even more significant, the pontil rod was widely replaced from around the middle of the nineteenth century by the gadget, a spring-loaded device that gripped, with a pair of claws, the base of the object to be worked. Thus a great many glasses of antique value have no pontil mark; this includes not only Victorian glass and some eighteenth century ware but much important art nouveau and art deco glass from the

present century. Pressed glass, which has been formed in moulds, will not carry a pontil mark either, yet a good deal of such glass is today highly collectable. Still it might be thought that if the pontil does appear, it is a fair indication that a piece is of pre-1850 manufacture. The truth is that it might be — but the pontil rod has been used right into the twentieth-century for some hand-made glass. Moreover, some reproduction antique glass wares have been made complete with pontil marks to complete their 'olde worlde' appearance. And finally, it will come as no surprise to the reader to learn that pontil marks have been deliberately faked to give old and not-so-old glass added value.

As the products of the Waterford and Cork glass houses (and the Benjamin Edwards firm in Belfast) date from before 1850, it is clear that genuine examples should carry a pontil mark, albeit one that has been ground away. The grinding away was generally done with a cutting wheel, which left a round, polished area in the centre of the foot. However, since the presence of such a mark cannot guarantee authenticity, you must consider the colour, weight, proportions and style of cutting before coming to a final decision about what you see.

As to prices, the suspicion that these may be set for a rise makes one slow to be dogmatic. At house clearances over the past couple of years a set of seventeen old Waterford goblets made £600, a set of fifteen old Waterford claret glasses made £700, and an Irish cut-glass salver on foot with a set of six cut liqueur glasses sold for £500. A very fine rummer — a drinking-glass with a large bowl and a thick but rather short stem — engraved with a cartouche and monogram, with the stem containing an Irish 1803 bank token, sold recently for £260. In general, old Irish drinking glasses tend to make around £40 or so each when sold in sets of from six to fourteen, with singles or twos being got for around £15 to £20 each. Good rummers fetch more — around £200 apiece. Irish unmarked cut-glass bowls and dishes start at about £70 and go up according to size, with pairs making more. This also applies to decanters, which can be bought from £80 to £100 for singletons, while early cut-glass claret and water jugs make about £200.

That said, the watchful collector, buying at house clearances, especially outside Dublin, can often pick up old cut-glass pieces for less than these prices. Marked pieces are, of course, rare and cost much more; inscriptions to look out for include *Penrose Waterford; B. Edwards Belfast; Cork Glass Co.;* and *Waterloo Co. Cork.* Some Irish glass retailers also marked pieces with their company name; they include *Francis Collins Dublin* and *Mary Carter & Son, 80 Grafton Street, Dublin.* But take care: these marks have sometimes been faked, and pieces with clear, crisp wording should be examined with particular attention.

TOP: Victorian silver mounted ruby glass claret jug.
CENTRE: Late Victorian star cut decanter.
BOTTOM: Late Victorian claret jug.

Coloured Glass

Coloured glass has had a long history throughout Europe, but after the popularising of clear, transparent glass there was a long period in which it fell out of favour. During the sixteenth century the Venetian glassmakers began to manufacture coloured glass, particularly in red, and soon afterwards blue glass production began in Germany and Holland. During the eighteenth century the German recipe for cobalt blue glass came into the hands of a Bristol porcelain maker named William Cockworthy, and although the glass was soon made at a number of centres, it became known as 'Bristol blue'. The Industrial Revolution brought along the techniques for the production of a range of new colours, including yellow, green, and orange, while from Bohemia came the method of manufacturing the type of yellow glass that was called vaseline glass. In Ireland too a number of glass houses produced coloured wares, including both the Waterford and the Pugh family works. However, much if not most of the coloured glass the Irish collector sees today is English and dates from the latter half of the nineteenth century. Continental glass, much of it French, is also frequently encountered.

Eighteenth-century coloured glass is not commonly seen at Irish sales, and it is expensive. A good pair of Bristol blue decanters from, say, 1790 and with their original stoppers could set you back about £800. At a sale in Co. Meath four Bristol blue comports of baluster form, on circular feet, sold for £800, and a set of ten finger bowls was £240. Amethyst or purple glass is very spectacular-looking on a table, and a good deal of it appears to date from roughly the Regency period - around 1790 to 1820. It tends to be expensive also. A set of eight Regency wine cooling bowls, in amethyst glass with gilded rims, was sold at an English auction for £2,800; in Ireland a pair of amethyst circular salts was sold with some lesser objects for £300.

The good news is, however, that a great deal of Victorian coloured glass is still relatively inexpensive and is both decorative and collectable. For example, plain green glass Victorian bowls can be got at auction from about £30, and single green wine glasses for £10 and less. With matched sets prices can rise. Expect to pay around £150 for sets of six and for a set of twelve to fourteen green glasses with a matching decanter the price could rise to about £500. Blue glass, even from the Victorian period, tends to be pricier, in particular blue drinking-glasses, which seem to be relatively rare. Single items are cheaper, and for a run-of-the-mill blue Victorian decanter you will pay around £80. Vaseline glass is cheaper: recent prices include a set of six tumblers with a jug at £45, a large bowl on circular foot for £35, and a box and cover for £30.

Ruby or cranberry glass, as it is sometimes called, is my own favourite, and it often comes a little cheaper than blue or green pieces. This is especially so if you buy at salerooms other than house clearances, where housewives have a sharp eye to the decorative possibilities of this lovely ware! But even here there can be value to be had; I bought what I think is a beautiful Victorian ruby glass and gilt bowl for just £50 at a Dublin house sale. House sales also often yield nice long sets of cranberry drinking glasses, which can be very tempting. Sets of fourteen or so can reach over £300, but at salerooms you may be lucky enough to find a set of six from about £50. Very attractive oddments can also be found; I recently saw a fine Victoriancranberry glass dish and cover sold with two cranberry jugs for just £110, and a ruby and gilt vase for £20. Ruby drinking-glasses can rise in price when accompanied by a matching tray or decanter; for six glasses and a decanter you could pay up to £200, and with a tray, six glasses would probably cost around £150. Vases seem to be the cheapest of all, and even the nicest can usually be bought for under £60.

One problem for the dedicated collector of Victorian coloured glass is that not a lot of it appears on the Irish market. However, a good deal of it comes up for auction in England, and the real glass enthusiast could consider buying there. Most of the major English auction houses hold specialist glass sales from time to time, and glass is not very difficult to bring back in a suitcase if you happen to take a holiday there. Just remember to wrap it well! Everyday clear glass and even cut, etched and engraved colourless glass from the Edwardian and Victorian periods is still very inexpensive — often significantly cheaper than new glass. I think it is worth buying. Go for matched sets, the larger the better, and don't buy chipped or cracked pieces. Because it is so cheap you can afford to buy the best, and I wouldn't be surprised if such pieces, carefully bought, showed notable appreciation in the years ahead.

Bohemian Glass

Among European glassware it often seems that the one you most frequently come across is Bohemian glass. In fact a proportion of what is described as Bohemian glass is German; many of the techniques of the Bohemian makers were shared by the Germans, and in both countries during the seventeenth and eighteenth centuries splendid enamelled glass was produced. Even the fine cutting and engraving for which Bohemia was famed during the eighteenth century was often matched by several of the German glass houses at places like Potsdam and Kassel. The early enamelled ware is a very specialised area of collecting, whether the pieces are German or Bohemian; prices are high, and there are many fakes and even more late nineteenth and twentieth-century reproductions, so great care is needed when buying. A German or central European humpen (cylindrical glass beaker) dating from the seventeenth or eighteenth-century with enamelled decoration could easily cost £6,000. The fine engraved works of the eighteenth-century Bohemian factories can command the same kind of prices; particularly in demand on London and European markets are large Bohemian goblets from the first half of the eighteenth century.

Most of the Bohemian glass offered for sale in Ireland is from the nineteenth century, when, although much ware was mass-produced, Bohemia became particularly noted for high-quality ruby glass. Much of this was produced using a technique called 'flashing', by which a thin layer of red glass (other colours could be used too) was applied to clear glass, after which the red was cut or engraved through to highlight the pattern in clear glass against the red background. This flashed glass is often confused with what is called 'cased' glass, also produced in large quantities by the Bohemian makers. On cased glass the applied layer is thicker than on flashed glass. The outer layer is then cut away so that what is left appears as a design carved in relief. Occasionally more than one layer is applied so as to achieve an almost three-dimensional effect. Not only colours were used for cased work: opaque glass, which had a white frosted effect, was often applied, and the raised panels were frequently gilded as well as engraved. The Bohemian glassmakers for a long time made the technique of casing glass into something of a trade secret; this was cracked by British and French glassworks around the middle of the nineteenth century, and soon local versions of the Bohemian product were on sale. One form of cased work that the English makers seem to have made almost uniquely their own was cameo glass, which, though mainly dating from the late nineteenth century, was heavily classical in inspiration.

Good nineteenth-century Bohemian glass is relatively expensive, with cased and engraved items such as jugs, vases and goblets costing several hundred pounds apiece. Even very ordinary vases in ruby glass with some gilding but without engraving or flashing would probably cost over £100 a pair at auction. As with the older Bohemian pieces, highest prices tend to fall to elaborate goblets; recently a red flashed goblet, almost two feet high, very finely engraved with an elaborate landscape and stags and hounds, was sold in London for £6,000, despite being of fairly late nineteenth-century date. Often within the reach of the

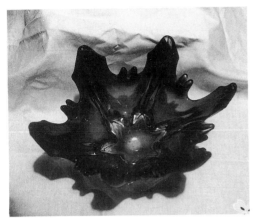

Art Deco amber glass vase.

Edwardian silver plated cruet stand with original cutglass bottles.

modest buyer, though not exactly cheap, are Bohemian glass lustres, coloured glass stands, usually flashed, out of which hang a number of glass prisms. These are now reaching over £400 for pairs, with English and French ones about a hundred pounds behind.

A variety of glass that is connected to Bohemian glass and that should be within the means of the small collector is that known as Mary Gregory glass. The story goes that an American woman in Boston, Mary Gregory, who worked as a glass decorator and enameller, decided to adapt to her own taste some of the patterns she saw on Bohemian glass, and began decorating the ware on which she worked with figures of Victorian boys and girls playing in flower gardens and the like. The technique was widely copied in England and was copied back by the Bohemians, who had invented it, and indeed Czechoslovak glass factories have been making varieties of 'Mary Gregory' glass ever since! Nineteenth-century examples whether from England, Bohemia, or elsewhere, should cost £50 or so, but it is all too easy to be caught out with one of the modern versions. So watch out!

French Glass

For many people, French glass means paperweights. Although this is rather unfair to the wonderful output of many of the glassmakers in other fields in France, it is true that the work of the three great factories associated with paperweights — Baccarat, Clichy, and Saint-Louis — has exerted enormous fascination over collectors everywhere. There are collectors — some of them exceedingly wealthy — who collect nothing else. The rarest paperweights fetch many thousands of pounds, and sometimes it is only a tiny feature of the design, all but invisible to the uninitiated, that marks out the rarest and the most prized.

These weights were first made during the 1840s, and the Saint-Louis factory seems to have been the first to produce them. The most popular design was 'millefiori', made by gathering clusters of coloured glass cane into a heavy glass dome. The canes were frequently arranged together in such a way as to form the effect of a bunch or carpet of flowers - hence the name. The best weights can contain as many as two hundred individual florets. Millefiori, although synonymous in the minds of many collectors with paperweights, was far from being the only pattern. It was most commonly employed at Baccarat, which was the largest factory and devoted about 60% of its paperweight output to millefiori designs. Central flower motifs were often used, and primroses and pansies seem to have been among the most favoured. Specially prized by collectors of Baccarat weights are those — and they are rare — that feature snakes. Of the flowers, the rarest appears to be a light mauve dahlia-type blossom.

Simple millefiori patterns seem to have formed the bulk of Saint-Louis' early production; later they became associated with the making of weights in which a single flower (or sometimes some fruit), in very strong colours, is displayed on a *latticinio* background of white honeycombed glass. Of these, those that feature a fuchsia or a geranium are probably the most attractive; pansies were also commonly used. Facet cutting to increase the appearance of depth in bouquets of flowers is also characteristic of the Saint-Louis factory.

The Clichy factory also manufactured a high proportion of millefiori weights, and is also known for its two-toned swirl designs. Also well known to collectors is the famous Clichy rose cane, which seems to occur in about 30% of the firm's weights. Designs featuring interlacing garlands of flowers are a fairly distinctive Clichy type. Among the rarest and most

Collection of 19th century Irish cutglass jugs.

sought-after Clichy weights are those that feature bouquets of flowers, sometimes on a background of muslin.

Some weights are marked with date and place of origin, but in practice it can be quite difficult to tell apart the work of different factories. Sometimes factory symbols are worked into the pattern of the weight and can be hard to pick out. Clichy weights tend to come in very striking colours, and I have an impression that blue is particularly common among them. The Clichy rose can provide an indication but is probably not used often enough for definite attribution. The same applies to the occasional use of facet cutting, and in any case all three factories made use of this. Saint-Louis weights tend to be rather high-domed, and sometimes — not as often as collectors would like — the letters *SL* may be found. Some Baccarat weights have the letter *B* on the base, and a few have a small star. The great majority of nineteenth-century French paperweights were produced during the 1840s, with fewer being made in the 1850s. Some paperweights are dated; Baccarat weights carry a number of dates from the late 1840s as well as from 1853 and 1858. Saint-Louis weights were rarely dated, and Clichy weights not at all.

Not all paperweights were French. They were produced in England as well, notably by the Bacchus company and by the Islington Glass Company. The collector also needs to bear in mind that when paperweight collecting became popular during the 1920s a number of English firms began to make copies of French pieces. You also need to know that French factories are still producing paperweights, some in nineteenth-century styles and some with new designs. Most Baccarat examples of the late twentieth century have *Baccarat France* on the base, but other pieces will not be so definitely attributed. Many of these modern pieces are of excellent quality and are as sought-after as the older weights. Paperweights are of varying worth, as can be imagined. At auctions, prices start at around £50, with good nineteenth-century examples tending to fetch £200 to £300. On the London market, the more desirable pieces from all three French factories tend to fetch around £1,000. Date and, more importantly, rarity are what dictate prices in this field, and you need to do plenty of serious research before you spend substantial sums of money. This is not always easy in Ireland, where the best examples don't often come up for sale and where those who offer them may not know as much about them as the collector would like. However, there are some excellent books on the subject (some are listed at the end of this volume) and no paperweight collector should be without at least one good, well-illustrated work on the field.

Apart from paperweights, it is the art nouveau and art deco periods that nowadays exert the greatest fascination for collectors of French glass. It is true that from around 1880 until the art deco period was in full swing during the 1930s some of the greatest glassmakers France has ever known were flourishing, and the idea that a piece of glass could be seen as a work of art resulted in the production of wares that were both new and exciting. The three great names, and those that now fetch the highest prices in salerooms around the world, are Gallé, Lalique, and Daum of Nancy, and individual rare pieces can now reach £50,000 and more. In Ireland none of the products of these factories is all that commonly seen — I have rarely seen a sale that contained more than one or two isolated examples — and of the three by far the most frequently encountered is Lalique. Because many Irish buyers are not very knowledgable about French art glass, it is sometimes possible to pick up simple Lalique vases and bowls for a few hundred pounds. For good pre-1945 bowls, however, prices are more likely to start at around £500; recently at a Kilkenny auction an opaline glass leaf bowl from this period was sold for £700. At the same sale a rarer Lalique blue ground vase (signed *Lalique*, which put it into the post-1960 period) was sold for £2,600. The Lalique firm was famous for the production of glass car mascots, the most celebrated being the one called 'Victoire, the Spirit of the Wind'. Prices for mascots fall into the £1,000 to £8,000 range.

As with French paperweights, as a collector of art glass you owe it to yourself to do some research, bearing in mind that although ignorance of the field among saleroom buyers can result in bargains for the knowledgeable, it can also result in prices for routine wares that are far beyond what they would be worth on international markets. It is essential as a collector of Lalique, for example, to familiarise yourself not just with the marks to be found on this glass but with the styles as well, for there are many fakes and copies about. This is all the more important because the present-day factory still makes pieces in earlier designs, and for the collector of older wares it is useful to be able to tell the difference. Before 1945 pieces were marked *R. Lalique*, in a variety of scripts and sometimes in capitals. Often the word *France* was added. After 1945 the *R.* was dropped and the mark read *Lalique France,* often, though not always, in capital letters. After 1960 the mark usually read *Lalique* in capital letters. Not always, though: there is one mark used after 1960 that is almost identical to one that appeared in 1945-60. Finally, some Lalique ware was unmarked, so that anonymous pieces that stylistically appear to be Lalique should be given careful consideration.

There is no doubt that glass is one of the most absorbing areas of collecting today. The fact that the glass market has been quiet for so long must mean that there are some exciting items lying in attics and sitting-rooms just waiting to be discovered. With the current interest in early twentieth-century glass there must be many people who harbour among wedding presents of the 1920s, 30s and 40s pieces of some worth. There is the chance too for the modest collector to get into some areas that are just beginning to attract interest and where prices are still reasonable. One such area would be Victorian pressed glass, for which prices start at as little as £10. The market is certainly one to watch with interest over the coming years.

Left to right: Cutglass decanter, possibly early Waterford; cutglass decanter, possibly Cork; decanter with triple ring neck and mushroom stopper, possibly Cork; rare early Cork decanter engraved with the arms of the city of Cork; triple neck decanter, probably Cork c.1810.

Georgian chest on chest — but is it a marriage? Note the canted corners on the top section which are not shared by the base. The grain of the wood on the top drawers seems to differ from that on the base. The bun feet are certainly later additions. Only careful examination can resolve or confirm the doubts.

Chapter Six

FURNITURE: the Early Years

urniture is the most important area of the antiques trade — because there is more of it, because more people are interested in it, and because more people buy it than anything else. A country's past is what dictates the kind of antique furniture one sees there, and Ireland is no exception. For much of its history the great majority of Irish people were exceedingly poor and had little resources to spare for furniture. So it is not too surprising to find that, even allowing for differences in population, there is far less quality antique furniture in Ireland than there is in England, France, or the Netherlands. And the situation is getting worse all the time, because of the amount of antique furniture being exported from Ireland to Britain and America. Estimates vary, but I was recently told by an experienced dealer that about 70% of the top-quality furniture from house clearances and other sources of fresh goods is ultimately finding its way abroad.

The proof of this is that in relation to the quantity of goods circulating in the Irish trade the retail business done is really quite small. Antique shops spring up in cities and towns, but many shut their doors within a relatively short time. In the longer-established businesses around the capital, stock is quite slow in turning over, and even here a good many of the buyers are foreign. Whenever I visit the antiques area of Francis Street in Dublin I am struck by the number of familiar dealer faces that I see in the shops. These dealers are most often there to sell, not buy, and the fact that they seem to regularly outnumber the private customers tells its own sorry tale. This is not, it seems to me, the fault of the antique dealers and shop owners. They are happy to sell to any comer, regardless of nationality. The problem, they claim, is that too often the Irish buyer is unwilling to pay the going rate. This is not, they say, because the Irish buyer is necessarily poorer than, say, the British buyer. 'The trouble', grumbles one dealer, 'is that when a thing is old, people seem to think it should be cheap. I've had customers who think nothing of spending a couple of hundred pounds on a suit of clothes exclaim in horror when I tell them that the price of a good set of Edwardian chairs is £500. And yet the suit will be in bits within the year.' Another dealer who nowadays buys for export told me of the experience he had when, some years ago, he decided to open a shop. 'I often sat there for days', he recalled, 'and never took in a shilling.'

In the end, the only way the public can stop the country's antiques from going abroad is by buying them themselves. They musn't expect to buy fine Georgian, Victorian and Edwardian furniture for nothing. Too

Early oak joint stool.

many collectors in other countries are far too eager to lay their hands on what is an ever-diminishing supply of goods for that to happen. But it doesn't mean you have to pay the earth either, for, as has been suggested earlier much antique furniture can work out just as cheaply as new, and it won't lose its value in the way new, mass-produced pieces do. There is antique furniture to suit almost every pocket. The one invariable advice is to go for quality. Don't allow shortage of funds to drive you into buying something that's large but shoddy, heavily infested with woodworm, or (worst of all) a composite of two or more articles. It's best, too, to avoid pieces that have more repairs than can fairly be called restoration.

Of course, if you decide to buy a good antique set of chairs, a dining-table, or a bookcase, it is true that considerable expense may be involved. So it pays to know as much as possible about the kind of thing you want to buy and to have some idea of the price band for such pieces. For the modest buyer, Georgian pieces will generally, though not always, be too expensive. An occasional small piece may be all that you can hope for. For major pieces you will find yourself choosing from Victorian and Edwardian furniture. One of the earliest surprises you will probably have is when you discover that certain Edwardian pieces have recently become much more expensive than Victorian furniture. This applies particularly to the fine Edwardian reproductions of Sheraton and Adam-style furniture fashionable at the turn of the nineteenth century and that feature decorative woods such as satinwood and floral marquetry inlays. A good Edwardian display cabinet with long, slender legs, made in mahogany or satinwood with inlays or stringing, would set you back about £2,500 nowadays, while the tiny painted

17th century carved oak coffer.

satinwood tables so popular around 1900 are now making up to £1,000. But if, like me, you prefer plain brown furniture anyway, you're not going to be too troubled by that, and there is plenty of nineteenth and early twentieth-century furniture around at reasonable prices.

One of the first things you need to know if you are planning to invest money in old furniture is how to date a piece accurately. As with all areas of learning, this is not as easy as it sounds. Good reference books will certainly be of help in identifying the principal features of design at particular periods, but they do not help you a great deal in distinguishing reproductions from genuine pieces. Furniture of almost every period has been widely reproduced at other times, but, as with fashions in clothes, the copies are never exactly the same as the first time round and it is through the differences that you can distinguish the originals of one era from the reproductions of the next. It is by constant handling of pieces that you will finally develop the expertise to tell the difference. That's why, even if you have no intention of attending any particular sale or of buying anything there, it's still a good idea to go to the viewing. You can look at furniture in museums and good antique shops, but nowhere else than at a viewing can you turn the pieces inside out and upside down in the way that you can there. If you really want to learn about antique furniture it really is important to go to as many viewings as you possibly can.

Old Oak Furniture

Until well into the eighteenth century the rooms of most houses, rich or poor, were relatively sparsely furnished and what furniture there was was generally made of oak. Even after the arrival of walnut and, later, mahogany, many everyday pieces continued to be made in oak, especially pieces made in the provinces and those supplied to the less well-off home. On the antiques market these pieces for a long time really aroused very little interest. Old oak tended to be a rather specialised market, appealing most strongly to those with an interest in sixteenth and seventeenth-century domestic history and who were less concerned with the decorative properties of such furniture than with its ability to provide a link with the past and to reveal more about how people lived. That has begun to change. During the last three or four years there has been a noticeable increase in interest. There has been a consequent rise in prices; I've noticed that between 1988 and 1991 the prices for seventeenth and eighteenth-century oak coffers in general rose about fourfold. The coffer is, in fact, probably the most common item of old oak to be seen in Ireland, turning up occasionally in salerooms and most often at country house sales. Other pieces are less frequently seen and almost always at house sales, especially those that are advertised (more and more seldom these days) as 'undisturbed contents', though indeed it must be said that the most fascinating selection of old oak to come on the market in recent years was a collection put together by a man who was wise enough to buy such things before they became as sought after as they are now.

For many centuries the coffer, also referred to as the chest or kist, was the most important item of furniture in the household. It was originally made by simply gouging out the centre of a portion of tree and hewing out a lid to go on top. By the middle ages coffers were being made out of a number

1600
Elizabethan
Turned

1605
Stuart
Baluster

1690
Spanish

1695
William
and Mary
'S' Curve

1700
Trumpet

1700
Portugese
Bulb

1700
Mushroom

1705
Inverted
Cup

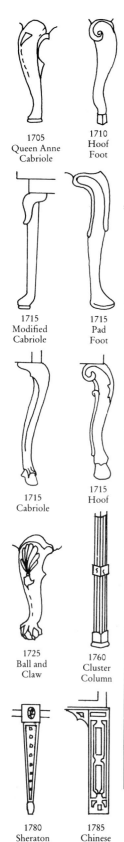

1705
Queen Anne
Cabriole

1710
Hoof
Foot

1715
Modified
Cabriole

1715
Pad
Foot

1715
Cabriole

1715
Hoof

1725
Ball and
Claw

1760
Cluster
Column

1780
Sheraton
Tapered

1785
Chinese
Chippendale

of fairly rough planks riven together by means of wooden pegs. By the sixteenth century the method of construction was more refined with panelled carcases and carving that was often highly skilled. Another design for panels was termed 'linenfold', a pattern carved in imitation of folded cloth. During the second half of the seventeenth century new kinds of furniture began to be more widely available, and such chests as were made over the next hundred years became plainer and more functional than before; possibly they were by then used mainly for bedroom storage.

Not many early coffers come up for sale in Ireland. The unsettled state of the country, especially in the two centuries between 1500 and 1700, ensured that not very much of the furniture of that period survived. The coffers you see will generally date from the eighteenth century and occasionally the seventeenth. It's important to remember, too, that during the nineteenth and twentieth centuries some coffers continued to be made for use as blanket chests and can easily be mistaken by the novice for earlier examples, and recently it appears that some fakes have been made. In fact I recently heard it jokingly remarked that there are now more seventeenth-century coffers in Britain than there were in the seventeenth century! Features that may denote early examples are the sight of wooden pegs at the top of the rail — more correctly called a muntin — separating the panels; short legs, perhaps showing some rot at the base; designs that appear to have been punched into the wood; iron locks and strap hinges (though these will often have been replaced on genuine pieces); and candle boxes fitted into the side of the interior (though these often occur on nineteenth-century pine coffers as well). Check the lid to see that it is original — I recently examined a coffer to discover that its 'lid' had an interesting-looking lock in one corner, indicating that it had started life as some sort of panelled door. Look to see that the back is genuinely old timber; because these pieces spent their lives against a wall, the backs tended to rot, and many of them have been replaced. The base or floor was also very prone to rot and worm and may also be a replacement.

The decision whether to buy a coffer with a major restoration like this is a moot one. Personally I would not buy a coffer that had its back or side replaced, but I would give consideration to one on which the base was a replacement, providing all else was well and the feet had not been subjected to some form of unpleasant butchery. If you see a coffer you like that has had major repair or replacement work you may decide that the piece is still so unusual that you are prepared to live with some degree of imperfection — perhaps even major imperfection. The decision is really up to you. But you should only pay top price if the piece is reasonably near perfect. This would include coffers with original lids; a long crack across is fairly common but, in general, it doesn't seriously devalue an otherwise good coffer. Rot in the feet may have rendered some attention necessary in the past; but provided the repair is discreet there should be no problem. Replacement locks and hinges will often have been needed during the life of a piece, and for many collectors this would not be a reason not to buy.

With regard to prices, it's probably true to say that in Ireland a plain or simply carved oak coffer dating from the late seventeenth or first half of the eighteenth century will cost between £500 and £900. At this price your coffer should be pretty near perfect. For very finely carved examples (and watch out — some coffers were newly carved during the nineteenth century) the price will probably go up to around £2,000, perhaps more if the piece is of really top quality. Yet it's difficult to give totally reliable guidelines for pieces that simply don't come up for sale all that often, and you could get a nice example for less than you might expect. For example, last year I saw an eighteenth-century coffer in need of re-waxing sell for just £180; certainly the purist would object to the loss of the coffer's original patina (it looked as if it might have been chemically stripped), but all its sides were there intact and there was no worm and no major repairs. A few days' work would have made it into a very nice, serviceable piece. I have also seen plain or modestly carved coffers with perhaps some worm, a bit of dry rot at the back and a couple of loose boards at the base fetch between £300 and £400 at house sales. I would rate this as fairly good value. On the other hand, at a Dublin sale lately I saw an eighteenth century coffer with both replacement lid and back sell for £650, which I would not think an especially good buy.

If you do happen to buy a coffer that has some signs of wear and tear, such as worm or rot, loose boards, and so forth, do not attempt to embark on any ill-considered restoration. Replace loose or broken boards with a minimum of carpentry. Treat worm and rot, but don't put in any fresh bits of timber. Leave locks and hinges alone unless they are threatening to cause cracking in the piece because of strain. Don't strip off the old wax in order to restore it — on the piece mentioned above all the wax was gone anyway, so nothing was lost by re-waxing, but to destroy the patina of an antique even where some damage exists is, in my book, an unforgivable sin. And finally, don't repair cracks on the lids of coffers with wood filler, nails, chunks of metal, or any other means. Just leave them alone!

Other Oak Pieces

The coffer was the ancestor of a number of different types of furniture, including the chest of drawers, the sideboard, and the armchair! Its closest relation is, as the name suggests, the chest of drawers. It was not a great step to extend the feet of the coffer, close down the top and provide pull-out sections for greater convenience in storage. At first these drawers were considered unsightly and were covered by an outer door, but during the seventeenth century the door began to be omitted and the chest of drawers as we know it today was born. By lengthening the legs still further and providing two doors to the body of the piece instead of a lid, what was called a food hutch or aumbry was made, close ancestor to the sideboard.

By the sixteenth century the coffer had also begun to develop into a chair by the addition of a straight back and a pair of arms. Single chairs were called 'box chairs' and longer ones 'settles', and for a long time they retained the feature whereby the seat could be lifted to disclose a storage area beneath. It would be rare nowadays to see a box chair outside a museum, but seventeenth-century settles are occasionally seen, and they continued to be made in pine as kitchen pieces until well into the nineteenth century. Early ones are generally made of oak and range in price from about £800 to many thousands; the last good seventeenth-century settle I saw sold took £5,200 at auction, while a much more modest one fetched £900. You will not come across many of these. Later pine ones can be got, however, and

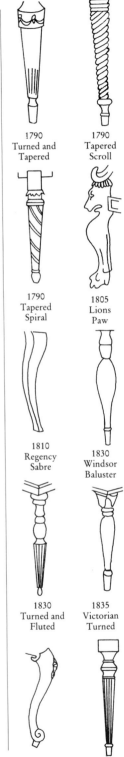

1790
Turned and
Tapered

1790
Tapered
Scroll

1790
Tapered
Spiral

1805
Lions
Paw

1810
Regency
Sabre

1830
Windsor
Baluster

1830
Turned and
Fluted

1835
Victorian
Turned

1840
Victorian
Cabriole

1865
Victorian
Reeded

1810
Thomas Hope
'X' Frame

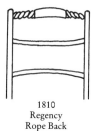

1810
Regency
Rope Back

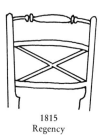

1815
Regency

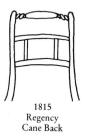

1815
Regency
Cane Back

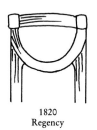

1820
Regency

nineteenth-century examples start at around a couple of hundred pounds. I think they make a very interesting addition to the kitchen that can accommodate them.

There are two kinds of dining-table that concern the oak collector: the refectory table and the drop-leaf, gate-legged variety. Refectory-type tables came first, but they were continued on into the seventeenth century and in provincial areas until well into the eighteenth. During the Elizabethan era these tables had huge bulbous legs; these were frequently copied in the nineteenth century. During the seventeenth century the legs slimmed down and were usually of a turned or baluster type, although country-made pieces often just had plain square legs. These later types are generally referred to as Jacobean (after King James I) or, if nineteenth or twentieth-century copies, as being in the Jacobean style. Prices for such tables can be high. In the week of writing a good one dating from about 1660 was sold at one of Sotheby's provincial rooms for £7,500, despite some restoration. I have seen one make almost £4,000 here in Ireland, and in Britain even very plain ones make £2,000 to £3,000.

Oak gate-leg tables are less expensive, though they have been rising in price. They are small and came into fashion towards the middle of the seventeenth century when the master and mistress had begun to take their meals away from their halls and their bevies of servants and to enjoy their dinner in the privacy of a small chamber. Legs on such tables are generally twisted or are of the slender baluster type. Prices range from about £600 to £1,400. Always check that flaps are original.

Early oak cupboards rarely appear for sale at auction, and when they do they are expensive. In Britain prices start at around £6,000 and then go up in an almost open-ended way; fine Elizabethan ones have made as much as £20,000. These early cupboards were elaborate pieces, generally richly carved, and divided into two or three sections, with a combination of open shelves and recessed cupboards. The definitions or names of these cupboards cause some difficulty for collectors, and they are variously described as court or livery cupboards. They were used for general storage purposes, the one with railed or slatted doors to their recessed sections probably being used for food, especially 'liveries', that is, the daily ration of food and drink for the servants. In Ireland a seventeenth-century court cupboard has made £2,600 and an early eighteenth-century oak cupboard £2,300. Because these pieces have always fetched high prices they have become a target for fakers, and there are many honest nineteenth-century copies as well. Many early pieces have also suffered the indignity of having been 'improved' during the nineteenth century with extra areas of carving.

Apart from box chairs, some other early oak chairs do appear occasionally at auction. They are often called 'wainscot' chairs, because their panelled backs and, frequently, sides resemble the panelling used on walls. Prices for good ones that have, perhaps, a carved lozenge or some other motif on the back panel start at around £1,000, plainer armchairs at about £550. Unadorned single chairs without arms from the seventeenth and early eighteenth centuries can often be bought for much less than this, for they are not much sought after by the decorating fraternity. A form of early seating that you will also spot from time to time at auction is the joynt or joint stool. It may be that this was the most common form of seating in homes before the late seventeenth century, and they probably served also as occasional tables. Construction was very simple, with the various parts pegged together, yet they were surprisingly sturdy, so that quite a few have survived relatively intact until the present day. They probably continued to be made until the eighteenth century, and in fact, because the method of construction scarcely changed over the years, they can be quite hard to date. For such small pieces they are quite expensive at auction, with prices ranging from about £500 for plain ones in good condition to as much as twice that for those with carving along the frieze.

1820
Empire

The Age of Walnut

This really covers the period between the restoration of King Charles II in 1660 until some years after the death of Queen Anne in 1714, and it encompasses quite a variety of furniture styles. My impression is that in Ireland very little quality walnut comes up for sale, especially from the earlier part of this period; both in England and Ireland and in America too, such furniture commands a very high premium.

1820
Regency
Bar Back

With the restoration of King Charles, everything, it seemed, that was redolent of the grim years of Cromwell's Protectorate had to be swept away. France and French fashions became all the rage. From carriages to cookery, all the appurtenances of the life of the wealthier classes had to be in the French taste. Though the diarist John Evelyn might complain of the 'luxury and intolerable expense' of it all, the styles in clothing, silver, interior decoration and furniture became extremely flamboyant, with the London furniture makers receiving a welcome fillip to trade when the Great Fire of 1666 destroyed most of the buildings in the heart of the city. During the massive reconstruction the demand for new furniture was, naturally, enormous. Many of the nobility seized the chance to rebuild their town houses in greater style and size than before, thus stimulating the furniture trade. Much of this furniture was very large, made from walnut and various exotic woods, decorated with fancy veneers and marquetry and often with painted surfaces as well as gilding, silvering, and japanning in a manner after the Chinese. Cabinets on stands were extremely popular, the stands being richly carved and frequently gilded. Chests of drawers were beginning to take over from the old coffers and were now generally made in walnut, often with decorative inlays and veneers. Bookcases had arrived, and writing-cabinets on stands with pull-down fronts. Chairs were high-backed, often caned, and often had sugar-barley twist rails and turned legs.

1825
Regency
Bar Back

During the William and Mary period, after 1688, styles became rather more restrained and actually much more elegant. Marquetry, especially the dense, two-toned style termed 'seaweed', was still popular, as were decorative veneers, but a great deal of the gilding and carving disappeared. New items of furniture continued to appear. The neat fold-over card table made its debut, as did the small kneehole bureau; the growing popularity of such small pieces testifies to a more intimate style of life, with the middle and upper classes separating themselves in their homes from their servants and no longer eating and entertaining with a band of servitors as had been done in the halls of mediaeval and Tudor times. The chest on stand tended, after around 1690, to evolve into the chest on chest, or tallboy, an item of

1830
Regency
Bar Back

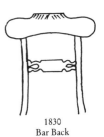

1830
Bar Back

1660
Charles II

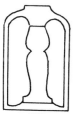

1705
Queen Anne

1745
Chippendale

1745
Chippendale

1750
Georgian

1845
Victorian
Bar Back

1850
Victorian

1860
Victorian

1870
Victorian

1875
Cane Back

furniture that has remained popular and much reproduced ever since. The William and Mary ones are usually found with walnut or oyster veneers. Similar to these pieces and generally made in the same kind of woods was the chest on stand, in which the latter was fitted with one long drawer. It usually had sugar-barley twist legs, finishing with bun feet and serpentine stretchers.

The Queen Anne period continued many of the older styles, but there were several important innovations. The cabriole leg was its most distinctive feature and, with the exception of the bureau cabinet, may be found on almost all kinds of furniture. At first it was smooth and plain, but later it became more decorative, with carving especially at the knees. Another characteristic Queen Anne piece was the lowboy, basically the one-drawered stand from the chest on stand, now with a smooth cabriole leg and an arrangement of short drawers. Queen Anne chairs are universally elegant. The best ones have strong curving front legs with perhaps a shell carving on the knee. There may be a pad foot or sometimes a claw and ball. The back legs are also curved, with a good 'kickback' to support the chair; they often have a well-moulded pad foot. These were called 'bended back' chairs and they were skilfully carved, usually from solid walnut, with slender, curving side rails and a centre splat, also curved. Seats were drop-in, the best over a deep frieze with central shell carving. They were exceedingly comfortable, with excellent support for the back. Queen Anne examples tend not to have stretchers; these began to return during the early Georgian period, which retained many other features of Queen Anne chair design.

Not a great deal of this later seventeenth and early eighteenth-century furniture appears at Irish sales. Much of what there once was has been exported long ago, many pieces disappearing as the great houses were broken up during the years between 1922 and 1960. You will come across occasional chests on chests and chests on stands dating from around 1700. Prices start at around £2,000 for those in walnut veneers, but you could pay up to £20,000 for a really good one. You will often see chairs in a Charles II or William and Mary style, but by and large they will be nineteenth-century imitations made in oak. A very good set of eighteen sold at a sale in Co. Offaly a couple of years ago for £4,500 — not bad value, I think. Good marquetry tables from the late seventeenth century don't appear too often either; the last one I saw so described was certainly not genuine, for its thin

1830
William IV
Bar Back

1830
William IV

1835
Lath Back

1840
Victorian
Balloon back

1845
Victorian

veneer betrayed it as a nineteenth-century copy. It made just over £1,000; clearly the purchaser knew what he was getting, for a genuine example would have cost at least four times that.

Queen Anne and early George I furniture is more often seen. Sets of dining-chairs are rare and expensive: for six, prepare to make out your cheque for at least £7,000. Singles are sometimes found at more reasonable sums. I once saw one sell at a poorly advertised house auction for just £45 — proving how necessary is the presence of dealers to maintain good prices at sales — but don't count on that happening too often! A more realistic expectation would be to pay £400 upwards for fairly routine examples, rising to £2,000 to £3,000 for really good ones. Pairs make more, and fours more again.

If paying high prices, do keep a weather eye out for nineteenth century copies; check for the presence of dowelled joints rather than pegs or mortise-and-tenon joints, for dowels indicate a period after the eighteenth century. Joints often loosen slightly, particularly at the point where the back of the seat rail meets the stiles, and if you pull the chair into a good light you can often see whether the joint is tenoned or dowelled. Look, too, at the carving, especially at the knee and foot of the cabriole leg; it has often been added later. The giveaway is that such carving tends to look very flat, rather than standing proud of the leg. This is because it had to be cut into the leg; were it original it would have been carved from a piece of wood thicker than the final leg, with the straight sweep of the leg being finally shaped by cutting away from the carving. This lent a definite impression of height to the carved area. It's important to be able to tell the difference between original and added carving, because the quality and quantity of carving influences strongly the prices paid for early eighteenth-century chairs.

You may find Queen Anne lowboys, probably used originally as dressing-tables, appearing at auctions. Again, many are later copies and will be honestly described as being 'in the Queen Anne style'. In general, the copies will be made in mahogany, originals in walnut or oak. Some early lowboys made in the George I and II periods were made in mahogany; they will generally be described as being of their correct period and will often be just as desirable as Queen Anne pieces. It's also true that there are some oak Victorian lowboys about, made perhaps as honest copies but possibly as fakes! So take care if paying high prices. Early pieces generally start at around £2,000, with walnut sometimes, but not always, fetching more than oak. On the international market, American examples tend to make the highest prices, with sums as high as £20,000 being reached. On the converse side, prices for very plain examples can dip as low as £900.

The Age of Mahogany

By the eighteenth century, the furniture people used had increased greatly both in variety and quantity, and in Ireland, as peace settled on the country during the years that followed the Williamite wars, the survival rate of furniture began to improve markedly. The Anglo-Irish ascendancy, prosperous and secure, began to build their great palladian mansions, while in the towns and cities the middle class began to erect their own, more modest, town houses. These comfortable classes were anxious to obtain the

1750
Hepplewhite

1750
Chippendale

1760
Rococo

1760
Gothic

1760
Splatback

most fashionable furniture for their new homes, and they began both to import pieces in large numbers and to commission furniture in Ireland.

Early eighteenth-century pieces, as we have seen, were generally made in walnut, but a particularly severe winter throughout Europe in 1709 killed off almost all the remaining walnut trees. Existing stocks of seasoned timber began to be exhausted around 1720, and from then on mahogany became the most important wood for furniture. In 1725 Ireland imported just one-third of a ton of mahogany; by 1750 this had risen to 200 tons. Of course, this was still not an immense quantity, and although the years 1740 to 1770 have been seen as the golden age of furniture making, it is clear that much of Ireland's needs were met by imports. The most characteristic Irish piece of this period is generally agreed to be the rich, dark mahogany mask table with elaborately carved apron, incorporating festoons, tassels, shells, flowers, and grotesquely carved heads and faces. However, although Irish furniture did exhibit certain features of its own, makers generally reflected the prevailing English taste, and, as with glass, it is difficult to distinguish genuinely Irish furniture from English, unless it has been signed by the maker or displays stylistic features known to be associated with Irish craftworkers.

The eighteenth-century furniture makers soon discovered that mahogany had many advantages over the more familiar walnut. It was very hard and almost impervious to pest infestation and rot, and it displayed a range of rich tones and figures, that is, the swirls of decoration that appear naturally along the grain of the wood. It was an ideal timber for high, crisp carving, and in the early years of its use it was possible to obtain planks so wide that a table could be made with a smooth, unbroken top. Most of this mahogany came from Central America, and the earliest to reach Europe was the dense, heavy timber from Jamaica, soon to be followed by the highly figured Cuban variety, ideal for use in the solid and as a veneer. By the second half of the eighteenth century world stocks of these fine timbers were already becoming exhausted, and furniture makers were forced to turn to Honduras mahogany. This wood is much lighter than the other mahoganies and has a rather dull grain with little figuring. Initially used for drawer linings (sides) and for cheaper furniture, by the latter part of the nineteenth century it had virtually replaced the finer woods.

Mahogany was not the only new wood to reach Europe during the first half of the eighteenth century, although it was the most important. There was rosewood from Brazil and Ceylon, used both in the solid and for veneers, and there was ebony, kingwood, tulipwood, purpleheart, and many other exotic woods that could be used in the increasingly elaborate patterns of marquetry and inlay. During these years a host of new decorative and useful methods of furniture enhancement were developed. Upholstered chairs became common and a wide range of new fabrics appeared. Colonial trade, technological advance and relative peace had enormously increased the prosperity of Europe, and the furniture craftworkers, inspired by access to new materials and techniques and the increased number of wealthy patrons, burst into a period of creative exuberance never seen before or since. This period reached its height during the 1750s, and the style that epitomised it is called rococo. In Britain, its greatest proponent was Thomas Chippendale, who produced his famous book of designs, *The Gentleman and Cabinet Maker's Director*, in 1754.

Georgian brass bound plate bucket.

18th century carved oak side chair.

Charles II style upholstered side chair.

The Chippendale Era

Thomas Chippendale was a man who felt it important to be able to mix in what was then called polite society. Born at Otley, Yorkshire, in 1718, he probably retained some of his rough edges throughout his life and was not as readily accepted as an equal among his wealthy customers as he would have liked. How much more, then, would he have relished his posthumous fame and especially the manner in which the period of his career and the manner of his cabinet making are described as Chippendale rather than being named, as is usual, after the reigning monarch!

Many people have the impression that Chippendale was a designer only and that he did not actually manufacture furniture. This is not true; Chippendale maintained a thriving workshop in London, where he carried out both cabinet making and upholstery. The range of his work is best seen by reference to the *Director*, versions and facsimiles of which have from time to time been published and several of which are still in print. Chippendale himself described it as a 'large collection of the most elegant and useful designs of household furniture in the Gothick, Chinese and Modern [rococo] taste.' The latter was the most important, and was distinguished by fine scroll carving incorporating shells, flowers, plants, and sometimes grotesque faces. If one feature could be said to distinguish rococo it was the curve. The *Director*, which had reached its third (and best) edition by 1762, included sixty patterns for chairs, using both straight and cabriole legs. Tables appeared with cabriole legs when in rococo style and with straight ones when the Chinese or Gothick style was employed. Among the latter were very

Chippendale

attractive 'breakfast' tables and drop-leaf tables with a curious fretwork cupboard underneath. There were also neat side tables, which are nowadays sometimes referred to as silver tables but which Chippendale described as 'china tables' and which appear to have been used for laying out tea things.

The intellectual life of the eighteenth century gentleman was catered for by the fine designs for bookcases, desks and other library furniture, and several such pieces made in a subtly restrained rococo style were supplied to great houses in England. These included the beautiful 'violin' bookcase purchased by the Earl of Pembroke and the famous library table made for Nostell Priory in 1767. Smaller writing-tables were shown in a number of different styles, and the fashionable chests of drawers known as commodes were offered in every conceivable pattern, from finely carved rococo to japanned examples in the Chinese style.

Collecting Furniture in the Chippendale Style

It often seems as though the most distinctive object from the middle of the eighteenth century is the Chippendale dining-chair. The basic pattern and shape devised by Chippendale has remained popular up to the present day — so beware! Few modest collectors will be able to afford sets of genuine eighteenth-century examples of the style; a set of six chairs in the simplest design with little carving and square legs costs between £3,000 and £5,000, with prices rising all the time. Singles, of course, are less and you might be lucky enough to pick one up for about £300. A harlequin set, that is, a set consisting of similar but not identical chairs, of Irish make could expect to fetch around £3,000 for a set of six. With elaboration of design, with rich carving and cabriole legs ending in scrolled feet, prices rise considerably, and a good set of six or eight could reach £10,000.

It is among the nineteenth-century reproductions, some of them very fine indeed, that as an ordinary buyer you will probably find what you seek. Such sets will be described in sales catalogues as 'Chippendale style' or, perhaps, 'George III style'. The best of these copies are not cheap, and fine sets can make as high a price as their eighteenth-century counterparts, but simply designed sets can be bought from about £800 for six. If you have some money to spend and are determined to buy only the real thing, do be

Careful
Examination

careful. Many sets of chairs from the George III period include ones that have had some restoration. Examine each chair, slowly and carefully, from top to bottom, looking out for fresh timber, fresh nails, and sections that do not quite tone in with the colour and texture of the rest of the piece. Look at the carving, especially on chairs that feature a cabriole leg. Is the carving crisp and high, standing clear of its surrounding surface? If it seems to sink into the chair, it is probably a later addition. With straight-legged chairs, the absence of stretchers will suggest that the chair is not a genuine eighteenth-century example. However, their presence isn't necessarily a guarantee that it was made then as stretchers sometimes feature on later copies. Finally, go back over every chair, carefully checking that each one is identical and that a slightly different one has not been slipped into the set. Only if you are satisfied that the set is without major flaw should you pay the top price. Of course, furniture is made to be used, and it's very likely that a set of chairs will have been subjected to a variety of repairs during the

ABOVE: A young boy's uniform of Hussar Colonel with sabretache, belt bag, hat and plume, mess jacket and boots with original Mameluke sword. BELOW: Georgian double break front bookcase with Gothic moulded pediment over six brass mesh doors. Gilt mirrors in George II style, and a pair of William IV library chairs.

This oil on canvas by George Hall is in a pseudo Jacobean style but was painted in 1871. It is entitled 'Historical Scene with Young Lady in Elegant Yellow Dress about to hide in a chest'.

ABOVE: George II Irish punch bowl, chased with shells, leaves and foliage in Rococo manner. By William Walshe Dublin c. 1750. *Top left*: George IV coffee pot by W. Nowlan of Dublin c. 1822. it is still redolent of the Rococo style, with chased birds, fruit, flowers and scrolls. *Bottom right*: Baluster shaped coffee pot made in Cork by John Nicholson c. 1770.

Collectable green glass including decanter and water jug and four large finger bowls. The four cutglass salts with folded rims and square bases may have been made in Waterford.

LEFT: Eighteenth century continental ash dresser.
ABOVE: One of a pair of Irish George III mahogany
bookcases with Gothic style glazed upper doors.
BELOW LEFT: William IV rosewood breakfast table on triform
base. Stamped by Williams and Gibton.
BELOW RIGHT: Edwardian painted and satinwood bureau
with classic scene decorating its cylinder top.

Georgian flip top tripod table.

Red lacquered 18th century bureau
in Chinese style.

Georgian mahogany bureau bearing the trade name
Walsh & Sons, Bachelor's Walk.

course of its life. It may even be that at some stage a chair or two became irretrievably damaged and that a number of chairs from the set were dismantled and, with the addition of some new parts, extra chairs generated from the pieces. There is really nothing wrong with such sets. They are still useful and attractive and may represent a very good buy for your home. The point is that such shortcomings should be reflected in the price you pay.

It is also possible to find Chippendale-period two-seater settees in a similar style to the dining-chairs. Again, care is necessary in the purchase of such pieces because of the great numbers of them made during the latter half of the nineteenth century. A really good genuine one could cost as much as £10,000; nineteenth-century ones can be had for far less. The elaborately carved Irish mask tables of the eighteenth century owe a good deal to Chippendale's influence, although the carvings are frequently more profuse than those on the English versions. It is hard to put a reliable price on such objects. They do not come up for sale very often, and when they do, demand can be keen; whether they appear in Dublin, London, or New York. A simple one might fetch £5,000 to £7,000 but when one is dealing with the best examples, it is not unlike trying to price a fine painting. The quality of the timber, its figuring, its colour, the beauty and quantity of the carving, the provenance, the general condition and the heat of demand on the day can push prices into many thousands of pounds. A very fine one, which was once at Castle Morres in Kilkenny, sold at Christie's in July 1992 for £52,000. Good 19th-century reproductions are expensive too, although small ones can be bought for around £2,000; but even top-quality modern copies can be very highly priced as can be seen from the chapter that follows.

It was inevitable that the increasing flamboyance of the rococo style of furnishing would eventually produce a demand for simpler lines. This happened, quite suddenly, around 1765 in England and a little later in Ireland. During the 1750s two brothers, James and Robert Adam, went on a grand tour of Europe. The serious study of archaeology had recently begun, and at Pompeii and elsewhere the brothers were able to view the excavated remains of the artefacts and buildings of classical times. On their return home they began to produce designs for furniture and architecture in what they called the 'neo-classical' style. A new era had begun.

Irish Mask Tables

Chippendale style dining chairs.

Chapter Seven

FURNITURE: NINETEENTH AND TWENTIETH CENTURIES

The Regency Period

he immediate effect of the neo-classical movement was that furniture became slimmer, straighter, and less fussy. The beauty of furniture was held to lie primarily in the wood itself. Mahogany and rosewood continued to be widely used, but satinwood, introduced to Europe from the West Indies around 1770, made an increasingly frequent appearance. Used as a veneer, it was an ideal timber for highlighting the slender lines of the new furnishings.

In 1788 the widow of George Hepplewhite issued *The Cabinet and Upholsterer's Guide*, containing more than two hundred of her late husband's designs for household furniture. Hepplewhite, unlike Adam, was not an architect but a cabinetmaker who, in his youth, had been apprenticed to the famous firm of Gillows at Lancaster. His designs show a softening of Adam's rather severe classical lines and aimed to 'blend the useful with the agreeable'. As well as including patterns of his own, Hepplewhite's *Guide* seems also to have brought together a range of designs that were already popular among London's cabinetmakers and his easy-to-live-with pieces, especially the distinctive shield-back chair, have been produced and reproduced right up to the present day.

An even more important designer was Thomas Sheraton, whose name became almost synonymous with the new style of home furnishing from the 1790s right through to the 1820s. The restraint of many of his designs indicates that in his *Cabinet-Maker and Upholsterer's Drawing Book*, published in 1793, Sheraton was aiming at a middle-class clientele as well as at aristocratic patronage. It is significant that many of the subscriptions to his *Drawing Book* came from provincial cabinetmakers, indicating that in districts beyond the capital there was an increase both in the demand for good furniture design and in the money to pay for it.

The new fashions in furnishing appear to have reached Ireland around 1782, when William Moore, a cabinetmaker from the London firm of Ince & Mayhew, arrived in Dublin and began to make classically styled tables and commodes. Ince & Mayhew was one of London's most prestigious cabinetmaking establishments and was noted for its very high prices. Not surprisingly, its craftsmen had an exceedingly high reputation. Moore was enthusiastically patronised by affluent Dubliners engaged in the building of town houses, and he was also the maker of the famous Titania's Palace.

Heppelwhite

Sheraton

Moore

Regency
mahogany
sideboard.

Mid Victorian stool. Note the height of the carving which though not unduly elaborate is of good quality.

Strictly speaking, the term 'Regency' ought only to be applied to the period between 1811 and 1820 when, owing to the madness of King George III, his son, later George IV, was obliged to take his place, under the title of Prince Regent. However, for most collectors the term is rather loosely used to describe the period between 1780 and 1820, when the prince and his set were among the most influential arbiters of fashion. The prince himself favoured a far more elaborate style of furnishing than that laid down by the Adam brothers, and after he became king there was a trend towards increased heaviness in furniture. However, there was no sharp break in style, and it can often be quite difficult for the collector to decide whether a piece was made in 1810 or in 1825.

Sideboards

As the Chippendale chair seems in some way to characterise the period before 1770, it often seems that the piece most redolent of the Regency period is the bow-fronted long-legged sideboard, most often made from mahogany or with satinwood in veneer. It was in fact James Adam who invented the sideboard as we know it, around the year 1775. Such sideboards usually have six tapering legs, often ending in a spade foot, and although it was generally held that the elegance of a sideboard must rest in its lines and proportion, some pieces feature inlays of exotic woods.

There is a wide variation in the price of such pieces on the antiques market. Width, height, timber, inlay and general style and condition all influence potential buyers, and most examples fall into the £1,000 to £5,000 range. Especially desirable are small sideboards and ones with square rather than turned legs; the latter tend to indicate a date close to the end of the Regency period.

When you are examining a small sideboard, check that its depth has not been reduced. This may have been done by unscrupulous dealers, who know that smaller pieces make better prices, but the depth may also have been honestly cut down by a previous owner who found it too great for a small room. Examine the piece to see that its height and width are roughly in proportion to its depth. Pull out a drawer. The area behind the drawer at the back of the sideboard, because it is exposed to the air, should have darkened over the years; if it looks very light it may be that the darkened portion has been cut away. Check the back corners for any signs of fresh timber or nails, and look at the back of each drawer to ensure that the sides, or linings, have not been reduced in size.

It may be that you decide that a reduced sideboard suits you because your home is too small to take a large one anyway. This is fine, so long as the price you pay is reduced to fit the condition of the piece. Bear in mind too that the value of such a piece will not appreciate at all to the same extent as a sideboard that has not been tampered with. Many collectors would not touch such a piece, and if your aim is investment as well as pleasure you would do better, if you are seeking a small sideboard, to wait until such a one appears on the market and be prepared to pay the going price.

Another alteration that can be carried out on Regency sideboards is the replacement of the legs. Sometimes turned legs have been replaced with the square, spade-footed variety to make the piece more salable; frequently,

Examining
Sideboards

repair has been made necessary by breakage. Examine each leg carefully; the place to look for unauthorised joinings is at the point where the body of the piece meets the leg. Check that lines of inlay or stringing applied at this point are not covering up a join, by ensuring that the timber above the inlay matches that below.

Chairs

The most distinctive type of Regency chair is that which features sabre legs and bar back; but the style has been much imitated during the last thirty years or so, so be careful not to confuse reproduction with antique. It's a general, though not infallible, rule that the genuine period chair will be heavier than the modern one. It will also have a soft patina quite unlike the bright shine of the modern piece, and the grain of the timber will usually be more complex. The reproduction will often be meanly proportioned; a genuine Regency sabre leg, for example, should have a good 'kick-out' in front.

Viewing a
Set of
Chairs

When viewing a set of chairs, take time to check each one individually. Look out for fresh timber and nails and for parts whose colour does not match the rest. Don't forget to turn chairs upside down, as this often reveals repairs you might otherwise miss, as well as the presence of pest infestation or rot. Finally, set the chairs out in a row, if you can, to ensure that they really are identical and not just similar.

The prices of all nineteenth-century chairs have been rising steadily during the last few years, with few really good sets being bought at much less than £2,000. For a set of six Regency mahogany chairs of the kind referred to above you could expect to pay somewhat more than that — perhaps as much as £3,000. For very finely crafted ones with special features such as spiral turned bars or inlays you could pay very significantly more. Square-legged chairs are just as expensive, but those with turned legs from the latter end of the Regency period can be got for less; you could be lucky enough to buy a set of six for around £1,500, but prices for these too are rising. Bear in mind that the more chairs in a set the higher the price will

Edwardian period wine cellaret in Adam Revival style.

Mahogany brass bound peat bucket.

Late Georgian dressing table.

be. Sets of eight are considerably more expensive than sets of six and by the time you have reached sets of twelve you could be looking at a figure in excess of £8,000. The presence of one or two carvers makes a set of chairs more than usually desirable and even more expensive; a set of ten Regency chairs, including two carvers, with their original upholstery and with an unusual X-shaped centre splay, were sold not long ago for £34,000! This was a particularly fine set in tip-top condition, and it was the special features and the almost perfect original upholstery that pushed up the price.

One piece of good news if you like Regency chairs but happen to be rather short of funds is that single chairs quite often turn up at sales and are sold for around £50 or even less. This means that if you have patience and are prepared to live with a collection of unmatched chairs, you could buy enough to go around your table for as little as £300. Such chairs also make very attractive hall and bedroom pieces, and I think they are a very good buy.

Early Nineteenth-Century Occasional Furniture

The Regency period saw a great increase in the number of small pieces of furniture offered to the customer. It is at this time that canterburies, davenports, small tripod tables, sofa tables, pembroke tables, small open bookshelves and work or sewing-tables became popular. Just because such pieces are so small they are now much in demand, and prices are high, often so high that they seem hardly commensurate with the usefulness of such

Occasional Tables

objects. I always feel that there is really very little one can do with an early nineteenth-century fitted work-table or wine cellaret, but I am in a minority, it seems, and the market is willing to pay as much as £2,000 for a fine work table and even more for a good brass-bound cellaret.

Small early nineteenth-century occasional tables are both appealing and useful. The small drop-leaf table with dummy drawer called a pembroke table can fetch prices of up to £2,000 and more for the best ones, but you will often come across plain ones, perhaps in need of some restoration, and these can be relatively inexpensive, with prices starting at around £350. A sofa table is wider than a pembroke table, with most of its width in the centre portion and the leaves rather narrow. The very earliest sofa tables were made without stretchers so that they could be pulled over a sofa for use as a tea or writing-table, hence the name. However because they lacked a stretcher such tables tended to be fragile and the legs often worked loose. Most of the early sofa tables we see today have two legs with splayed feet and a stretcher uniting them. Later in the period such tables were often made with a centre pedestal support. Regency sofa tables are somewhat more expensive than pembroke tables, with good ones being priced at between £2,500 and £5,000. However, if you like this kind of piece it is possible to buy Victorian versions with four turned legs from around £400.

Dressing-Tables

One sort of Regency piece that is still quite reasonable in price is the dressing-table. The more elaborately styled ones are lovely things, with pull-up mirrors and sliding shelves and drawers and lots of intriguing little fitted compartments. These appear to have been designed for the dressing-room of the man of the house, with the mirrors ideally placed for shaving or for tying the cravat. If you are very lucky you could buy one of these at auction for £600 to £800, but prices have been rising of late, and better ones have begun to fetch prices in excess of £1,000.

Another bedroom fashion that began during the George III period and continued into the early nineteenth century was the two or three-tiered corner washstand, usually with splayed feet and often featuring inlay or stringing. A few years ago these pieces were very cheap, but of late they have begun to reach between £400 and £800 at auction, depending on quality.

Plain dressing-tables with an apron round the back and sides, on rather long legs and with one or perhaps three drawers, are still inexpensive and are ideal for use as hall or writing-tables in the modern home. These continued to be made until well into the nineteenth century, but the Regency ones can usually be distinguished from later ones by the rings on their turned legs or by legs which are reeded or fluted. It should be possible to buy a well-made mahogany one from the Regency period for around £400. Victorian ones, which generally feature a simpler turned leg, often with a ball at the top, are even cheaper, and can be bought at auction from as little as £100 and sometimes less.

The Age of William IV

The accession of King George IV led to a period of more extreme opulence in furniture fashions, especially in the homes of the wealthy. The overthrow of Napoleon and the restoration of the Bourbons in France led to a new enthusiasm for things French, and there was a strong revival of Louis XV styles. Brass inlay and vast gilded mounts were applied to furnishings, and the legs of chairs and tables were frequently contorted into grotesque representations of crocodiles, sphinxes, dolphins, and lions' heads.

The middle class and gentry did not aspire to such lavish display, but even among their furnishings the move from simple classical lines had begun, and during the reign of William IV, which lasted from 1830 to 1837, many of the features common in Victorian furniture were making their appearance. Sideboards became large and rather square and were often in the double-pedestal style that became extremely popular during the Victorian age. Large library tables were fashionable, in mahogany and rosewood, with trestle-style supports and scrolled feet. Round breakfast tables with tip-up tops were popular for informal meals in the breakfast parlour; here too the most favoured woods were rosewood and mahogany. The Regency bar-backed dining-chair continued in vogue, but the sabre leg was universally replaced with the turned leg, which already showed the rounded chunkiness that was to become more pronounced during the 1840s and 1850s. Also seen was a heavier type of dining-chair with a rather wide squared back, which was occasionally upholstered. There was a fashion for cane seats, especially in the making of light, open armchairs, and the library chairs known as bergères.

At auction, sets of William IV bar-backed chairs tend to make more than the square-backed style. A set of six bar-backed ones could set you back by as much as £2,000, depending on condition and quality, but you could be lucky enough to find a set of the square-backed ones for around £800 for six. Library chairs, whether caned or otherwise, are extremely sought-after at present, and for a good one, £1,000 would not be a surprising price. Pairs and fours — the latter are seen at auction but they are rare — are even more expensive.

The round breakfast-table of this period is popular now, as it is ideal for the modern home. Prices depend on quality and the timber used, but it

At Auctions

Regency period
rosewood canterbury.

Three particularly fiine Victorian chairs; the one in the centre is known as a prie-dieu.

Chiffoniers

is possible to buy such tables, especially mahogany ones, for a sum comfortably less than £1,000. The rosewood ones tend to fetch a bit more.

The variety of smaller pieces continued to increase during the 1830s as sitting rooms began to acquire that cluttered look that reached a peak of popularity between 1860 and 1880. It would appear that the canterbury was the most fashionable of these pieces. Originally designed to store sheet music, they are in strong demand on the antiques market and fetch very high prices. A simple mahogany or rosewood canterbury, with a single drawer at the base and with the usual pattern of curved or vertical slats, about eighteen inches high, above, could now be expected to fetch £1,000 or more. Those with one or two extra shelves and a gallery top regularly make twice that. The latter style is generally referred to as a canterbury whatnot. These pieces usually feature round wooden handles, or occasionally cone-shaped ones, and they continued to be popular into the Victorian period. Later canterburies are frequently made in walnut or walnut veneer and are often not of the quality of earlier examples. In general, however, prices for the later ones are not much less than those paid for 1830s pieces. Fine ones especially, are in demand, whatever their age.

As well as the large sideboard for use in the dining-room, small sideboards called chiffoniers were used during this period, probably in the drawing-room. These first appeared during the Regency and were rather richly made, with brass inlays. The William IV pieces are simpler and therefore a lot less expensive, though prices have been rising, and chiffoniers that you could have bought a year or two ago for around £800 are now making almost twice that. Chiffoniers continued to be made during the Victorian era, but the Victorian ones are quite easily distinguished from the earlier pieces. The William IV ones, very often made in rosewood, generally

Victorian credenza of ebonised timber with boulle door and ormolu mounts.

have a straight, shelved back; during the Victorian period they were usually made in mahogany and had a curved back with applied moulding. At the time of writing, Victorian chiffoniers can be bought for less than £600, but here too prices are rising, and particularly fine examples are already making a good deal more than this.

If you have formed the impression that the styles of the William IV period tend to merge into those of the Victorian era, you are quite right, and it is very difficult to distinguish many William IV pieces (particularly chairs, I always think) from early Victorian ones. It also has to be remembered that in Ireland and in provincial England many designs remained in fashion until long after London had moved on to the next craze. It is therefore perfectly possible that chairs that seem indubitably to have been made during the 1830s date in fact from the 1850s. However, this is not a problem likely to affect the collector of everyday nineteenth-century furniture. Accurate dating is much more important at the very expensive end of the market, as for example when highly priced objects of eighteenth-century French furniture need to be distinguished from nineteenth-century copies, or when a piece is fetching a very high price because it has been attributed to a particular maker.

Dating

The Victorian Age

In approaching the subject of Victorian furniture I have to confess that I'm coming to my own favourite period. I have often had the feeling that there is a faintly intimidating quality about fine Regency furniture: its sleek, elegant lines seem to suggest that you ought to be able to live up to it. To be seen to advantage it needs a certain austereness in decor; dust and grimy walls do not live happily with it! Victorian furniture, on the other hand, makes no such demands. Its darker, curvier surfaces tolerate the knocks of daily life with relative good humour, and — provided the more massive pieces are avoided — it is extremely comfortable to live with. Unfortunately for the small collector, it seems that quite a number of people are coming round to this point of view, and pieces of Victorian furniture that would have been despised five or ten years ago are now making substantial prices. Nevertheless, it would still be possible to furnish a house with Victorian pieces at no more than the cost of new furniture of good quality.

Desks

Davenports

One piece of Victoriana that is expensive at auction today is the davenport. These small desks with lift-up tops and drawers to the side have been something of a price phenomenon of late. Up to four or five years ago you could easily have bought one at a Dublin saleroom for around £500 — indeed a friend of mine bought one about nine years ago for less than £100. Now, however, even a very plain davenport can cost as much as £1,000, with the very best ones making as much as £3,500 and more — although lately it seems that prices have been slipping a little. In general the very simple boxy ones are the earliest and belong to the Regency or William IV period. Victorian ones were more elaborate, often inlaid with novelty woods, with raised or pop-up stationery compartments and richly carved legs to the front. The early davenports mainly come in rosewood and, to a lesser degree, mahogany; during the Victorian period, although mahogany was used, walnut and walnut veneer was the preferred timber for these pieces. Thanks to their greater elaboration, Victorian davenports make prices just as high as the older examples, and in fact it would often be possible to pick up a Regency or William IV piece for less money than a Victorian one, simply because it is so plain.

If you are one of those who would dearly love to own a davenport but cannot afford it, all you can do is take comfort from the fact that, rationally considered, the davenport, which generally lacks a sensible degree of space for the knees, is actually quite uncomfortable to work at and has little storage space. Much better value is a functional Victorian pedestal desk or roll-top bureau, which should be obtainable for something between £650 and £1,300, depending on size, quality and fittings.

Dining-Tables

Another Victorian piece that has shown a substantial increase in value over the last couple of years is the good-quality D-end dining table of the kind that has a deep frieze about the top and sturdy turned or cabriole legs. Such tables have lately been making £2,500 to £3,500 at auction. However, it is perfectly possible to get Victorian tables far cheaper than this. One style that I would consider to be very underrated is the plain, solid mahogany drop-leaf table with turned legs. These regularly sell for around £400, and you couldn't buy a modern table approaching this quality for that kind of money.

Round Victorian breakfast tables, usually of mahogany and with a tripod or pedestal leg, are regularly seen at auction in Ireland, and the price band is fairly wide. My own impression is that the pedestal style is a little less popular with buyers, and it's possible to buy a mahogany table of this kind for around £600; in poor condition you could get it for a good deal less. Really fine tripod-leg examples can fetch up to £2,000.

The Centre Leg

When buying tables with a centre leg, whether pedestal or tripod, check very carefully that the leg really belongs to the table top. These tables are a favourite for the furniture marriage-broker, and such deceit is easy to hide unless the prospective buyer examines it thoroughly. If in doubt get the auctioneer to go over the table with you. With a tripod leg, make sure that each foot is securely attached to the centre pod; feet regularly break away and are replaced or repaired. I would avoid at any price a table that has been the subject of such a repair. The point at which pod and foot meet is one of extreme stress, and if the joint has broken once, it is inclined to happen repeatedly. Round tables are also prone to developing cracks across the surface. Whether to buy such a table is something you must decide for yourself. You may decide that you are not too concerned about short cracks or, perhaps, chips in a walnut or rosewood veneer. However, I would avoid tables with long or very open cracks; they look ugly and are not easy to restore.

Chairs

The most characteristic style of Victorian dining-chair is the balloon back. Before about 1860 these were generally made with the turned leg popularised during the late Regency period; after 1860 the curved cabriole leg was more common. Mahogany was the commonly used wood, but sets in rosewood, walnut and beech will also be found. Beechwood chairs should be the least expensive to buy, but remember that they are often mistaken, even by

Neat boulle side cabinet of a style which, even in a modern house, can add something spectacular to a room.

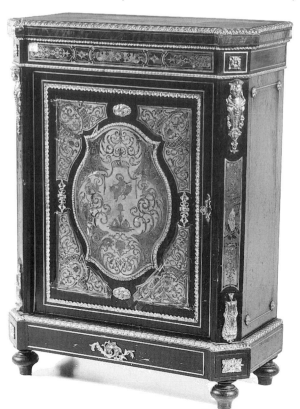

auctioneers, for mahogany. When viewing, look carefully at the grain of the wood on the curved top rail. Mahogany has a much denser and busier grain than beech; often beech seems to have hardly any grain at all save for a few occasional dashes. At some inconspicuous place on the chair press the wood slightly with the tip of your fingernail. If you see a slight indentation, the timber is unlikely to be mahogany. Walnut chairs tend to develop a warm chocolate-coloured patina, and the grain has a soft-streaked appearance. Rosewood also has a streaky grain, but it is much darker than that of walnut, and the almost-black swirls stand out strongly from the background hue of the timber.

Good sets of six or eight Victorian dining-chairs have been on the rise of late and now make between £1,200 and £2,000 at auction. I have the feeling that the cabriole-leg style is more favoured by buyers. For those who feel daunted by such prices, I think the solution is to buy two sets of three or four reasonably similar chairs. Such sets can be got for as little as £300, and they come up quite often at sales. Victorian easy chairs come on the market at a great range of prices. Pairs of button-back ladies' and gentlemen's chairs can now make up to £1,000 a pair, but singletons can be bought at prices starting from as little as £150. Chairs needing upholstery and perhaps a re-polish can be got for even less than this.

The chaise longue was a highly popular item for the Victorian drawing-room. The Victorian lady was a martyr to a range of ailments, real and imaginary. Unrelenting childbirth was the dominant fact of her existence, and many women died of it. For some, the claim of 'delicacy' was the only way to avoid the sexual overtures of their husbands. Others, damaged by ill-managed pregnancies and deliveries, developed chronic gynaecological problems that made activity an ordeal. A few, frustrated at the lack of opportunity for women, developed symptoms of what we would now recognise as clinical depression. And finally, many Victorian women succumbed to what they called consumption and what we knew as tuberculosis. Upper-class women spent a good deal of their day propped up on their chaise longues, in graceful poses, with an elegant little bottle of smelling salts close to hand should they chance to have an attack of the 'vapours'. Here they could receive their callers without exertion.

Today, chaise longues can be bought from about £60 for very plain ones requiring restoration to about £600 for the best examples in good condition. If you are thinking of buying one, however, do bear in mind that, although they take up as much room as a settee, they are really only comfortable for one person to sit upon.

The Chaise Longue

Bedroom Furniture

Victorian chests of drawers are most usually to be found with straight fronts, round wooden handles, and bun or sometimes bracket feet. They can be bought from around £200 to about £800 for the very best. If you have room for them, very large 'Scotch' chests can be excellent value, as most buyers tend to go for the smaller ones, and if you have a really big bedroom you could, for an outlay of some £350, become the owner of a well-made Victorian chest capable of accommodating jumpers, shirts and socks for an entire household!

Very late Regency period sofa table with spiral twist legs. This style, though more usually with turned legs, was very popular throughout the 19th century. Earlier examples, however, which have trestle supports tend to fetch the highest prices.

Simple but good quality Georgian fold over card table on cabriole legs with pad foot. The front outline, with its recessed centre, is known as a reversed or inverted breakfront.

Victorian wardrobes too can often be surprisingly inexpensive, at prices from around £50. Rather massive Empire-style wardrobes of a very high degree of workmanship were exceedingly fashionable during the late nineteenth century and are seen quite often at house sales. They sell for around £500 to £660 — not especially cheap, perhaps, but for this money you can make yourself the owner of a finely crafted carved or inlaid piece at a price that compares very favourably with the cost of a new fitted wardrobe. When buying wardrobes, try to check for woodworm at the back. This is often made of soft pine, which is prone to infestation. A little woodworm, even a little more than a little, can be effectively treated, but extensive infestation, affecting all or most of the back, is not desirable.

The Edwardian Era

Although Queen Victoria was not succeeded by her grandson Edward until 1901, a number of the changes in furniture fashions that we associate with the Edwardian age had already well established themselves. By around 1890 heavy carving and generous curves began to fall out of favour, to be replaced by what was called a 'Sheraton revival'. Furniture became slim and sleek again, and novelty woods, especially satinwood, became popular. Luckily for the collector who finds it difficult to distinguish such pieces from late eighteenth-century examples, the satinwood used in late nineteenth and early twentieth-century furniture differs somewhat from that used in the older pieces. The West Indian satinwood used at the turn of the eighteenth century had a rather short grain similar to mahogany, but the East Indian satinwood used in the later copies has a striped grain that gleams in the light. There was a great fashion for painted satinwood, which was applied to many display cabinets and occasional pieces. Such pieces are now extremely expensive, and a small occasional table of painted satinwood could cost as much as £1,000 with painted satinwood bookcases reaching up to three times as much. Leggy Edwardian display cabinets, known as vitrines, in

Satinwood

ABOVE AND OPPOSITE PAGE: Very typical Victorian mahogany balloon back dining chairs. They are very well made and probably date from around 1850 but their uncompromising plainness might deter some buyers and highest prices tend to go for those with finely carved backs.

satinwood or inlaid mahogany can fetch around £1,000 to £3,000, depending on quality and often appear at auction in pairs.

Late Georgian fashions were perhaps most closely followed during the Edwardian period in the production of fine side tables. Often made in pairs from mahogany or satinwood and incorporating cross-banding and inlays of exotic timbers like tulipwood and yew, such tables can more than equal the craftsmanship displayed a century earlier. Prices tend to hover about the £2,000 mark, and of course pairs are the more desirable.

Another kind of piece crafted in the Adam style during the Edwardian age for which collectors are willing to pay very high prices indeed is the Carlton House desk. These elegant objects have a leather-topped writing surface that is surrounded at the back and sides with a superstructure of drawers and pigeonholes. Standing upon long, slender legs, they are frequently seen in satinwood with marquetry or brass inlay. You would be very lucky to obtain one at auction for less than £6,000.

Chairs

Such very high prices for Edwardian furniture apply, in the main, to the sophisticated productions of the Sheraton revival. Everyday Edwardian furniture is not particularly expensive and often compares very well in price with the cost of new pieces.

On dining-chairs the balloon back was superseded towards the end of the nineteenth century by a straight padded one, often carved across the back rail. Both mahogany and beech were used, but a surprising number turn out on close inspection to have been made in walnut. Sets of six are very common and I think underpriced at present, often selling at auction for around £300.

Another useful buy for the modern home is the Edwardian salon suite. This generally consists of six chairs, which are perfect for use as dining-chairs, along with two easy chairs and a chaise longue to complete the ensemble. There is no problem in obtaining plain mahogany or walnut sets for well under £1,000, although the very best ones have lately begun to make a bit more. The furnishings of the elegant Edwardian salon often included a number of highly ornamental occasional chairs. Many of these had paintings on their backs or decorative pads made of satin or damask. Although the slender lines of such pieces are redolent of the Regency period, the general style is really quite unlike anything made at the earlier time. By and large, very thin cabriole legs and a highly decorated back will suggest a late nineteenth-century date rather than a late eighteenth-century one, although there are exceptions, especially with regard to Continental furniture. Prices for such chairs, particularly those that have arms, tend to hover about the £400 mark.

Sideboards

Edwardian sideboards tend to be of the square mirror-backed variety. The range of prices for these is rather wide and can be unpredictable. I have seen a hotly contested one reach a price of £1,600 at auction and, not very long afterwards, seen a smaller but not greatly inferior one sell for £40! These two extremes apart, the price tends to be determined by the timber used and by the extent and quality of the inlays displayed. They can most frequently be found at between £350 and £500. They are usually made in mahogany but occasionally in rosewood. The latter are rare and always in demand when seen. Whenever you are startled by the price paid for a mirror-back Edwardian sideboard, check that it isn't rosewood. Depending on style and size, these can make up to £2,000 at auction.

Smaller Pieces

The Edwardians had a great love for rather 'gimmicky' small furniture. Such objects include dressing-tables and work-tables with attractive and often unexpected fittings, small music cabinets, and coal cabinets with pull-out boxes and finely inlaid doors. The prices for such pieces can be rather hard to gauge; often when examining such an item you will find that you haven't seen anything quite like it before. However, in my own experience pieces of this sort tend to make around £500 or a little less.

Also very popular during the Edwardian period was the revolving bookcase. Usually these are simple affairs of mahogany or oak with three or four slats at the end of each section of shelf to keep books in place, but very occasionally one comes across a highly decorated satinwood example. These can fetch up to £2,000 at auction, but the plain ones make around £300, with very big ones fetching significantly less, owing to their very definite unwieldiness. Check the condition of such bookcases very thoroughly before you buy, for their design makes them inherently fragile. Always turn them upside down to ensure that the leg and turning mechanism hasn't been seriously damaged or replaced. Look carefully under each shelf for fresh timber and nails, for here too lurk areas of frequent repair. Having carried out your inspection, you must now make your decision whether to buy a repaired piece. It has to be admitted that the nature of the revolving bookcase is such that, on most of them, repairs have been necessary at one time or another. If you decide to buy, remember, as always, that deficiencies should be reflected in the price you pay.

The Twentieth Century

During the final decades of the nineteenth century oak furniture became popular once more. At first its use was associated with the Victorian gothic revival, when much furniture was made in a style that mimicked the windows and gables of churches, while bookcases and buffet sideboards revived the heavy carving and turned baluster supports seen on Tudor pieces. Unless a definite attempt has been made to fake genuine Tudor pieces, there is no difficulty in distinguishing these imitations from the real thing. The appearance of the oak used in the nineteenth-century pieces is smoother, shinier, paler, and lighter in weight. The mock-Tudor buffet sideboard does not seem to be especially popular with the Irish buyer at present and, at prices that often hover around the £400 to £500 mark, they can, if they're not too massive, offer good value to those who like them.

From 1900 onwards oak was increasingly used for everyday furniture. Much of this was made to satisfy working-class and middle-class demand, and a good deal of it was shoddily made. However, a large number of quality

Oak Furniture

pieces were made also, especially by manufacturers who had been influenced by the arts and crafts movement, initiated during the late nineteenth century by William Morris and others with the aim of bringing back a high standard of craftsmanship to the making of everyday objects.

Good-quality oak furniture continued to be made during the 1920s and 1930s, and, apart from the occasional arts and crafts style piece firmly attributed to a particular designer, much of it is ridiculously cheap today. I would go further and say that I don't think this state of affairs will last, and if I were giving a collector on a limited budget a tip for the future I would suggest that if you bought some solid oak furniture of the 1930s at the prices made at today's auctions, you might, in years to come, have reason to feel very pleased with yourself. At worst, you will have bought yourself some very nice and serviceable furniture at considerably less than the price of new pieces. In the last year or two I have seen a 1930s Jacobean-style sideboard for £155, an attractive 1930 oak writing-desk for £145, a set of four slat-back oak chairs for £100, and several arts and crafts style sideboards with carved decoration on the doors being knocked down for less than £40.

The 1930s were also associated with the art deco movement. This style almost defies attempts to describe it in words. To define it as an attempt to explore the effect both of geometric form and of movement in the visual arts is both inadequate and, perhaps, meaningless to anyone who has not had the opportunity of seeing objects made in the art deco mode. Yet if you have seen a few examples of the style it is quite easy to recognise again. It was, above all, startlingly, boldly, refreshingly modern, and even today art deco pieces still have the power to amaze.

Flip top breakfast table dating from about the late 1830s. This sort of pedestal base often suggests the William IV rather than Victorian period.

Although some notable furniture designers and makers produced furniture in the art deco style, it influenced furniture rather less than it did glass, ceramics, and sculpture. Such furniture as was made was often created to the order of wealthy customers and naturally remains expensive today in London, in America, and on other international markets. Unfortunately for lovers of art deco furniture, one doesn't really come across a great deal of it in Ireland. No doubt the economic situation here during these years meant that demand for expensive furniture and new designs was limited. Now in the Irish antique market there seems surprisingly little interest in such pieces as do appear, and it's worth keeping an eye out for things that combine good craftsmanship with decidedly modern design and that may have been made during the 1920s and 1930s. Occasionally an unassuming, unnamed piece can make its way into an auction and sell for quite a modest sum. I recently came across a magnificent art deco dining-suite in a Dublin auction room. It consisted of long sideboard that contained drawers, a wine rack, some cupboard space, and a shelved area. There was a hanging unit to go with it. A magnificent table, made of walnut and wonderful golden bird's eye maple to match the cupboards, was the centrepiece, and eight sturdy chairs, well upholstered in cream leatherette, completed the ensemble. After some agonising I decided that despite its beauty there was no escaping the fact that it was too large for my dining-room. Mixed feelings were my lot when it failed to make its tiny reserve of £300 and remained unsold! At the same

Art Deco

This fine davenport bears the label of Strahan of Dublin. It is made of walnut with inlays of hollywood and boxwood and its satinwood lined interior is fitted with drawers and pigeonholes. (Photo courtesy Adams)

sale a fine walnut-framed art deco style chesterfield suite sold to some discerning bargain hunter for just £210.

You will have noticed that our account of antique furniture has brought us surprisingly close to the present day. The truth is, of course, that as older pieces become scarcer the frontier of what is considered antique is inevitably going to be pushed further and further forward. As well as that, it's clear to anyone who attends auctions regularly that very fine reproduction furniture, even that made during the last thirty years, is eagerly sought after. In this connection the firm of James Hicks ought to be mentioned. This cabinetmaking establishment was founded by Hicks in 1894 at 5 Lower Pembroke Street, Dublin, to restore old furniture and to make copies of Chippendale, Adam and Sheraton pieces. The reproduction work of the firm is so fine that collectors are prepared to pay virtually as much for it as for the real thing. After the death of Hicks in 1936 the firm continued to exist until the 1970s, so many of the pieces seen are really of very recent date. Hicks's best work was probably in the Chippendale style, with heavy mask tables, dining-chairs, tables and writing-desks all being made.

Prices are high, and they seem to be rising. In late 1988 a Chippendale style mask table with central frieze mask and a mask at the top of each elaborately carved cabriole leg, the frieze itself carved with flowers, scrolls, and swags or garlands, fetched £10,500 at a Kildare house sale. Just two years later, at a Kilkenny saleroom, a similar table by Hicks, possibly not quite so interesting in that it lacked the masks on the legs, was sold for £15,740. A set of Chippendale-style dining-chairs by Hicks would be expected to reach anything from £14,000 to £18,000 for sets of ten and twelve. A large Georgian-style dining-table by Hicks, D-ended and with square, tapering legs, has sold for £9,500; I have seen period tables, of no worse quality, sell for less. Regency-style pieces by Hicks also sell well, though not as spectacularly as the mid-eighteenth-century style examples, and generally not so expensively as period furniture. For example, single tea and card tables sell for between £550 and £900, with simply styled writing-tables making a bit more. But even with regard to these Sheraton-type pieces, if the items come in a pair, or if there is fine inlay or marquetry, prices rise dramatically. A pair of George III style demi-lune side tables, inlaid with foliage and a yew-wood fan, recently sold at auction for £11,000, and a pair of inlaid satinwood carvers has made £3,000. One of the finest lots of Hicks furniture ever to appear at auction in Ireland was offered at the dispersal sale at Humewood in Co. Wicklow in the summer of 1992. It was not actually part of the house contents but came from another private collection, and comprised a pair of satinwood, mahogany and marquetry side tables with gilded friezes and legs. They were made, sometime after 1894, in the style of the eighteenth-century cabinet maker, William Moore, and not only did they reflect the design of the earlier period but the same method of construction was employed. They fetched £28,000.

For reproductions to fetch this kind of money they must be of the very best quality and made of solid timbers or the very finest veneers. Chipboard and fibreboard are out! But for the really good piece, old or even not so old, there is, it seems, a ready market.

James Hicks

19th century country pine dresser.

Everything is in readiness for a house contents sale.

County Down Bookbinder, Sydney Aiken, working on the Blackstaff Press edition of Richard Dunscombe Parker's *Birds of Ireland*. (*See also illustration below*) Parker (c.1805-81), regarded as Ireland's Audubon, remained unpublished until this modern fine edition was published in the 1980s.

Art Nouveau style binding of decorated vellum by Cedric Chivers (1901).

Chapter Eight

BOOKS

wise old book collector once wrote that he who succumbs to the lure of bibliophily becomes 'the victim of the least vicious of hobbies.' I am not so sure. Victim the collector may certainly be, but whether book collecting is quite so harmless a hobby as may be imagined is doubtful. The trouble is that book collecting lends itself rather readily to obsession. Unlike tables and chairs and cabinets, there is always room in the house for another book. If you run out of shelves you can put up some more. If you find when you put them up that there are now, after all, some extra spaces, well, you could always buy some more books ...

The trade has a name for a collector like this. He is called a bibliomane, an overenthusiastic gatherer of books. If he prizes them so highly, he will permit no-one else to read them, he will put them under lock and key and become known as a bibliotaph. If he loses the run of himself completely, buying books because, as a great climber said of Mount Everest, they are there, he will find himself falling into bibliomania. The most famous bibliomaniac was Sir Thomas Phillips, a nineteenth-century collector, whose aim was to acquire a copy of every book ever written! Strangely enough, as he filled his shelves with every conceivable form of written material — books, documents, old bills, account-books and letters — he actually raised the consciousness of historians and others with regard to the importance of keeping old books and written records. So despite his eccentricity, his career in collecting was useful after all.

Sir Thomas Phillips

For some reason, it would appear that the majority of book collectors are male. Why this should be so I have never been able to discover, but the fact remains that whenever I attend a book auction I find myself one of perhaps just two or three women present. Even at book fairs and in antiquarian and secondhand bookshops most of the customers are men. They are not just any men either. They are solid men, of a certain maturity of years. They are well dressed, but not flamboyantly so. They rarely wear jumpers but may sometimes be seen in what were once called sports jacket and flannels. The less sartorially elegant are inclined to favour cardigans.

There are those who will immediately cry 'Nonsense! Plenty of young men at book sales.' Indeed, there are. But get into conversation with them and find out what they do for a living. Ten to one they are booksellers or dealers, not true collectors. The private collectors, the real collectors, are more or less as I describe. I often wondered what they do for a living, and I think I know. Some, I suppose, are businessmen, some may be bank managers. Some are certainly teachers. But most, I suspect, are senior or retired civil servants. Many of these men, I would guess, grew up in the years when education and book learning were hard to acquire. Families made sacrifices to get boys into secondary school, to get a Leaving Certificate, in order to achieve that most glittering of prizes, the civil service job. In the end it was their knowledge and love of books that got them those jobs, and it's not surprising that many of them held onto this love and in their later years turned to the gentle sport of bibliophily. I may be completely wrong, of course. These book collectors may very well be dentists, artists, builders, retired sportsmen. But I should be surprised if they were.

Winds of Change

Having said all that, I think there are certain signs that winds of change may be about to blow through the book world. General antique dealers have begun to appear at book auctions, the prices of the most valued books have been rising, and it may be that the investment buyer is about to make a serious impression on the book trade. I cannot say that I welcome this development, for I have a fear that the price of old books for the small collector who buys to read and enjoy will be pushed up by those who wish to buy in the hope of making profit. While it would, of course, be ingenuous to suggest that many present collectors don't buy in the hope that their purchase will maintain or increase its value, I think it's true say that this isn't generally their primary purpose, and it would be a pity if such collectors were edged out of the market by those whose first aim is investment.

What to Collect

The collector who would like to acquire a small library of fine or interesting books but isn't sure how to go about it may ask: what should I collect? The answer to that is simple: anything you please. While it is true that there are quite well-defined areas of book collecting and a range — enormous, I can assure you — of books that it is generally agreed are worth collecting, it is also true that there are thousands of collectors who follow quite individualistic lines and buy books that no-one else has yet thought of collecting. Many of them hope that what they are collecting, at modest prices because few others want them, will some day be more in demand and that they will have the satisfaction of having acquired something valuable at a very low price, or of selling at a pleasing profit.

This will not happen, of course, if what they buy is rubbish, if the books are torn or dirty or lack pages or if they are the umpteenth impression of worthless editions. The books you buy ought always to be good in themselves, no matter how modestly priced they are or how little anyone else beyond yourself values them. Your book should be written by someone with something worth saying in a volume that is clean, with dust jacket where possible, and containing all its original text and blank pages. As to what the book is about, that is up to you. The most satisfying form of collecting is when you come to an author through genuine interest in what he has to say. His subject could be something you have studied at school or college, it could be about a hobby or the field in which you work. You may simply decide to buy copies in fine editions of books that you have enjoyed over the years. Any motive is valid.

This chapter will deal mainly with books in which, for the moment at least, a significant number of booksellers and collectors are interested. This is for reasons of space, needless to say, for really the subject is infinite. I think it is also the case that book collecting is just as subject to the caprices of fashion as other areas, and what is valued by one generation may not be so highly regarded by another. For example, up to fifty or so years ago a wide range of religious texts could command good prices, as could certain works in Latin and Greek. Nowadays a collector might happily be paid to take away many such volumes. It is worth mentioning in this context that very few Bibles are worth a great deal of money. Many people imagine that the old, well-thumbed family Bible must be valuable; sadly, only very important editions and richly bound Bibles are of interest in today's market.

The market at present includes among its chief areas of interest: fiction from the eighteenth to the twentieth century; drama from the sixteenth to the twentieth century; poetry from the eighteenth to the twentieth century; history; natural history; travel; topography; and children's books. There are other fields of interest of course, such as gardening, farming, sport, transport, science, medicine, and many more, but it would appear that at present a very high proportion of the book trade is concerned with the subjects I have mentioned. Very few collectors would attempt to buy every book within their subject; what they do is choose an area of specialisation within their chosen field and concentrate on that. Most collectors have several specialist areas, and naturally, as their interests develop with the years, their collecting interests, too, will shift about.

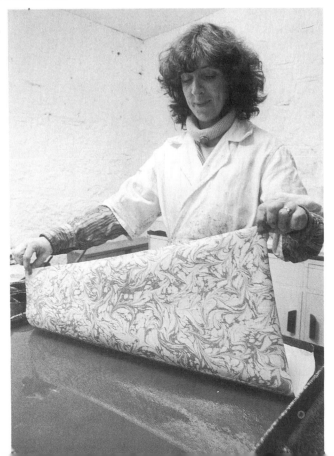

Marbler, Solveig Stone, making marbled paper for Parker's *Birds of Ireland*. (Photo courtesy Blackstaff Press)

Many collectors will be seeking their books in first editions. If a non-collector were to ask what is so special about a first edition, the answer would often have to be: well, nothing really. Nevertheless the fact remains that this is what the book market most values, and before you have spent very long dabbling in the area you will feel that this is what you must have too. There are instances where a second or specially bound or annotated edition may be as important as or more important than the first; research and experience will tell you when this is so.

When you first take up an area of interest you will probably have acquired a rough knowledge of the dates of publication of your favoured authors, but as time goes by you will find yourself having frequent recourse to bibliographies. These are huge and immensely absorbing volumes that give the dates of publication of every work of each author listed. The best all-round bibliography is *The British Museum General Catalogue of Printed Books to 1955* and its supplements, some of which are entitled the *British Library Catalogue*. (Unfortunately, you will not find this on the shelf of most public libraries, but research and university libraries have copies. To see these it may be necessary to write to the librarian to receive permission to use the library. The one easiest to get into is probably Trinity College Library. Ring before you go, however, to ensure that access will be permitted.) There are also many specialist bibliographies available — some are dedicated to the works of one author. For the collector of nineteenth-century fiction — a very

BELOW LEFT: A volume of Moore's *Life of Lord Byron* (1831) in half morocco binding with marbled boards.
BELOW RIGHT: A late 18th century full calf binding.

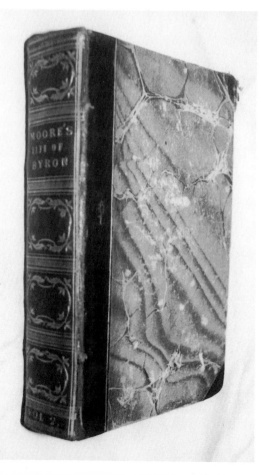

important area — the most useful bibliography is Michael Sadleir's *Nineteenth-Century Fiction*. I have not yet come across a really good bibliographer of twentieth century fiction, and in the case of many minor authors you will have to be your own bibliographer. (A list of some of the more useful Irish bibliographies is given at the end of this book.) An indispensable adjunct to the bibliographies is the *Book Auctions Record*, published annually and giving the prices reached by a wide range of books during the preceding year. It is rather weak on books of Irish interest, and for these you had best keep your own records; this is most conveniently managed with a card index, or perhaps a file on your personal computer.

So, having established the years of the editions that you seek, how are you to recognise them? With twentieth-century fiction and, indeed, very many twentieth-century volumes, there is no great problem. Most books nowadays obligingly include the year of publication along with the date of any previous editions or impressions. Many nineteenth-century and a reasonable number of earlier volumes also include a year of publication, and if you know the date of the first edition there should be no difficulty in distinguishing this from subsequent printings. Where dates are not included in a book, you will have to be aware of the various features that distinguish each edition, if indeed there was more than one at all. You will have to discover how many volumes the first edition contained, the kind and colour of its covers, the kind and number of the illustrations or maps included, and whether there were any mistakes or unusual features in the typesetting of the edition you seek. Other clues may appear within the books themselves as you examine them. For example, terms like 'First illustrated edition', 'First collected edition' or 'Preface to the first edition' all indicate that a volume is not of the first edition.

Having hunted down your quarry, you must now turn your attention to its condition. This should be as near perfect as possible. With twentieth-century volumes, condition needs to be all but pristine, with pages spotless and jacket in place, if there was one originally. There should be no scribbles or tears and no pages missing. To a certain extent this is a counsel of perfection, for many twentieth-century books are sold without jackets and at prices that suggest that the lack does not always seriously devalue an otherwise perfect book, especially if it is non-fiction. Before the twentieth century, books did not as a rule have jackets, and here it is the original binding that the collector seeks. With nineteenth-century volumes, you are generally looking for original publisher's cloth binding, particularly when this is known to have been especially decorative in some way.

With regard to books published between 1750 and 1830 you are keeping your eye out for the publisher's original boards, but you will not always find them! These boards were in fact intended as temporary coverings only; when a gentleman bought a book during the eighteenth-century it was generally understood that he would remove the boards and have the book bound in leather. A book bound in contemporary leather would scarcely be less valuable than one still in boards. A very late rebind, say from the middle of the nineteenth century or later, would usually result in a significantly smaller price. I say usually, because if an attractive rebind does happen to catch your fancy you may decide not to worry too much about authenticity. With regard to nineteenth-century books issued originally in cloth, too, my

Books Auction Record

Identification

Condition

impression from attending book auctions is that a good leather binding will not detract from the value of a book, and a really fine binding may enhance it. There is, after all, a good deal of personal taste involved.

Buying Books

The most usual way to buy old books is through an antiquarian bookseller; the most exciting way is at auction. Unfortunately, book auctions are relatively rare events in Ireland, although they are quite common in England and a book or two can make a very nice memento of a holiday! Dublin is now relatively well served by secondhand bookshops that carry an interesting antiquarian stock as well as the possibility of bargains buys. Other dealers both in Dublin and around the country operate from home and by appointment. These can be contacted through the classified phone book. The antiquarian booksellers publish a list of such dealers, and this is obtainable at many bookshops. Many of these booksellers supply catalogues to regular customers and will also try to find particular books for you. Contact can also be made through the book fairs that are now held regularly in Dublin and occasionally elsewhere.

Another way books can be bought (and sold) is through book magazines. None exist in Ireland, but there are several useful and entertaining English ones that can be ordered on subscription. They frequently carry 'for sale' and 'wanted' advertisements, and since much of this business is done by

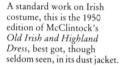

A standard work on Irish costume, this is the 1950 edition of McClintock's *Old Irish and Highland Dress*, best got, though seldom seen, in its dust jacket.

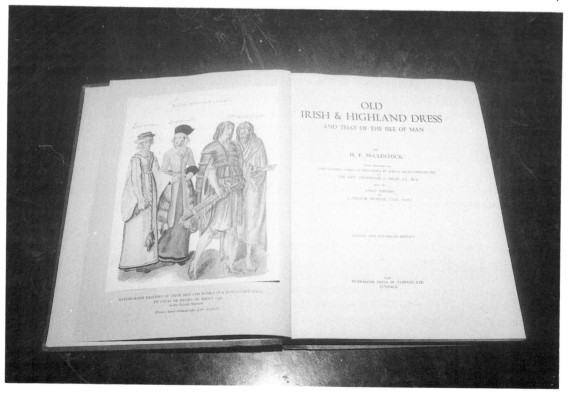

post in any case, the Irish buyer is at no particular disadvantage. These magazines are a particularly good way of obtaining copies of minor or less-collected authors.

At the time of writing, specialist book auctions are held in Ireland approximately twice a year. If you see one advertised, it is well worth sending for the catalogue straight away rather than waiting until viewing day. Book catalogues are rather densely packed affairs and really require leisurely study. Lots are not, alas, catalogued alphabetically, and very often a number of unrelated books are offered as a single lot. In this case it is very easy to miss something you are interested in until it is too late. It has happened to me more than once that I have noticed an interesting item for the first time just as it was being knocked down to somebody else! Having the catalogue in advance means that you will make a much more efficient and speedier job of viewing.

The conditions of sale at book auctions are similar to those at other sales. However, book catalogues do contain a number of terms and abbreviations that can seriously baffle the beginner and some of these are included in the glossary at the end of this book. Make notes in your catalogue of all the features you want to see in the books that interest you, and examine each book as carefully as you would a chair or a glass. Check the date first, and make sure that every leaf and plate, including endpapers, is present in any book you wish to buy. If it isn't and you decide to buy anyway, make sure, as always, that this is reflected in the price. Be aware, though, that flawed copies of books that are not especially rare do not appreciate in value as well as do fine copies. Extreme rarity, of course, can alter matters, and there are books that collectors are happy to see in almost any condition. But as a general rule, buy only the best you can afford, even if it means reducing the number of books you buy.

In general, you will get your books more cheaply at auction than from booksellers. It isn't always true, of course, and it often happens that if there is something you really want, the easiest way of acquiring it is to leave the details with your friendly dealer and allow him to get it for you. Naturally, you must expect to pay for this service and for the dealer's expertise. However, I have the feeling that the mark-up among reputable book dealers is generally not as much as the level of profit taken by general antique dealers. There are good reasons for this, in that with items such as furniture, single pieces of stock tie up more capital and more space than books do. If you do like buying at auction, don't forget to investigate the general auctions, especially house clearances. The days when unknowing auctioneers pushed large quantities of books into cardboard boxes and sold them as job lots are all but gone. Nevertheless, the fact that there are a few shelves of books in a house about to be cleared is not always advertised by the auctioneers, and if you are lucky you could be the only serious collector there. It's worth while, therefore, if you spot any likely-looking house clearances to ring up the auctioneer and ask if there are any books in the sale.

Book Auctions

Books of Irish Interest

It often seems as though the prime area of interest among collectors is Irish history, both national and local. There are a number of general histories of

This is the copper engraved frontispiece from Samuel Johnson and George Steevens' *Works of Shakespeare* (3rd ed. 1785). The rag pulp paper of volumes like this is immensely strong and a volume can be lifted by holding a single page: don't experiment with a valued volume, however!

Ireland that are of importance. These include Thomas Leland's *History of Ireland*, issued first in 1773 in three volumes. Prices for the set are between £120 and £160, depending on condition and binding. Contemporary leather would be most sought after here, but the £160 cited was in fact paid for a fine half-morocco copy of the first edition. There are a good many poorish copies of Leland about, and a copy of the first edition with, say, the joints of the spine cracked and in worn leather binding would cost about £70 to £90 at auction. Since the book is relatively common, it would be best to go for an edition in fine condition. If it's really a reading copy you're after then there would be little wrong with buying a well-bound copy of the 1814 edition at around £60 to £80.

Another early author who concerned himself with the history of Ireland was Sir James Ware. He lived during the seventeenth century and spent much of his life in antiquarian research and writing. Although he knew little Irish he was aware of the necessity for the inclusion of original documents in serious historical research, and he employed the Irish scholar Dualtach MacFirbhisigh to translate large quantities of papers for him. Most of his work, originally written in Latin, was not translated and published until after his death in 1666. The first collected edition of his work with translations by Robert Ware and William Domville was issued in 1705. A copy of this in good condition, with the original errata leaf, would be between £100 and £150. Rather more popular is Walter Harris's revised edition of Ware's *Whole Works*, published in three volumes between 1739 and 1764; good copies fetch £250 to £400 depending on condition. Walter Harris, was an important historian in his own right. He was expelled from Trinity College for participation in a riot, but the college had to eat its words when later in his life, it conferred upon him the degree of doctor of laws for his services to historical research. A copy of the first edition of Harris's *History and Antiquities of Ireland* published in Dublin in 1764 will cost about £160 to £180, while a copy of his 1766 edition of the *History and Antiquities of Dublin* would be in the same price range or a little above.

There are some key histories of Ireland written during the nineteenth and early twentieth century that are only now being challenged on the basis of usefulness by modern authors. These include Richard Bagwell's two histories, *Ireland Under the Tudors* (1885-90) and *Ireland Under the Stuarts* (1909-19). For the first three volume edition of *Ireland Under the Tudors* you would now pay close to £300. Although it doesn't carry as much weight in the area of historical analysis as modern scholars would like, it is rather racily written and based on research among vast quantities of State Papers, which Bagwell was among the first to explore seriously. As an indispensible compendium of facts about the sixteenth century it has yet to be bettered. The Stuart period is not at the moment entirely fashionable among historical researchers, so *Ireland Under the Stuarts* is a little cheaper than the *Tudors*, being around £200 a copy for the first edition. It also was published in three volumes.

The Normans are even less popular among students at present than are the Stuarts, so copies of the first edition of G. H. Orpen's useful four volume work *Ireland Under the Normans*, (1911-20) is slightly less expensive at around £180 a copy.

Other highly regarded histories that are sought after by collectors included P. W. Joyce's *A Social History of Ancient Ireland*, two volumes, 1903, priced around £90, and Eugene O'Curry's *Manners and Customs of the Ancient Irish*, three volumes, 1873, at around £350. On the eighteenth century there is J. A. Froude's prejudiced but entertaining account of *The English in Ireland*, three volumes (1872-74), which can be bought for £50 to £60 and deserves to be more, and W. E. H. Lecky's History *Ireland in the Eighteenth Century*, which can make as much as £80 for the rather dreary five volume edition of 1892.

History

Many local histories are most eagerly collected, principally, it seems, by the natives of the counties to which the books are related. The men of Meath may ponder over a first edition of Gogan's *Diocese of Meath, Ancient and Modern* (1862-70) for £70 to £90, Corkonians may prefer the 1750 first edition of Charles Smith's *Antient and Present State of the City and County of Cork* at £150 to £200, while lovers of Co. Wexford can purchase Hore's *History of the Town and County of Wexford*, published in six volumes from 1900 to 1911, for about £500, or the 1979 Oxford reprint for around £30. There are many fine works about the history of Dublin; expect to pay £150 or so for Monck Mason's 1820 edition of the history of St Patrick's Cathedral, around £50 for Myles Ronan's *Reformation in Dublin under Elizabeth*, first published in 1924, and up to £140 for *A History of the City of Dublin* by J. T. Gilbert, published in three volumes between 1854 and 1859. A good facsimile reprint of this work also exists, published by Gill and Macmillan in

Local History

J. T. Gilbert

1978 and for those who cannot afford the first it makes a very attractive alternative at £50 or so. Moreover, it includes a good index, a feature lacking in the first edition.

J. T. or Sir John Gilbert was a rather remarkable scholar, whose works could, indeed, form the basis of a very interesting specialist collection. He wrote and published the first volume of his history of Dublin before he was twenty-six, displaying an archival talent amazing in one so young. The Royal Irish Academy was so impressed by this work that they immediately elected him a member (although they had refused him a couple of years before because of his youth and inadequate academic record) and placed him in charge of the publication of facsimile versions of many of its manuscripts. Later he was appointed Secretary of the Irish Public Records Office and Inspector of the Historical Manuscripts Commission. Historians owe him a profound debt of gratitude for the manner in which he rescued Irish archives from the chaos that had reigned before his appointment.

The collector interested in Gilbert had better, I suppose, start with the biography of him published by his wife in 1905. In truth it is a rather tedious biography, its only redeeming feature the fact that it includes a list of Gilbert's works. A copy of this should be obtainable for £20 or so. After that, prices rise! Gilbert's useful *History of the Viceroys of Ireland* is around £60 for the first edition of 1865. His *Jacobite Narrative of the War in Ireland* was published in a limited edition of 200 copies, one of which would now cost £60 to £80. Less sought after is his *Narratives of the Marriage of Maria Clementina*, which, although limited to 150 copies in 1894 could cost as little as £40; however, it is of interest to Stuart enthusiasts. Gilbert was also responsible, together with his wife, for the editorship of the *Calendar of Ancient Records of Dublin*, published in nineteen volumes between 1889 and 1944. Full sets, in blue morocco-backed boards, do not come on the market often; the last one I saw was sold at auction for £340, which seemed extraordinarily good value for such a goldmine of otherwise quite inaccessible material.

Other collections of documents edited by Gilbert include *Documents Relating to Ireland, 1795-1804,* which in its limited edition (two hundred) of 1893 fetches about £200 and usually appears in a green half-morocco binding, and *The Charlemont Papers* (1891-94), which costs about £80 for its two volumes in their cloth binding. There are two expensive Gilbert works. One is the seven-volume *History of the Irish Confederation and the War in Ireland* (1882-91), which appeared in a limited edition of only twemty-five numbered copies; the last copy sold at auction made £625. Even more expensive is the *Facsimiles of the National Manuscripts of Ireland,* which appeared in a four-volume-in-five folio format between 1874 and 1884. It was originally bound in cloth and contains almost three hundred lithographic plates, making it virtually a work of art as well as one of historical interest. At a recent sale it made £3,000.

Another interesting area of collecting related to Irish history is that of the various rebellions. The 1798 rebellion, especially in Wexford, seems to attract the lion's share of collectors, but the others also have their followers. A good start could be made with Sir Richard Musgrave's *Memoirs of the Different Rebellions in Ireland,* of which there were two editions in 1801. The first could rise to £150, with the second reaching over £100, but for the more modest collector there is always the perfectly adequate third edition of 1802, which should not cost much more than £60 to £80. An interesting volume on the 1641 rebellion is Mary Hickson's *Ireland in the Seventeenth Century*, which was first published in 1884. Until a short time ago this used to sell at around £60, but on a couple of occasions recently it has fetched close to £150.

There is a wealth of fascinating material on the 1798 rebellion. One of the most sought-after volumes is Edward Hay's *History of the Insurrection of the County of Wexford*, first published in 1803. Hay was a rather interesting character who, while not himself directly involved in the rising, had a brother, John, who was executed for complicity with the rebels and had many friends who were deeply committed to the rebellion. After the Act of Union, Hay devoted his life to the campaign for Catholic emancipation. His *History* sells at between £80 and £100 for the first edition. Another *History of the Rebellion in Ireland in the Year 1798,* first published in 1801 by Rev. James Gordon, was condemned by Sir Richard Musgrave and others for its degree of bias. Nevertheless it pleases the collectors and sells for around the same price as the Hay volume.

Topography

Closely bound up with history is topography. There are three important works in this field that are especially sought after by collectors. They are Bartlett's *Scenery and Antiquities of Ireland*, which costs between £200 and £250 for the 1846 edition in two volumes; Samuel Lewis's *Topographical Dictionary of Ireland,* first published in 1837 and costing around £200 for two-volume cloth-bound sets; and *The Antiquities of Ireland* by Francis Grose,

The Waverley Gallery (1841) with fine engravings done under the supervision of Charles Heath in its original red morocco binding. Its rich gold tooling is typical of the period.

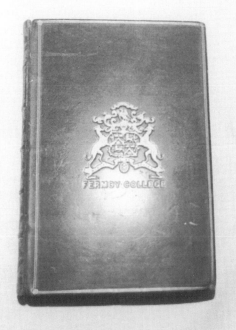

Prize binding from Fermoy College, Cork.

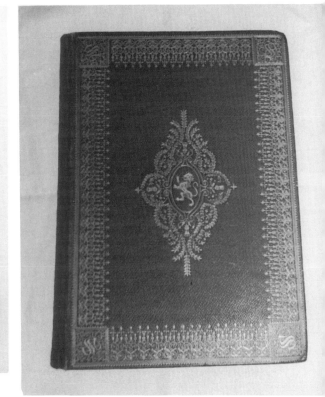

first published in 1791 and again in 1797. The first edition, which contains over 260 engraved plates, costs up to £400 or so at auction, with as much as £300 for the 1797 version. All these sets are fairly frequently seen at book auctions, and the aspiring owner shouldn't experience too much difficulty in obtaining them, but prices do seem to be rising fairly steadily. Another topographical set that is in almost as much demand is Edward Ledwich's *Antiquities of Ireland*, first published in 1790 and containing 37 engraved plates. This has made over £200 at recent sales.

Books relating to eighteenth and nineteenth-century roads and travel sell very well. Samuel Lewis published his *Atlas of the Counties of Ireland* in the same year as his *Topographical Dictionary,* and you will often find the two sold together. In its first edition the *Atlas* contained one large folding map and 32 county maps; on its own it fetches about £100 or a bit more. Taylor and Skinner's *Maps of the Roads of Ireland* in its first edition of 1778 appears at most major sales; price seems to vary a bit according to condition, but good copies tend to make between £200 and £300. When buying, check that all maps are present; there should be one large folding map and 299 others. Needless to say, the same check should be made on all atlases and topographical works, as missing plates do affect value, and if you are settling for imperfect copies do be careful of the price you pay. A little less often seen but in even more demand when it is is Bernard Scales's *Hibernian Atlas* in its first edition of 1776. This has an engraved title page and thirty-seven very fine hand-coloured maps, and it fetches between £450 and £600. The second, improved edition appeared in 1809 and is also expensive, generally making over £400.

A recently written follow-up to Robert Lloyd Praeger's attractive topographical work, *The Way that I Went,* has aroused interest in this author of late, and this volume, published in 1937, sells for up to £70. For his lesser known *Irish Topographical Botany,* published by the Royal Irish Academy in 1901, you could expect to pay a similar amount or a little more. Check that all six folding maps are present. Closely connected with topographical works are travel books, and a number of books of travel and observation were written in and about Ireland during the nineteenth and twentieth centuries. The most popular is undoubtedly the work of Samuel Carter Hall and Anna Maria Hall published during the first half of the nineteenth century. A copy of their *Week at Killarney,* published in 1843, sells for around £50. More often seen — and a great deal more in demand — is their *Ireland: its Scenery, Character, etc.,* first published in three volumes between 1841 and 1843. This set, often found in green morocco binding, should not cost more than £200, and is often found at around £140. However, it must be said that it sometimes makes as much as £400 and more at non-specialist or house clearance sales, presumably because the title is so well known that some private buyers imagine it to be worth more that it is. I would not pay such an amount for a copy of this work, for it is far too often and easily obtained for the lower sums at specialist sales. The same fortune, incidentally, often befalls Flora Mitchell's *Vanishing Dublin,* which has been known to hit £270 or so at general sales but would only make around £160 or so at a book auction. Going back again in time to a very popular coaching work, Wilson's *Post Chaise Companion or Traveller's Directory through Ireland,* we come to a volume that, despite its limited use to the modern motorist, continues in very high demand! It was first issued in 1786, and this edition fetches £100 to £130, but all editions are relatively expensive, with even the third, published in 1805, making as much as £75.

Irish Literature

Collectors of the Victorian novel are most concerned with English three-deckers, so called because many works were issued in three-volume editions. The Irish market for nineteenth century fiction is less developed but is still interesting, and there are some rarities. Until very recently it would have been possible to buy many of the first editions of Charles Lever's novels for £10 to £15 but there has been a noticeable increase in collecting interest of late. A copy of *The O'Donaghue: a Tale of Ireland,* first published in 1845 and with illustrations by Phiz, is making around £40 now, while rather less expensive are *Harry Lorrequer* (1839), *Jack Hinton the Guardsman* (1843), and *Luttrell of Arran* (1865). Like *The O'Donaghue,* these volumes are enhanced by the Phiz illustrations (Phiz, whose real name was Hablot K. Browne, was also the illustrator of a number of Charles Dickens's works). *The Confessions of Con Cregan* (1849) seems a little more expensive and may reach £50 or £60, while the priciest Lever lot I have recently seen was a copy of *Luttrell of Arran* in its original sixteen parts and with its original advertisements and twenty-eight titles and plates by Phiz; it made £300. Despite these relatively high prices, it is possible to find Lever first editions for less than this, and if it is reading copies you are after you could keep an eye out for the Chapman & Hall 1879 set of Lever's *Works,* which still sells for under £100 for sixteen volumes.

William Carleton

An author noted for his depiction of the Irish peasantry during the early nineteenth century, both in novels and stories, is William Carleton. A graduate of a hedge school, and a travelling scholar, he was, it seems, destined for the priesthood but confounded his family by joining the established church. His most famous collection of stories was his *Tales and Sketches of the Irish Peasantry,* several editions of which are of interest to collectors. The first appeared in 1825 and should cost about £60, with the edition of 1851 making, perhaps, a little over half that. The 'new edition' of 1843-44, in two volumes, containing a number of etched plates, is really the best, and this is reflected in the price, which would be comfortably over £100; it was recently sold for £160 in a fine binding by J. Larkin. There was a New York edition in 1862 that would make £30 or a little more, and finally there is a modern two-volume reprint, with a preface by the late Barbara Hayley, which sells at around the same amount. Rarer than the *Traits and Sketches,* but not as good, is Carleton's *The Squanders of Castle Squander,* in its 1852 first edition. Original cloth is blue with silver leaf and it contains ten plates; it would make £130 to £150.

Historical Novels

There was quite a vogue for historical novels in Ireland during the nineteenth century, and some are of interest. The Hon. Emily Lawless was the author of a number of novels of sixteenth-century Ireland; these sell for £15 or so. The very detailed *Irish Chieftains* by Blake-Foster (1872) is better and sells at around £90. There are in fact a number of relatively untrodden paths in the collection of nineteenth-century Irish fiction, and interested beginners would do well to consult a copy of Stephen Browne's *Reader's Guide to Irish Fiction*, published in 1910 and costing about £25.

Twentieth–Century Irish Fiction

Much twentieth-century Irish fiction can be collected at modest prices, with first editions by authors like Edna O'Brien, Kate O'Brien, Elizabeth Bowen and Annie M. P. Smithson obtainable for under £20. Edna O'Brien's *The Country Girls* in its 1960 first edition is more expensive, however, and would make £40 to £60; and of Elizabeth Bowen's works, *Bowen's Court* (1942) is most desirable at around £50. Brendan Behan's work is, not surprisingly, collectable, with *The Quare Fellow* fetching £70 or more and *Borstal Boy*, published in the United States in 1957 and in England in 1958, making around £60 for both versions.

Samuel Beckett's *Murphy* in its English first edition of 1938 would fetch about £100 but it is actually more desirable in its first American edition (Grove Press, 1938), which could make five times that figure if it were signed by the author. The novels of Liam O'Flaherty have become collectable, and many households must harbour copies of his first editions in good condition; prices for his most popular novels, such as *The Black Soul* (1924) and *The Informer* (1925), could be expected to fetch up to £100. Lots of unsuspecting

Large two volume edition of Wortley Axe's *The Horse* (L.n.d.) with nicely tooled spine, packed with fine illustration and still useful information.

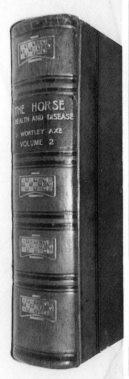

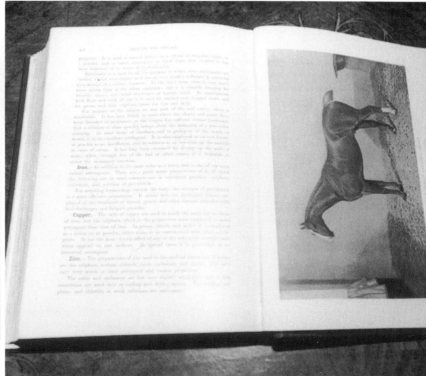

Wortley Axe — portrait illustration of 'Artist'.

homes, too, must contain copies of Flann O'Brien first editions and *At Swim-Two-Birds* (1939) makes around £100.

It is James Joyce who provides, by and large, the high spots of Irish fiction collecting, although his work tends to fetch more in Britain and America than it does in Ireland. Those who aspire to an important edition of *Ulysses* have need to do a little research, as well as dipping deep into their pockets, for there are a number of different first editions at very variable prices. The genuine first edition was published in Paris in February 1922 by Sylvia Beach's Shakespeare Press. It was limited to a thousand copies and they are numbered, and two different types of paper were used. Copies of this first edition have fetched as much as £25,000 in the United States.

The next edition of *Ulysses* was issued later in 1922. It was the first edition for Britain, but it was not printed there; to avoid the censor's eye it was, like the Shakespeare Press edition, printed in Paris. It was sponsored by Joyce's friend and patron Harriet Weaver, and published by the Egoist Press. This was limited to two thousand copies in blue wrappers and apparently numbered from 3 to 500, although one was sold in Ireland recently that was numbered 977. You could expect to pay £1,000 for a copy of this edition; the copy I have just referred to made £760 and lacked its errata leaves. It was bound in crimson morocco and had a cloth slip-case.

The third important *Ulysses* is the first edition printed in England. This was published by John Lane at the Bodley Head in 1936. It was limited to a thousand copies and had a buckram cover. This has made just over £200 in Ireland and almost double that in Britain.

Finnegans Wake was published by Faber and Faber in 1939 in a red cloth binding with a jacket. In top condition it would now make about £400. However, there was also a limited edition (425) that was signed by the author, with buckram cover and slip-case. A copy of this has made £1,750 at a book sale. *A Portrait of the Artist as a Young Man* was published in New York in 1916 and in England in 1917. Copies would be similarly priced to the regular Faber edition of *Finnegans Wake*. Copies of *Anna Livia Plurabelle* are scarce; published in New York in 1928, it would now make over £600.

Irish Poetry

It often seems that poetry generates more excitement among collectors than fiction, with W. B. Yeats, not surprisingly, sought after both at home and abroad. Prices are not always high, though, and the modest collector could build up quite a respectable collection of Yeats first editions, and other attractive editions, without enormous outlay. It would appear that Yeats, like Beckett and Joyce, fetches higher prices abroad than in Ireland. Not long after I saw a copy of *The Trembling of the Veil*, which was privately printed in a limited edition in 1922, sold for £55 in a Dublin sale, I spotted another copy of the same edition sell at an English auction for £140. In Ireland it would be perfectly possible to buy a selection of worthwhile Yeats items for around £50 or less.

The most expensive Yeats item at present appears to be 'Mosada'. This was a long dramatic poem published in the *Dublin University Review* in June 1886 and is rather a turgid tale of a beautiful Moorish girl who is ordered to be burned at the stake by her inquisitor lover, who discovers her identity

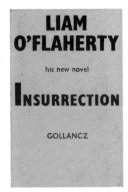

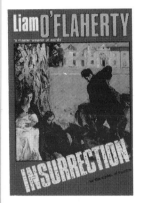

The first edition of O'Flaherty's *Insurrection* (Gollancz) and below the first Irish edition (Wolfhound).

too late to save her life. Yeats's father thought very highly of the piece and had it reprinted by Sealy, Bryers & Walker, selling it through subscriptions. This was in fact Yeats's first book, and the proud father presented a copy to the Jesuit poet Gerard Manley Hopkins, who, alas, wrote that he did not think highly of it. Such a view does nothing to deter modern collectors, who like best to see 'Mosada' safely between the clean covers of an untouched *Dublin University Review* of June 1886. For this prize they are prepared to pay around £1,200. A tattered copy could be reduced in value by up to half. Less desirable to the purist collector are copies of the June *Review* bound up with other copies of the same year. Such a volume would probably make around £750, but may well be actually more interesting to the student of Yeats's works, for the *Reviews* of the latter months of 1886 carried a number of pieces by Yeats, all published for the first time, including a number of poems and an attractive essay on Sir Samuel Ferguson, which appeared in the November issue.

After that prices drop! Yeats's *Four Plays for Dancers* would now make £150, a copy of his *Last Poems and Plays* (1940) should be got for about £40, and the very attractive *Stories of Red Hanarahan and The Secret Rose* first published in 1927 and illustrated by Nora McGuinness is obtainable for less than £60. A copy of the 1919 limited edition of *The Wild Swans at Coole* shouldn't be more than £30, with *A Full Moon in March* (1935) fetching around the same amount.

Poetry

Books about Yeats are as eagerly collected by some afficionados as his actual works, and some of them are quite expensive in their first editions. Among these would be Richard Ellman's *Yeats the Man and the Masks* (1949), which could make up to £20, and A. Norman Jeffares's *W. B. Yeats: Man and Poet* (1949), which could be got for somewhat less. Look for such volumes in good condition and with the dust jacket.

Most major Irish poets now appear to have a collector following, to the point, indeed, that even as new works are published it would be a good idea if you have an eye to the future to buy them in their first and add them to your library as they appear. Few such volumes will not show some appreciation in the years that follow. Poetry tends to be published in fairly small editions, but as the poet's reputation grows so does the demand for volumes of his works that may have become difficult to obtain. At present a copy of Patrick Kavanagh's *Ploughman and Other Poems*, published in 1936 as part of Macmillan's contemporary poets series, is making around £200. It is really quite scarce and should be looked for in its original printed wrappers. Volumes of Pádraic Colum's work don't fetch as much as Kavanagh's, but some are well worth collecting. For example, *The Children of Odin* (1922) and *The King of Ireland's Son* (New York, 1916) are attractive both for the text and for the illustrations by Willy Pogany, and neither volume would cost much more than £20. Austin Clarke too is still inexpensive. The Dolmen Press edition of *Collected Poems* (1974) is still under £30, while the enjoyable *Twice Around the Black Church* (1962) can be got for something over £20. More expensive, at around £65, is *Too Great A Vine* (1957), limited to two hundred copies, and signed by Clarke and the printer, Liam Miller.

Thomas Kinsella is a typical example of a poet whose reputation has grown enormously in recent years, and those who had the foresight to purchase his earlier work in first editions have much reason to be pleased with themselves now. The attractive edition of his *Poems, 1956-73,* published by Wake Forest in 1979 to a design by Liam Miller, is now up to £30 a copy. Make sure it has its rust-coloured jacket, which was made in very fine-quality paper. A fine edition of his poems was published in 1974 with drawings by Anne Yeats, and this now makes around £50, while a copy of *The Táin* published in 1969 and limited to 1,750 copies in slip-case would now fetch £120. Incidentally, there was another edition of this published by Dolmen in 1974, but this would make only about £20. A first edition of *Out of Ireland* (Peppercannister, 1987) is already changing hands for over £60, as is *St Catherine's Clock,* published in the same year and limited to a hundred copies. Séamus Heaney too is a poet well worth purchasing in first editions as they appear; *A Lough Neagh Sequence,* published by Phoenix Pamphlet Poets Press in 1969 is now making up to £75 for copies in good condition, while *Hailstones* (1984) in a signed limited edition of 750 is now around £60. Other first editions are still in the £10 to £20 range and I think represent a good long-term buy.

Special Editions and Presses

A number of small presses, specialising in Irish literature and history and producing volumes of very high quality, are now extremely collectable. These include the Dun Emer, later Cuala, Press, which issued much work by Yeats, and, of late, the Dolmen Press. The Dun Emer edition of Yeats's *Stories of Red Hanrahan* has fetched £60 in London, though it would probably make a little less here, and his *In the Seven Woods,* issued by Dun Emer in 1903, would be in the same price range or somewhat higher. A copy of Elizabeth Bowen's *Seven Winters* in the Cuala edition of 1942 should be £40 to £50, and similarly priced would be their 1921 edition of Yeats's *Four Years.* These are modestly priced Cuala editions, and some are a great deal more valuable than this. For example, the famous Cuala *Broadsides,* eighty-four of which were published between 1908 and 1915, with hand-coloured illustrations by Jack Yeats, are always hotly contested at auction, whether they come up as singles or in groups. I myself haven't yet seen a full set sold, but a large group of seventy-seven was sold a few years ago at a Dublin auction for £850, and I would expect a full set now to make very considerably more. Very recently at a Dublin sale four of them, framed, were sold at prices that averaged just over £50 each.

I've noticed that quite a few households have Cuala editions lurking about the bookshelves — the books and the broadsides often come up as singles at house clearances — and if you have any, you should be sure to have them properly valued before you part with them. The same applies to books issued by the Dolmen Press. This was only established in 1950, but already, as has been seen above with regard to poetry, many of its editions command good prices. Intending collectors would be well advised to consult *Dolmen XXV: an Illustrated Bibliography of the Dolmen Press.* This beautiful book, issued in a limited edition of 650 copies and a collector's piece in itself, gives full details of Dolmen publications during its first twenty-five years.

A number of quality presses in the recent past have engaged in the production of facsimile reprints of earlier books and documents, and many

Modern Irish Publishing
The recent revival in publishing in Ireland, in particular of small presses, must surely give rise to new opportunities for the collector here. Publishers such as The Gallery Press (and the earlier Tara Telephone imprint poetry pamphlets, now exceedingly rare), Blackstaff Press, Wolfhound Press, The O'Brien Press, the New Writers Press (no longer in existence), Peppercannister, Lilliput and others have produced an interesting output of contemporary Irish fiction, poetry and drama as well as a vast range of non-fiction titles of both specialist and general interest, and occasionally fine and limited editions. Which might become a 'collector's item' is of course subject to many variables, not least of which is the author's reputation and output. An example of the kind of possibility I mean is the first edition hardcover of an author whose reputation is growing internationally, Frank McGuinness, whose first play, 'The Factory Girls' was published in a short run initial hardcover edition (Monarchline/Wolfhound, 1982) and long out of print. First Irish editions of important writers could be an interesting area to develop, or modern Irish handbound editions or fine editions. Equally interesting might be first editions of Irish published children's books.

collectors wonder if they are a good buy. This is a question that's rather hard to answer. For example, a facsimile of the Taylor and Skinner atlas mentioned above has been sold for close to that of the real thing, although it was only issued by Irish University Press in 1969, but it was an especially fine edition. So too was the 1978 reprint of Gilbert's *History of Dublin* — in some respects, indeed, it is more useful than the original. Very often facsimile and reprint editions are expensive when first published, and you need to consider carefully whether they will maintain their value should you wish to re-sell. It has to be considered — and this is true also of the special issues of porcelain and other would-be collectables — that such an edition may be produced specially for collectors, and although it may be described as 'limited' it may in truth be limited only to the number of copies sold. Thus from the outset the demand for the volume may be fully met, at least in the short to medium term. Add to this the fact that collectors who purchase a specially issued and expensive book are very likely also to treat it with care, and you will realise that the book is unlikely to acquire scarcity value in the foreseeable future.

Some reprints of Irish interest have been issued in recent years with the aim, not so much of appealing to collectors, but of bringing out of print and rare volumes within reach of actual readers. Some of these reissues have themselves become collectable. Amongst these is *Ancient Irish Histories,* which includes the works of Edmund Spenser, Camion, Hamner and Marlborough and which was reissued in New York in 1970. It is now being offered for around £30. The 1979 reprint, in six volumes, of F. E. Ball's *History of County Dublin* (Gill, Dublin) is available from £120 or so. The very useful reprint of Dudley Westropp's *Irish Glass* issued by Figgis in 1978 in a very handsome green cover is now making £40 on the rare books market — I bought my copy for just £7 a couple of years ago.

Some out of print Irish fiction has also appeared in attractive reissues. An edition of *Peig* edited and translated by Bryan MacMahon and illustrated by C. O'Connor appeared in 1973 (Talbot, Dublin) and now sells for around £16 to £18. Wolfhound Press has reissued several novels by Liam O'Flaherty. The most expensive of these at present is their 1979 edition of *Famine* which is now fetching around £15. *The Wilderness*, with illustrations by Jeanette Dunne (1978), now costs around £12 with *The Test of Courage* (1977), illustrated by Terence O'Connell, fetching around the same price and Skerrett (1982) a little less.

If you find yourself attracted to an expensive facsimile copy, you should first satisfy yourself that the book is a true and fine copy, with top-quality paper and illustrations and a suitable binding. The next point is whether the original edition is so rare you are unlikely to acquire it at a price you could afford. You should then try to discover the performance of other facsimiles published by the same house on the rare books market and enquire how many copies of the facsimile edition are being issued to determine whether the price being sought seems reasonable; the fewer the copies, the higher the price. Finally, you should consider the content of the volume: if the material is of little intrinsic interest, the book will probably turn our to be a bad buy, no matter how beautiful it may be.

One could consider, for example, the Irish University Press edition of William Badcock's *A New Touchstone for Gold and Silver Wares*, a copy of which, though very attractive and limited to a hundred copies, sold, in its fine Niger morocco cover, at a recent auction for a mere £22, less than the cost of the binding. Another slow mover among IUP editions would seem to be Ilona Berlivits's *Illuminated Manuscripts of Hungary: XI — XVI Centuries,* which sells for under £20. On the other hand, the same press's edition of Pool and Cash's *Views of the Most Remarkable Buildings, Monuments and other Edifices* could cost up to £150, while even a moderately interesting reprint, William Morris's *Aims in Founding the Kelmscott Press,* may command a price of £60 or more. If, then, one were to single out any one priority in judging the value of a fine reprint or, indeed, any special edition, it would surely have to be this question of subject matter, for if the work is tedious or obscure no-one will be interested in it, no matter what edition it may be.

Some Irish first editions of Liam O'Flaherty titles are illustrated on p.120 (opposite), p.117 and p.126

Eighteenth-Century Irish Editions

A word should be said here about eighteenth-century Irish editions of previously published works, if only because many novice collectors imagine that when they see 'Dublin edition' on an eighteenth-century book they are holding a valuable and rare volume. This is not always the case. It's not very widely known that during the half century that preceded the Act of Union both booksellers and printers flourished in Dublin, publishing their own editions of the latest London books, at prices that were usually considerably lower than the English editions. (This was in the days before copyright laws: according to present-day principles these were pirate editions.) These books supplied much of the Irish book trade, of course, but significant quantities were exported to America, and some of them found their way back to England, where, to the annoyance of the London booksellers (and the authors!), a number of English buyers, reluctant to pay the London prices, subscribed for them.

Oliver Goldsmith and Samuel Johnson were among the authors whose works the Irish booksellers published in large quantities, but the works of Smollett, Fielding, Sterne and Gibbon were all issued in substantial numbers and in several editions. Collectors in this area should not be without a pioneering study of the eighteenth-century booksellers and their customers written by Richard Cargill Cole in 1986: *Irish Booksellers and English Writers, 1740-1800.* This book has been remaindered, and at the time of writing some few copies can still be found in one or two of the larger bookshops at around £5. Those who buy it now will secure not only an invaluable work of reference but a book that will surely itself rise in value in the years to come. As for the Dublin editions themselves, they come up at sales at prices that are fairly reasonable. For example, at a recent book sale a set of nineteen volumes (out of an original twenty) of *The Works of Swift* (Dublin, 1772) fetched just £150. This was issued by George Faulkener, one of the most important booksellers and a notable character of eighteenth-century Dublin. Boswell's *Life of Johnson,* apparently published in two Dublin editions during 1792, would fetch £50 to £100 for a copy of the version published by J. Rice, R. White, P. Byrne and nine others and printed by John Chambers. The other version, a large folio edition, has made £340 at a country house sale. The first Dublin edition of Edmund Burke's *Reflections on the Revolution in France* dates from 1790 and fetched £160 at a recent sale.

Non-Irish Material

Many Irish collectors confine themselves to Irish material, but it would be a mistake to think that all of them do. Far from it: there is a healthy trade in a very wide range of material in English and also in French. We will confine ourselves, however, to works in English. In this general area, history is rather less important than it is to collectors of Irish material, and here fiction, natural history and travel tend to be the most important fields. Good editions of Gibbon's *Decline and Fall of the Roman Empire* are, however, always in demand. The first edition appeared between 1776 and 1788 in six volumes, and a fine copy could fetch £1,000. Another useful history still widely collected is Clarendon's *History of the Late Rebellion*, which was published in 1702-04 and deals with the English Civil War of the seventeenth century. First editions would cost several hundred pounds, but there is a 1720 edition in one volume that can be found for around £50, and an 1849 edition in seven volumes that includes some material on Ireland. For this you could expect to pay somewhere around £100 at auction.

A number of nineteenth-century histories such as those of Macaulay and Carlyle, highly thought of in their time, are not now widely collected, and may be obtained, even in fine editions, for very modest sums.

The same fate has overtaken some Churchilliana, works relating to Winston Churchill and his family. Until the late 1970s this was quite a thriving area of collecting, especially in Britain, with books by Churchill such as *The Story of the Malakand Field Force (1898)* and *London to Ladysmith via Pretoria* (1900), making substantial sums. This has changed somewhat and, with the exception of a few select items, owners of Churchill-related volumes may be quite disappointed with prices offered. To quote an example: I recently purchased the first edition of Churchill's two-volume biography of his father, Lord Randolph Churchill (1906). It came as part of a boxed lot of thirty-five volumes costing £40. Fifteen or so years ago it would have made almost as much as that on its own.

In starting to collect English fiction one is entering a vast terrain, much of it uncharted, especially, with regard to minor authors of the nineteenth and twentieth centuries. The greatest excitement of the market is aroused by the high spots, that is, the very best books by widely acclaimed authors. Not so many years ago, as recently even as the late 1960s, it would have been possible to build up a collection of nineteenth-century novels that have become acknowledged classics, without spending a fortune.

Some volumes would always have been elusive and, when found, cost a great deal. It would be a lucky collector who would ever see, let alone buy, a first edition of *Wuthering Heights*, and first editions of Jane Austen have never been cheap. The 1811 edition of *Sense and Sensibility,* for example, still in original boards, was sold at Sotheby's not long ago for £9,500. In recent times Anthony Trollope has been much in favour, and highest prices are paid for first editions in original cloth. Some prices achieved at a recent London sale include: *The Claverings*, two volumes, 1867, £1,400; *Lady Anna*, two volumes, 1874, £1,900; *Ayala's Angel*, three volumes, 1881, £2,200 and *The Way We Live Now*, two volumes, £1,050. Of course this was a sale that had a number of high-quality Trollope lots and therefore brought out the devotees in large numbers. One dealer afterwards commented that he reckoned he had had fourteen interested competitors for one particular lot. It must also be said that the condition of most of the lots was excellent. Nonetheless it would be interesting to see the kind of prices reached by the same volumes in a more general sale held in the English provinces or in Ireland.

Dickens's works are, of course, always sought after, but the prices of many of his first editions are not as high as might be thought, because although he is popular his works have been issued in large numbers both as first and later editions. Some confusion among novice book collectors is caused by the fact that many of Dickens's novels were first issued as monthly parts, and these part issues therefore strictly speaking constitute the first editions. However, not only are these difficult to come across in a complete state but they are also a nuisance to read and something of a visual blight on the bookshelf. Accordingly, most collectors go for the first book edition, which was usually released as soon as all the parts had been issued. Original cloth binding is, of course, the most desirable and the most expensive.

At present it would appear that of Dickens's first editions, *Great Expectations* (1861) is the most expensive. During the summer of 1860 the magazine *All the Year Round*, which Dickens was then editing, was running a serial by Charles Lever called *A Day's Ride*. Sales of the paper had fallen off badly, and it was clear that Lever's novel did not please the public so, having secured the best terms for Lever to have the novel published in book form, Dickens replaced the serial with a novel of his own, *Great Expectations*, which he had originally planned to write in book form. Despite the change of format, *Great Expectations* proved to be one of Dickens's most successful stories, perhaps the most successful. A copy in book form, with thirty pages of advertisements, in a special binding by Sangorski and Sutcliffe, has made $26,000 at auction in the United States. Of course, this was a special copy from the important collection of Estell Doheny, and it would hardly make as much on this side of the Atlantic. Just the same, a copy of the second edition of later the same year has made £2,800 at auction in Britain.

The most expensive Dickens first edition that the ordinary collector is likely to see is *A Christmas Carol*. In 1843 Dickens, dissatisfied with his regular publishers, Chapman & Hall, decided to oversee the publication of *A Christmas Carol* himself, engaging the illustrator John Leech to provide four hand-coloured etchings and four wood engravings. The book was a publishing though not a financial success, with 6,000 copies sold before Christmas 1843 and 2,000 copies of the second printing sold by the middle of the following January. A good copy in its original cloth and with its two pages of advertisements could expect to fetch at least £1,000. Next most expensive is generally the first edition of *The Pickwick Papers*. Publication of *Pickwick* in parts began in April 1836 and continued until late the following year, and by the time it finished, over 40,000 copies of each part were being sold. By the end of 1837 the first edition in book form became available, and at auction today a copy in fine condition would make about £600.

Just as expensive (perhaps, of late, even more so) is *Oliver Twist*. Unlike most of Dickens's novels, this was not issued first in part form, so the first edition in book form is the true first. It appeared in 1838 in three volumes with plates by George Cruikshank. These illustrations, of outstanding quality, gave us the images of Mr Bumble, Fagin, Sykes and the rest that have passed into literary legend. Cruikshank was probably the greatest book illustrator of the mid-nineteenth century, and many people feel that his plates for *Oliver Twist* were his greatest work. What a pity it was, then, that he and Dickens should have quarrelled during the production of the book, so that Cruikshank never worked for Dickens again.

Prices for many other Dickens first editions are really quite modest. *David Copperfield* is one of the dearest of these; prices vary, but I have seen it make sums from £80 to £190. *Hard Times*, though small, is often quite expensive in its first book form of 1854; it could fetch up to £150. *A Tale of Two Cities* should be obtainable for between £200 and £300. First editions that should be available at around £50 to £80 include *Martin Chuzzlewit* (1844), *Nicholas Nickleby* (1839), *Dombey and Son* (1848), *Little Dorrit* (1857), and *The Old Curiosity Shop* (1841). *Bleak House* (1853) and *Our Mutual Friend* (1865) may be found to be a little more expensive.

People are often disappointed when their cherished sets of Dickens's complete works, often handed down through a couple of generations, turn out to be worth not much more than their value as pleasant reading books. The trouble is that as Dickens was so much in demand, even in his own day, sets of his novels have been continually and frequently published in very large numbers. I do think, though, that complete sets of Dickens in good-quality bindings are well worth buying. They often do not cost a great deal, and over the years good late nineteenth and early twentieth-century sets should maintain or enhance their value. Some Dickens sets are worth noting as being of higher value. The Nonesuch Dickens was issued in twenty-four volumes between 1937 and 1938 with one steel plate from the original illustrations. Up to recently the price for the set in its original buckram ran at around £1,500 for sets without the plate. However, a set made rather special by inclusion of three of the original steel plates used for the illustrations recently sold in Britain for £5,200. Whether that kind of price would be reached for an ordinary set at an ordinary sale is doubtful. Another set worth looking out for, although it is also fairly expensive at around £800 to £1,000, is the centenary edition of 1910-11. Nevertheless, house clearances in particular will yield from time to time perfectly respectable Dickens sets worth from £100 upwards.

One nineteenth-century novelist who is still quite affordable in many of his first editions is Sir Walter Scott. His novels are now felt by many readers to be rather heavy going, and copies of his first editions can turn up quite inexpensively at book fairs and auctions. In fact Scott is an author who sixty or seventy years ago might have fetched more, relatively, than he does nowadays. I myself bought the three-volume first edition of *The Fortunes of Nigel*, in contemporary full calf binding, for just £10 a year or so ago. The only real high spot of the moment seems to be *Waverley* (1814), which made £350 the last time I caught sight of it, which was, I think, in 1987. Even *Ivanhoe* (1820), which is still very readable today and incomparable in its description of mediaeval pageant, doesn't make more than £200 or so. Sets of the complete Waverley novels have a certain appeal, mainly, one suspects, as 'furniture'. I recently saw a fine set, published in Edinburgh in 1829-33 and consisting of forty-eight volumes in red morocco, sell for just £380 — a very attractive addition to any bookshelf, and a real feast for the genuine Scott lover. More recently, a set of forty-eight published by A. & C. Black of Edinburgh in 1860 with quarter calf binding was sold for £450. One thing to beware of if buying these sets — and it certainly affects the 1867 A. & C. Black set — is that some of these collections are typeset in double-column format, rather like that which is often used for bibles. This makes the text extremely tiresome to read, especially if the type is, as almost always, very small. If, like me, you actually enjoy reading Scott, you would be better advised to purchase a visually more comfortable layout, even if it means buying a less distinguished-looking set. Luckily, the first editions don't suffer from this problem.

There is just space to briefly mention some of the other prices that may be paid for important nineteenth-century fiction. Oscar Wilde's *The Picture of Dorian Gray* (1891) in the fine binding designed for it by Charles Ricketts would now fetch about £500; Jane Austen's *Emma* (1815) in a contemporary leather binding would make between £1,400 and £1,800; the first edition of Lamb's *Tales from Shakespeare* (1807) is now worth over £500 in good condition; and a copy of Jane Austen's *Mansfield Park* (1814) has made £1,200 for a copy in contemporary binding. The Brontë sisters tend to come expensive: at a major American sale held during 1990, Charlotte's *Jane Eyre* (1848) fetched over £10,000 in its original purple cloth, while *The Tenant of Wildfell Hall* (1848), written by her sister Anne, realised £19,000. However, a good seven volume set of the Brontës was published in 1889-92, and in a calf binding this has made £420 at an English sale.

Nineteenth-Century Detective and Adventure Stories

Both the adventure and the detective story were truly born during the nineteenth century. Needless to say, among such volumes Sir Arthur Conan Doyle and Sherlock Holmes are in highest demand. First editions come in the £150 to £250 price range, with *The Valley of Fear* (1915) being somewhat cheaper at around £70 and the 1888 edition of *A Study in Scarlet*, in its original wrappers, being the scarcest and dearest at over £1,000. Sherlock Holmes had made his first appearance, in this story, just a year before, in the *Beeton's Christmas Annual* of 1887. A copy of this elusive and precious item turned up at auction in Sotheby's of New York in June 1990, where it made $52,000, or £30,590 at the then rate of exchange. The very popular *Hound of the Baskervilles* (1902) comes in at about £250, depending on binding and condition. *The Moonstone* by Wilkie Collins, three volumes, 1858, is very rare and would set you back £1,000 to £3,000. Until lately, copies of the second edition were making around £50 but seem to have risen in more recent times.

A very fine nineteenth century exponent of historical adventure stories was William Harrison Ainsworth. He is not widely known these days but his

books are hotly sought after by the cognoscenti. His collected works of 1875 in sixteen volumes are not all that expensive at around £300, but first editions can be surprisingly pricy. In Dublin recently a copy of *Old St Pauls* (1841) sold with another, unrelated volume for £320; the Ainsworth book would probably have made £170 to £200 on its own. Works by Ainsworth are worth seeking out, even in subsequent editions, for their story value as well as their collectability. It was he who first popularised the adventures of the famous eighteenth-century highwaymen. Dick Turpin was the hero of *Rookwood*, one of the more attractive editions being the fourth, which includes plates, while Jack Sheppard is the dashing adventurer in the novel of that name published in 1839 in three volumes.

The expansion of the British empire during the second half of the nineteenth century gave birth to a crop of adventure novels featuring great white hunters and doughty seekers of hidden treasure. The heroes are good chaps, good shots, fine sportsmen, and awfully kind to the natives, whose main function is to lug our hero's gear around and help protect him from the nastier natives who would impede him in the shouldering of the White Man's Burden. One of the liveliest of this genre was G. A. Henty, who wrote over eighty novels between 1870 and 1910. Most of his first editions are dated on the title pages, and for serious collectors there is a bibliography: *G. A. Henty : a Bibliography* by R. L. Dartt (Sheratt and Son, 1971). This is an American publication and would not be easily obtainable in Ireland. Irish collectors may have to be satisfied with more general bibliographies. The most popular Henty title is *By Sheer Pluck* (1884, Blackie), which should cost around £40. Also much liked and a little scarcer is *The Young Colonists* (1885), for which you could pay up to £65. *With Roberts in Pretoria* should be about £45, but other Henty first editions should be obtainable between £25 and £40.

One word of warning : it has often seemed to me that Ireland is awash with reprints of Henty's books, which are often offered to collectors at prices that, given the plentifulness of such volumes, are really far too high. Henty reprints, even in good condition, should be obtainable at between £5 and £10; this is the 'going rate' in Britain and there is no reason why they should be any more expensive here. I recently saw a dealer at auction pay just £12 for a carton of eight Henty volumes in good condition, which included some first editions; and while I do not deny the dealer's right to a living and a fair profit, the private collector should be wary of giving too much for Henty reprints.

First editions of the best twentieth-century fiction can generally be obtained for less than the cost of fine nineteenth-century work. Editions were usually larger and many authors, especially the less popular, are not yet collected widely. There are some notable high spots, however. A copy of the first edition of J. R. R. Tolkien's *The Hobbit* (1937) would cost you about £3,000 and prices of all Tolkien first editions are high, while a first edition of William Golding's *Lord of the Flies* (1954) changed hands during 1988 for £1,000. The first edition of the first novel by Agatha Christie, *The Mysterious Affair at Styles* (1920), is now fetching in excess of £600 at auction and up to £1,000 when offered privately. Other Christie titles are not so expensive. You could pay up to £400 for *The Secret Adversary* (1922) and £300 for *The Murder of Roger Ackroyd*, but other first editions still remain at between £60 and £100.

Not all first editions of popular classics soar to such heights, and indeed, it is in the field of crime, adventure and suspense that prices seem to have risen most during the last decade. Other novels equally beloved by many can be purchased for modest sums. A copy of the first British edition of Margaret Mitchell's *Gone With the Wind* (1936) should be obtainable for around £300, though it is up to ten times that in America. W. Somerset Maugham's *Of Human Bondage* (1915) hovers around the £150 mark, while copies of the first edition of Daphne du Maurier's *Rebecca* come in at a knock-down price of around £25. If you are buying these more recent novels, do try to obtain copies with jackets if you can. For copies without, even very clean copies, you should pay significantly less than the prices quoted above.

Although for minor authors there is no comprehensive bibliography, for collectors of more popular twentieth-century fiction there is an invaluable guide called *Modern First Editions* by Joseph Connelly (Orbis, 1984) and recently reprinted. This splendid volume gives not only the date of the first British and American editions of every book listed but the current market price as well. Connelly concentrates on crime and action books and he is a little short on more literary works, but it is a goldmine of interesting and useful information just the same, and could suggest some unthought-of areas of collecting for the beginner.

Natural History

Natural history books, it seems, have rarely been more sought after than today. The real lure of such books is the fine coloured plates that often lurk between their covers and the best are very expensive. Books about birds lead the way, and a copy of the first edition of James Audubon's *Birds of America*, issued in four volumes between 1827 and 1838 is the most sought-after work. The book contains more than four hundred engraved aquatints coloured by hand, and at auction would be expected to reach about £1.6 million. In Britain the first important bird book was John Gould's *Birds of Great Britain*. Originally published in twenty-five parts between 1862 and 1873, it will most often be encountered in a five-volume set that contains more than 350 coloured plates and that could be expected to make £25,000 at auction. These are prices far beyond the reach of the ordinary collector, but bird buffs will be glad to know that a volume published by Methuen in 1967 entitled *Birds of Australia* by A. Rutgers includes 160 plates by Gould and should be obtainable for £100 or less.

Not all antiquarian bird books are so expensive, and many useful and attractive ones can be bought for a few hundred pounds and less. Included among these is the work of a real genius named Thomas Bewick, who revived the mediaeval art of wood engraving for his illustrations. His *History of British Birds* was published in two volumes, one in 1797 and the other in 1804. The price for this could rise to £500 to £600, but I have seen a copy of the 1826 third edition sold for just £90. This was in 1987, and as this is a desirable edition in which some of the woodcuts appear for the first time, I would expect the price to have risen since then. Other good-quality but more modestly priced bird volumes to be sold in the recent past include A. G. Butler's two-volume *Birds of Great Britain and Ireland*, which contains 115 coloured plates and would cost around £210, and a run of Sir William Jardine's *Naturalist Library* volumes, comprising seven books on birds, which reached £250. Jardine's *Library*, the full set of which consists of forty volumes, was issued at Edinburgh in 1833-43 and could cost up to £2,000. The fourteen volumes on birds, especially the two on humming-birds, are highly prized.

Botanical volumes rival the prices made by bird books. Some more modest works include E. J. Lowe's 1861 edition of *Beautiful Leaved Plants*, which contains sixty fine plates and should cost around £150 at auction, and the same author's 1867 edition of *Natural Ferns,* which should be about the same price. A particularly fine botanical illustrator was James Sowerby, who, with the botanist John Edwin Smith, issued between 1790 and 1814 thirty-six volumes of *English Botany*. A first edition of this work is now about £2,000 but admirers of Sowerby's artistry need not despair, for a third edition, edited by John T. Boswell Syme in thirteen volumes between 1863 and 1892, now fetches around £400. A set with eleven volumes was sold in 1988 for £220 at auction.

One of the most outstanding producers of natural history books during the late nineteenth century was the French writer Comte Georges-Louis de Buffon. His intention was to bring current knowledge on natural history before the general public, and his work appeared in many editions during the next hundred years. The first edition of *Histoire Naturelle,* published in forty-four volumes between 1749 and 1804, now runs to several thousand pounds. However, the Paris edition of fifty-eight volumes, 1774-78, made £750 during 1988, and there are several still cheaper editions about. One of these is the 15 volume English translation by J S Barr issued between 1797 and 1798. This would fetch somewhere above £100 and would really be of more interest to the non-French-speaker than the earlier, more expensive editions. It includes engraved plates.

Books on travel and exploration from the eighteenth and nineteenth centuries now form an important part of the book market. Books connected with the eighteenth-century explorer James Cook are particularly sought after, and first editions of his *Voyage Around the World*, published in two volumes in 1781, could now reach as much as £1,000. Another of his works, *A Voyage to the Pacific Ocean*, edited by James King and published in three volumes in Dublin during 1784, would now be expected to reach over £250 at auction. Books on Africa are extremely collectable. One of the most enlightened explorers of the continent was the Scottish surgeon Mungo Park, who was murdered in 1805 while on an expedition through the Niger valley. His *Travels in the Interior Districts of Africa* was published in 1799 when he was just twenty-eight. It still reads well, and should be obtainable for around £200. Polar exploration has always captured the imagination, and books in this field are steadily collected. Sir John Franklin perished on an expedition to the North Pole in 1847. He had

earlier published a *Narrative of a Journey to the Shores of the Polar Sea* in 1823. A first edition would cost about £400, but the second edition is not a bad substitute at about a quarter of the price. The tragedy of Captain Robert Scott at the South Pole is, of course, even more widely known than that of Franklin, and the 1913 two-volume edition of *Scott's Last Expedition*, edited by Leonard Huxley, is much collected and costs £150 or so.

Collectors of exploration books shouldn't forget that adventurous expeditions are still being undertaken, and accounts of these can be added to the bookshelf as they are published. First editions of books by the climber of Everest, Sir John Hunt, and by adventurers such as Chris Bonnington and Tim Severin, are well worth collecting with the future in mind.

I conclude this chapter with so much left unsaid and so many books unmentioned. But perhaps this is just as well, for book collecting really demands that you plough your own furrow. Because it is less expensive than more general antique collecting, you can afford to take more chances, set your own fashions, and build up a collection that is unique to you. The one universal criterion is quality: a worthwhile text in the very best condition you can afford. Remember that the really bad mistakes are made when you pay a high price for a book that is seriously damaged, especially if it lacks plates or text. Patience when viewing is the answer here: never feel too hurried or embarrassed to go through a book slowly, looking at a page at a time, if you feel that's necessary. Leisure is, after all, the keynote in book collecting, both in the gathering and in the enjoyment of your collection.

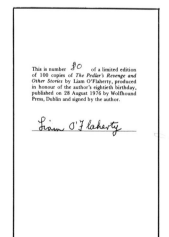

This is number *80* of a limited edition of 100 copies of *The Pedlar's Revenge and Other Stories* by Liam O'Flaherty, produced in honour of the author's eightieth birthday, published on 28 August 1976 by Wolfhound Press, Dublin and signed by the author.

Liam O'Flaherty

Chapter Nine

PICTURES

erhaps the most important thing to bear in mind when considering pictures is that no one medium is intrinsically superior to another. Oil paintings, watercolours, drawings and prints of quality are all desirable works of art. There is no sense in which a watercolour should be seen as a poor man's oil painting, or a print as a cheap alternative to 'genuine' art. By and large, it is true to say that the medium was deliberately chosen by the artist as the manner in which he wanted to create that scene or that statement. Even where prints have been made from original paintings, it was often the case that the artist was involved with the printmaker in the creation of the new version of his work.

This is reflected in the prices and values of pictures. A fine print by Rembrandt could cost hundreds of thousands of pounds, while a poor and dingy oil painting by a poor and dingy artist would scarcely command £20. As always, it's best to buy quality, but the dictums of many art experts and books on art to buy only the best in whatever field you're operating can fall with a hollow ring on the ears of the art lover who is decidedly slender of pocket. But there's no need to be downcast. The modest collector can still have lots of fun with pictures of all kinds in the £50 to £300 price range, where you will be buying pictures that, if not always first-rate, are still decorative in the home.

This is not a mandate for buying bad pictures! 'Buy the best you can afford' must still be the watchword. It is true that the best oil paintings do tend to be expensive — and some, as we all know, fetch millions — and in a general way it probably has to be admitted that a cheap oil is usually a bad oil; but even for sums less than £100 it is still possible to buy small, well-executed watercolours and drawings by unknown amateur artists. Good prints of the eighteenth, nineteenth and twentieth centuries were often issued in sets, and it's often possible to acquire single items from such sets for just a few pounds. There's no sense in imagining, naturally, that such pictures will greatly increase in value in years to come. They may, of course. Your unknown watercolourist may be unexpectedly 'discovered' by the cognoscenti of the art world (this happened to owners of watercolours by Mildred Anne Butler and paintings by Norah McGuinness), or your print may turn out to be rarer than you thought, engraved perhaps by a printmaker previously unknown to you. But don't count on it. The chief value of such purchases, apart from their decorativeness, will be what you learn through them about the various art forms.

Before you even think about buying watercolours, or indeed anything of visual art that interests you, read as much as you can about your favoured areas, and go to the National Gallery and other collections on public view and see the work of the best artists. Many galleries and cultural bodies offer lectures on aspects of the arts: make use of them. Go to the viewings of the art sales, and even if you can't attend the auctions personally, ring up afterwards and find out the prices of any pictures that caught your interest. Don't neglect the many opportunities offered by small commercial galleries to see exhibitions of recent, and even not-so-recent, work. These establishments are very often staffed by knowledgeable and enthusiastic people who, even if they are aware that you won't be buying today, are still happy to discuss the pros and cons of the artist on display. Some of them too, if you do decide to buy, will offer you a deal whereby, during at least the reasonably foreseeable future, if you wish to re-sell your purchase they will take it back from you at the price at which you bought it. Eventually, by viewing as many paintings and prints as you can you will develop an eye for quality, for good execution and draughtsmanship, for skilled use of colour, and, perhaps more than this, an appreciation of the moment at which a fine painting ceases merely to be an attractive composition and becomes a work of art. Even on a limited budget you will probably find that, in the end, you can reach a working compromise between your taste and your pocket.

Watercolours

In the minds of many people, watercolours are associated with the notion of amateurishness in art, with the leisuretime doodlings of ladies of fashion or idle housewives of long ago. The fact is that although many such artists were women and were amateur, some of them attained to a considerable brilliance in the execution of their work, and the best of them are now highly priced in today's art market. Moreover, the majority of watercolourists were male, especially before the nineteenth century, and up until modern times most of those who earned their living with their brush were men.

As with several other areas of collecting that we have noticed, in the field of watercolours there is particular interest among Irish buyers in artists who have painted Irish subjects or were themselves Irish. During the later 1980s there was considerable price inflation of the works of some artists, especially women, of Irish origin, but of late things seem to have settled a little, albeit after a number of unsuspecting fingers were burned. Such price 'hypes' can be created by astute dealers and collectors who, having decided to 'discover' an artist, buy up as many paintings by that person as possible (at fairly low prices, of course), and then, having publicised the artist by means of an exhibition or catalogue, proceed to release paintings onto a now eager market, making a considerable profit by so doing. Gradually other owners of works by the same artist try to cash in too, until the market reaches saturation point and prices take a dive. There is nothing wrong or illegal in such activities. Many artists thus discovered and popularised are genuinely good artists. But as soon as an artist becomes fashionable, and the papers are writing him or her up with increasing hyperbole as price record after price record is set, the wise collector will stand back a little and take stock. If, despite what you read, you have the hunch that paintings of no less quality than those by the newly trumpeted artist are making hundreds rather than thousands of pounds because they carry a different signature, you would do well to keep your money — or spend it on the cheaper paintings. After you have educated yourself as fully as you can in the artistic fields in which you have a particular interest, your best shield against disappointment is to buy or enjoy what *you* like, not what others tell you you ought to like, nor what the popular press tells you everyone else likes. You should not buy with the sole, or even the chief, aim of making money, remembering that though the art world may ring with stories of those who have made a fortune buying and selling paintings, it is a little more reticent about those who have lost one. Buy what you can afford, and buy to enjoy, and you won't go far wrong. And buy a fashionable artist if you like him and can pay the price; but remember that if you buy at the height of a craze you will probably find that the value will slip, even if later, as will probably happen if the artist is a good one, it begins to move very slowly upwards again over a longer period.

Irish
Watercolours

Returning to the Irish watercolour market, it is a fact that Irish artists and subjects have dominated the market in recent years, with quite a strong demand for such works in the London houses as well, though many of them have been bought by Irish collectors and dealers to sell or keep at home. The 1980s saw a fashion for rather sugary landscapes and rustic farmyard scenes, epitomised by Mildred Anne Butler (1858-1941), working in watercolour, and Frank McKelvey (1895-1974), painting in oil. As to prices, both these artists had reached rather dizzying heights by the end of the eighties but have now slipped somewhat as public taste seemed to turn to more robust works. Prices for Butler's work vary quite widely, depending on subject, size, detail, colour, and general quality. They tend to start at around £600 for smallish works, rising to about ten times that for the very best. Favourite subjects are cattle standing in groups by ponds, and hens running about farmyards. Floral scenes seem a little less popular, though some of them are rather attractive.

An artist who did much better things in watercolour than Mildred Butler and many of whose works are no more expensive was Andrew Nicholl (1804-86) of Belfast. He was a regular exhibitor at the Royal Academy during the early and mid-Victorian period. He concentrated almost entirely on landscapes, but made a number of gloriously detailed studies of wild flowers on grassy banks. For fine examples of these you could pay more than £6,000 but attractive works by Nicholl have been sold at auction for £1,000 or a little less.

In the same price range, sometimes more expensive, is John Luke (1906-75). His works show an extraordinary strength, all the more remarkable when seen in watercolour (he also worked in oil). He painted landscapes but also experimented with other subjects. One of the most interesting watercolours by him offered for sale recently was a sketch for an unfinished mural he painted at Millfield Technical College, Belfast, during the 1960s. In one sense the work, 'Industrial Belfast', is primitive, as murals tend to be, but it is an arresting depiction of the industrial scene.

Not all good watercolours are as expensive as this, and many fine artists can be secured for sums below £500. One of my favourite watercolourists is Bingham McGuinness, and although his larger, more important watercolours can now make several thousand pounds, there are many good ones to be found for quite modest sums. Especially attractive is his use of

Irish
Watercolours

light, often shaded in tones of grey and ochre. He painted many street scenes. His *Street in Bruges* made £2,800 at a sale in Dublin during 1989, but I have seen a number of works by him fetch between £190 and £500 at salerooms. A watercolourist who produced many rather indifferent landscapes but who has certainly increased in popularity of late is Alexander Williams (1846-1930). A couple of years ago I saw watercolours by him — 'Road to a Bog on Achill Island' and 'View of Glendalough' — fetch just £190 each in a Dublin saleroom. At a house clearance sale some time later there was a collection of his watercolours on offer, landscapes and seascapes all, and they fetched on average £600 apiece, with the most expensive making £1,100. This trend seems to have continued in subsequent sales. An artist of far better quality was Helena J. Maguire; I have seen just one watercolour by her in a recent sale. Entitled 'A Quiet Moment', it showed a young woman sewing by a French window with a flower garden beyond. It fetched £1,150, around a quarter of what was made by a (for me at least) vastly inferior Mildred Anne Butler that sold on the same day.

Attractive watercolours that are unsigned or whose signatures are, alas, unknown to the art world can be bought at prices that start at just a few pounds. Here you must buy on the basis of quality and the appeal of the work to you personally, but don't expect these purchases to appreciate significantly in value. Many such watercolours will have been painted by just the sort of amateur referred to at the beginning, but this doesn't necessarily mean that they will be bad work. Surprisingly, book sales can be quite a fruitful source of watercolours of this sort, because many of them were painted or mounted in albums and can be purchased within their own covers or, sometimes, in loose folders. The albums containing such watercolours were sometimes themselves quite elaborate and can cost several hundred pounds at auction; often, however, a quick calculation will reveal that the paintings work out at perhaps £10 each. If you are looking for something to hang on your wall, these collections may not provide what you seek, for, of course, in many cases it would be nothing short of vandalism to break up an album in order to frame and hang its contents. For such purposes you had best stick to loose collections; in these instances, where the artist is unnamed or unknown, the individual items will work out really quite cheaply.

Individual framed watercolours can be found at house clearances, but in general I find that saleroom auctions provide the best selections and the best opportunities for buying something attractive at modest cost. The firm of James Adams of St Stephen's Green, Dublin, begins many of its regular sales with a nice run of such items, and there will generally be some good value among the lots on offer. Prices generally start at around £30.

Oil Paintings

It has been said that it was the Renaissance Flemish artist Jan van Eyck who invented oil painting, but it would appear that during his lifetime a number of artists had begun to work on some of the same processes that he was using. From that time, it has been in this medium that the world's greatest paintings have been executed. Most have been painted on canvas stretched across a wooden frame called a stretcher; others, as the new collector will quickly notice, have been painted on boards, usually made of a hard wood such as

The sort of topographical work which can be afforded by fairly modest collectors. This one is unsigned but of good quality, and depicts Athcarne Castle, Co. Meath prior to the alterations of 1830.

mahogany. The attraction of painting in oils for many artists is the greater complexity that can be attained in the medium, as it allows a picture to be built up in layers, using a variety of tones, strokes, and details. When it is finished it is left for about six months to allow the paint to dry, after which it is varnished, both to protect the work and to enhance its colour.

Having first educated your eye by visiting the top galleries and exhibitions, you will quickly find when you transfer your attention to the saleroom that there are an awful lot of bad oil paintings about. Luckily, there are sufficient good ones to keep most collectors happy and even under, say, £2,000, there is plenty of attractive work from which you can choose. If you can afford to buy the occasional oil in the £1,000 to £2,000 price range, you will find that many country house sales will offer you a choice of good-quality works by artists of some repute. There may, of course, be the temptation at this level to purchase minor or even rather poor works by major artists, but this can be a mistake. It is often far better to go for high-quality works by lesser-known artists. These have a rather greater chance of appreciating in value than the work of a major painter on his off day, and they will be pleasanter to live with.

The very large house clearance with a substantial picture section is often the right place to pick up good-quality oils at a fairly keen price. This is my experience, at least, and I'm not quite sure why this is so. The larger art dealers, of course, always attend such sales in some numbers, but they tend to be after the more valuable and expensive works. The modest buyers may only be interested in bidding for small watercolours and prints, and very

Where to Buy

often, I've noticed, there is a group of paintings in the middle range for which there is not all that much competition at all. This is where, if you have saved up a few pounds to buy one or two good paintings for your home, you can hope to score.

I saw precisely this phenomenon on a very hot day in the summer of 1990, and some very fine paintings were knocked down to a few discerning buyers who hadn't allowed the overpowering heat to put them asleep, as it had some of the attendance. A very fine pair of oils on canvas by Colin Huntes depicting horses in a landscape was sold for just £950; not only were they of good quality but they were of good size as well and would have made wonderful centrepieces for anyone's sitting-room or dining-room. On the same day a fine study of horses and poultry in a stable by A. Lemon after J. F. Herring was sold for £700, and the quality of the work would not have been unworthy of Herring himself. On that day, too, a colourful and well-executed still life by F. May was purchased for just £575 — and that was only one of a number of very attractive signed and unsigned oils that were got for around the same price.

Portraits

There are some kinds of oil painting that are not very popular with the public because of their subject matter but that in themselves are examples of high-quality work. If you can live with such subjects, you will find that you can often purchase them at surprisingly low cost. One of these groups is that of portraiture, especially of people whose names are not well known to history but who may have been painted by highly competent portrait painters. Sometimes, too, copies were made, even hundreds of years later, of portraits of famous people made by equally famous artists, and these can also prove reasonably priced. Buyers, it seems, are not all that keen to acquire portraits of someone else's ancestors. The cheapest works in this group are Victorian portraits of gentlemen in black coats, closely followed by fat Victorian ladies in black dresses. If you like them, they can often be yours for around £100. The prices go up according to quality, and if the faces are well painted and the costumes elaborate or colourful, such works could reach between £1,000 and £2,000; but if you keep your eyes open you will find that there is plenty of choice at the £500 to £700 range.

Portraits from the sixteenth to the eighteenth centuries can be rather more expensive, especially if they are attractive ladies, but you will find that some of them are quite affordable, too. For instance, I recently saw two eighteenth-century copies of seventeenth-century portraits sell for £360 and £250, both of which were well executed and certainly of interest to the historically minded. The more expensive was a small half-length portrait of Oliver Cromwell by an unknown artist but quite well done, and the other was an oil on canvas of an unnamed Williamite officer — one could have had some fun trying to discover who he was. Not, I suppose, a very great painting, but still one of some historical interest was another work I saw lately being knocked down for just £240. This was a portrait by an unknown seventeenth or early eighteenth-century artist of Patrick Russell, Archbishop of Dublin and strong ally of King James II.

Another subject the public fails to warm to is that of dead animals, and if you have a strong stomach you will often find that you can buy very well-painted oils of tablefuls of dead game or of animals killed at a hunt or some such thing. The two most recent examples that I have seen offered at auction actually failed to sell (both featured deceased pheasants hanging on hooks), but who knows what bargains might have been had if a properly appreciative art lover had happened along? I have also lately seen a charming composition — it was well painted — depicting a dead cockerel and hen fetch £480 at auction. It was really quite large — almost two feet by three and in a gilt frame. Signed by J. Fyt, it was no doubt good value to anyone who could live with it.

Good still lifes can bebought by the modest collector, with prices for **Still Life** good ones starting at around £500, but prices of the very best, even those that are unsigned and attributed to some 'school', have been rising, and fine unsigned ones, particularly if they are of large size, have been making between £3,000 and £5,000 of late. These are even more desirable if they appear in matched pairs, as they sometimes do, and at a recent house clearance in Co. Dublin two still lifes of fruit, nineteenth-century and unsigned, fetched £3,800 over an estimate of slightly less than half that figure. At the same sale a really fine French nineteenth-century study of flowers and a butterfly in a stone niche made £1,800. However, elsewhere an almost equally good one by Joseph Furst of flowers in a vase on a marble ledge was sold for just £850; and at several sales lately I have seen good still lifes of smallish size being sold for around £250 or so.

Good landscapes, especially good large landscapes, tend to be **Landscapes** expensive. Bad landscapes of all kinds abound, so do examine work carefully before you decide to buy. In general, I would say that the modest buyer who fancies a landscape would be better to go for a watercolour than an oil, as you will be more likely to find a decent one within your price range in that medium. Still, good small landscape oils can be found in the £400 to £700 bracket, and within this range it is also possible to buy the occasional topographical work or landscape featuring some house or antiquity. For example, a very nice topographical scene of Athcarne Castle, Co. Meath, dating from the early nineteenth century, was recently sold for £625. It was of fairly small size — just over ten by fourteen inches.

Seascapes, too, are popular with artists, and many of these are very **Seascapes** poorly executed. Prices tend to start at around £200, but many at this price are really quite dreadful and best avoided — nasty, blobby turquoise skies and sea, blurry beige beach, and, far off, a single tiny yacht. The best ones to look for are those of named ships at sea or entering harbour; for example, at a Co. Carlow sale lately a view of the *City of Liverpool* entering harbour by R. Pald cost only £400 and, I think represented very good value. At the same sale a topographical-type view of, possibly, a bay in the Crimea and showing a regiment awaiting battle on the shore was a very interesting buy at £650. Stormy seascapes, especially with ships, are much in demand with buyers, but before you part with anything other than a modest sum of money do consider carefully the quality of what is on offer. In general, you will probably find that it is difficult to purchase a good seascape for under £400.

If you like religious paintings you may discover that this is another area **Religious** in which it is possible to purchase good work at relatively small cost, for this genre has tended, in recent years, to lose favour with buyers, except in the case of work of very exceptional quality. I have often seen, for example, nice Madonnas with Child and portraits of the Virgin in small sizes sell between £200 and £300.

Oil on canvas 'Blacksmith Shoeing a Bay Horse' after Sir Edward Landseer.

Animals

Moving in the opposite direction on the scale are animals, not so much horses, which seemed to reach their peak some years ago, but portrayals of cats and dogs. Strangely, paintings of hens in farmyards seem also to have caught buyers' imagination lately, with Edgar Hunt's hens and ponies being especially popular. Hunt's paintings range from about £3,000 to £10,000, but it is possible to buy work 'in the style of Hunt' for significantly less. Dogs and cats show no sign of slackening off in popularity, so good-quality ones bought at reasonable prices could prove to be rather good buys even (or maybe especially) in the short term. The nicest one I've seen of late was a William Osborne painting 'Receiving a Deputation', which depicted a venerable old bloodhound listening to some weighty plea being put by two rather impudent-looking younger dogs. This painting made £12,000, and it deserved to; you will find that the more interesting or unusual the activity in which the dogs or cats are engaged, the more the price will rise. However, simple head studies can be got from around £200, while a good-quality portrait of a dog or cat seated on a chair or floor could fetch twice or three times that. I'm speaking here, of course, of unsigned work; compositions by named, accomplished artists would cost more. Paintings of dogs engaged in outdoor work such as hunting or retrieving at a shoot are very much in demand at present and can be fairly expensive, with prices for much good work lying between £600 and £4,000. I suspect, too, that this particular genre has some further way to go in the future as far as values are concerned.

A word should perhaps be said here on the subject of restoration and cleaning of paintings. In most cases, dirt and discoloured varnishes can be removed from oil paintings without too much difficulty — but only, I must stress, by a professional. It is all too easy to ruin a good picture by the use of solvent and other cleaning methods, and even easier to destroy a watercolour. If a picture you fancy appears to be in need of rather extensive restoration, you need to think about this when considering the price you are prepared to pay. It may also be that your oil painting has some tears in the canvas or, worse, tearing or cracking because the stretcher behind it is in a state of collapse. In this last situation it may be that the picture will need to be re-lined, that is, have the painted canvas attached to a new one at the back in order to prevent further tearing. With oils on board you may find that there are some cracks that need professional attention. The real dilemma arises if, when you are buying good-quality but not very highly priced work, the cost of restoration looks likely to exceed the price of the painting. If you are buying from a good auction house, its staff should be able to advise you on the cost of restoration. The decision whether to buy must then be a personal one, and you may well decide that even if the cost of restoring brings the final price of the picture to beyond what it would ever hope to reach should you re-sell, you still like it enough to bear the expense.

In general, though, if a relatively inexpensive and not very high quality painting needs professional attention beyond that of cleaning, it is probably best avoided.

Restoration and Cleaning

Prints

It often comes as a surprise to modest collectors to learn that there are many different kinds of prints, and that one of the first things you need to understand is what a print is not. It is *not* an illustration put onto paper by purely photographic means. Such pictures, often very attractive copies of great paintings or watercolours, abound both in department stores and antique shops and may often be described as prints. They are, however, more properly termed photo reproductions or, as auction catalogues often describe them, coloured reproductions. Occasionally, very finely produced photo reproductions may have been acknowledged by the artist and signed by him, and in such cases the buyer can expect to pay somewhat more for them. Nevertheless, such pictures are really no more valuable than, say, a magazine illustration that has been signed by the artist. They should not be confused with genuine prints, although the prices I have seen paid for items like coloured reproductions of eighteenth and nineteenth-century hunting prints suggest that they all too often are.

To be considered genuine a print must have been created by means of an impression taken from an inked block. Upon the block — which may be made of copper, steel, wood, or indeed a variety of materials — an original design or copy of an artist's drawing may be engraved. The paper is then passed over it and the print 'pulled' by hand.

The buyer needs to be able to tell the different kinds of prints apart, as well as all the different kinds from the photo reproduction. This is by no means easy. To do this, you need to handle prints, out of their frames, as often as you can, and you need some background knowledge of the main techniques used. A good magnifying glass will help as well.

Woodcuts

The oldest print technique is the woodcut. This is made from a wooden block on which part of the wood is cut away with a knife to leave the design standing up in relief. This portion is then inked over and the required number of impressions on paper taken from it.

This method of illustration was probably first used for playing-cards and religious pictures, but by the late fifteenth century its history had become closely bound up with the printed book, because the inked block could be set up with the type, and the picture and text printed onto the page at the same time. The first important depiction of Ireland by the woodcut method can be seen in John Derrick's *Image of Ireland*, published in London in 1581. A fine facsimile edition of this work was published at Edinburgh in 1883, limited to 286 copies. It is not often seen for sale in Ireland; the last one I saw was sold at auction for £80 a couple of years ago, and I imagine the price would be significantly above that by now.

Image of Ireland

A number of important artists, including Albrecht Dürer (1471-1528) and Hans Holbein (1497-1543), produced designs for woodcuts, but it is unlikely that such items would come the way of the modest collector. Pirated copies of Holbein's work were issued from as early as the sixteenth century, and occasionally some of these turn up at sales. Keep your eyes open!

Thomas Bewick

The woodblock technique fell out of favour during the seventeenth century, but during the eighteenth century Thomas Bewick restored it to new popularity by his method of wood engraving. Bewick used the end grain of a very hard wood such as boxwood and engraved his lines with a burin, or graver, rather than cutting away with a knife. The portion that was inked was still that standing up, but the resultant design was much more fluid and varied than had been possible with the old methods. The actual lines engraved were, of course, left white, and it was for this reason that Bewick's technique was dubbed the 'white line' method.

Bewick's methods were employed in the illustration of his natural history books, and it was for book illustration that wood engraving remained most widely used during the following eighty years. Though there was, inevitably, much hack work, the best artists, too, contributed illustrations both to books and periodicals. These included Myles Birkett Foster, whose watercolours are now also highly prized, John Millais, Dante Gabriel Rossetti, and Holman Hunt. For the modest collector this often means that

Malton print 'Powerscourt House'.

fine examples of the work of such artists can be acquired at fairly reasonable prices. Particularly sought after is Moxon's 1857 edition of *The Poems of Tennyson*, which included illustrations by Hunt, Rossetti, and Millais, while the 1854 edition of Thomas Gray's *Elegy in a Country Churchyard* had illustrations by Birkett Foster.

Many of these prominent artists supplied only the drawings for such illustrations, the actual wood blocks being worked by professional engravers. Among the most notable engravers were George and Edward Dalziel who not merely engraved themselves but maintained a whole company of craftsmen. Their firm worked on the Moxon Tennyson, and although this is among the most sought-after of Victorian illustrated books, it does not, it's probably true to say, contain their best work. Some of this may be found in a volume of *Parables of Our Lord*, published in book form in 1863. It is true that the success of the Dalziels' work here owed a good deal to the talent of John Millais, who prepared the original drawings, but it cannot be denied that the engravers did very well by their artist. The book was not at the time a financial success, and copies are nowadays quite hard to come by. Another relative rarity well worth looking out for is the 1851 edition of *The Story of Jack and the Giants*, with drawings by Richard Doyle and engravings by the Dalziel brothers.

Although it is perfectly possible to buy much Victorian wood-engraved illustration at modest cost, the collector may find that much of the best material has become rather expensive in recent years. You need not despair, however, if you can't afford copies of such work, for some of the very best wood engravings appeared in the popular journals of the period, including the *Cornhill*, the *Illustrated London News*, and the *Graphic*. These are often

The Dalziel Brothers

found at auction in elaborate bound sets, which can be expensive. A bound set of the *Illustrated London News*, with forty-three volumes for 1842-68, recently fetched £1,450 at auction. But fine single copies of the *Illustrated London News* can cost as little as £10 and sometimes less, and odd copies of the *Graphic*, which contained some of the most interesting wood engravings of the period, can be got for as little as £1.50 in mint condition. What works of art of nowadays can be obtained for as little as that?

Engraving on Metal

While the popularity of wood engraving waxed and waned, the use of engraving on metal both for books and for loose pictorial prints remained constant from the seventeenth to the nineteenth century. Five techniques chiefly concern the collector: etching, copper line engraving, steel engraving, mezzotint and aquatint. These differ from the woodcut in that they are intaglio methods; that is, the design is cut into the metal plate and it is into these incisions rather than the surface that the ink is poured. The plate is then wiped clean of surplus ink, and dampened paper is forced, by means of a press, into the lines to take the impression. It is certainly open to the modest collector to obtain examples of work in all these media, although you may find the very best etchings, mezzotints and aquatints beyond your reach. This will be particularly the case if you like coloured prints, for that is what the market mainly demands at present. But if you should happen to have the good sense to acquire a taste for black-and-white engravings, then you will find that a far greater range of really good work will come within easy reach of your pocket than if you stick only to coloured examples. In fact at present, because many people find black-and-white prints unacceptable for decorative purposes, and also because many general dealers and auctioneers know little of this particular field, there are bargains to be had if you have done the research necessary to enable you to recognise quality work by lesser known engravers and even, from time to time, more important craftsmen, whose names are all but unknown nowadays to many of the collecting public.

Steel Engraving

During the seventeenth and eighteenth centuries virtually all line engravings were done on copper. Steel was introduced at the beginning of the nineteenth century and the hardness of the metal, which enabled the printer to take many more impressions from the plate than he could take from the softer copper, meant that it quickly became widely used. It can be very difficult, especially for the novice, to tell a copper and a steel engraving apart, and very often only your knowledge of the artist or engraver, the date of the print and the name of the printer or publisher will enable you to decide accurately. In general, finer lines were possible in steel than copper, and the engravers took pride in running these fine lines closer and closer together, with the result that whereas a print from a copper plate tends to have a very perceptible network of lines, the fineness of the steel lines can result in a rather smoother effect. But this is not an infallible rule, and only experience (and a magnifying glass) will perfect your judgement.

The prices paid for copper and steel engravings vary enormously, and the modest collector will find many opportunities of buying something worthwhile for a reasonable sum, especially, as has been suggested, if you go for black-and-white examples. French copper engravings of the seventeenth

Malton print 'St. Stephen's Green'.

century are quite often found loose in folios, particularly at book sales, and you will often come across them, framed, in antique shops. Beware, though, of rather small ones which may have been cut out of books and framed in such a way as to conceal the fact. Among portrait engravers the work of Robert Naneuil stands out; subjects engraved by him included Cardinal Mazarin, Queen Christina of Sweden, and Marshal Turenne. Other celebrities of the day were interpreted by Antoine Masson. Many French engravers, particularly during the eighteenth century, prepared plates after the work of landscape artists such as Nicholas Poussin and Claude Lorraine. The appeal of such engravings, often rather large in size, is more limited than that for portraits, and for those who like them there is often value to be had. I have seen five unframed prints after French old masters sell for just £50, a collection of eight sepia-tinted prints after Claud Lorraine knocked down for £18, and a large portfolio of various seventeenth, eighteenth and nineteenth-century engravings after Chasteau, Poussin, Scotin and others go under the hammer for £60. Mind you, it is my own opinion that much French engraving, particularly that after the seventeenth and eighteenth-century landscape painters is dull in the extreme and not to be compared the fine portrait work of the engravers, both English and Irish, who worked in London at the same period. But there is no doubt that if you like it, it is possible to build up an interesting collection for a relatively modest outlay.

In England, most of the best eighteenth-century portrait work was done in mezzotint rather than line engraving, but some line artists stand out as worthy of the collector's attention. The best-known is probably William Hogarth, who was both a painter and a line engraver, but most of the great prints associated with him were engraved by other craftsmen after Hogarth's

Portrait Work

Hogarth

drawings. One of the very best, and my own personal favourite, 'The March to Finchley', which depicts an unforgettable scene from the 1745 campaign of Bonnie Prince Charlie, was engraved by Luke Sullivan, one of a very important group of Irish engravers who worked in London during the eighteenth century. He was born in Louth but brought up at the English estate of the Duke of Beaufort, where his father was a groom. His engraving of Finchley was published in 1750, and he also worked on other plates for Hogarth.

Perennially popular is Hogarth's series of prints, 'Marriage à la Mode', which has been copied in many versions right up to the present day. The buyer who seeks out original eighteenth-century prints of Hogarth's work has much need of homework, or you run the risk of paying too much for what can be very recent copies. For those who enjoy Hogarth's work but cannot afford original prints there are a number of nineteenth-century books on the life and works of Hogarth that include engravings in steel of his work. There is a set published by Rev. J. Hogarth Trusler, *The Works of William Hogarth* (1824), which contains two volumes and a selection of plates; this sells at £40 to £50. Rather better is an 1880 London one-volume edition of *The Complete Works of William Hogarth*, containing 150 engraved plates and, when last seen, costing £70 at auction in Kilkenny.

As with the wood engravers, much of the work of the nineteenth-century steel engravers was done for illustrated books. Some craftsmen continued to work on copper plates for loose pictorial prints after old masters and on genre scenes. One such engraver whose work is well worth looking out for is G. T. Doo, who lived from 1800 to 1886. He worked after a number of artists, and I have a fine genre scene by him after Norton, in mint condition, which I purchased for £40. Another name to watch for is that of William Finden, who did some good portrait work, including one of King George IV after Lawrence.

Many of the books for which steel engravings were made were of a topographical nature and are rather uninspired, but some are more interesting, and they are not always expensive. One such set, rather despised by collectors today but most interesting to anyone keen on nineteenth-century engraving, is *The Royal Gallery of British Art*. It was produced by William Finden and his brother, who by the 1830s were specialising in elaborate but mass-produced picture books for the gift market. Published in parts between 1838 and 1849 at the then fantastic price of £63 for a proof set and £20 for a less exclusive edition, it went down with the public like the proverbial lead balloon and left the brothers bankrupt. Today, it shouldn't cost the buyer much more than £80. Indeed, it's generally true that Victorian 'gallery' books included a number of volumes that can only be described as pulp illustration, but aside from the *Royal Gallery*, which is of interest, albeit as a curiosity, there were one or two good ones. One of the very best was *The Waverley Gallery* published under the auspices of the engraver Charles Heath in 1841. With engravings by Stodart, Hopwood, and others, and a rich binding of crimson morocco with gilt tooling, it is an attractive piece of Victoriana that shouldn't cost you more than £20. There are illustrated editions of major English poets that are also worth looking out for, as they contain good steel engravings. One of these, and it is not expensive, is the 1857 illustrated edition of Byron's works, which contains a large number of engravings after Birkett Foster and Kenny Meadows, among others.

Etching

To make an etching, a copper plate is heated and covered in wax. When this has cooled and hardened the engraver makes the design by cutting through the wax with an etching needle to expose lines of copper. The plate is then immersed in acid, which bites at the copper lines but leaves the waxed areas untouched. The etcher can control the depth of the lines by varying the time he leaves certain areas in the acid. If he is satisfied with the depth in one section but desires more biting in another, he removes the plate, covers the finished section with wax, and returns the plate to the acid bath for a further period. Prints made by etching generally have a smooth, flowing appearance, not unlike a pen-and-ink drawing. The method was frequently used in conjunction with line engraving, the last being used to lend more strength to figures and other important features in the foreground of the print.

Etchings were first made early in the sixteenth century but the technique is still used today in the making of specialist art prints. Of antique etchings, the work of Rembrandt is the most expensive, with prices starting at around £100,000 for the best impressions. If you want one you will probably have to travel to London, for not many come up for sale at Irish auction rooms. Other fine old master etchings include work by Albrecht Dürer and Wenceslas Hollar; such prints would not be as expensive as Rembrandt, but hardly come within the scope of the modest collector.

In truth, the collection of all good-quality etchings by well-known artists, including those of the nineteenth and twentieth century, is quite an expensive business. However, at salerooms you will often come across simple etchings by lesser-known or unknown artists that may be quite attractive.

Prices for such items start at around £10, going up according to quality. Occasionally, you may come across later copies or imitations of etchings by or after the old masters, which may be reasonable. At a Dublin saleroom recently an etching in the manner of Rembrandt fetched £570. It's probably true to say that the collector wishing to obtain, at reasonable cost, prints by

Coloured print after Snaffles 'Great Banks There was Below in the Fields'. Signed.

Cont. page 144

Mezzotints

The mezzotint was a variation on the copper engraving, whereby the copper plate was roughened by means of a rocker to give the impression on paper of a dark, velvety surface. The engraving was carried out by simply scraping areas of this 'burr' and, for highlights, polishing it brightly. The method was ideal for portraiture, as it lent a subtle softness to the finished print. Mezzotints can usually be fairly easily distinguished from line engravings by this soft, slightly mottled effect.

Although they worked mainly in London, a number of Irish engravers were prominent in this work, largely concentrating on portraits of contemporary celebrities. One of these was Andrew Miller, who, although of Scottish origin, came to Dublin to set up an art school with John Brooks, who had established a publishing house in Cork Hill. Among the many mezzotints prepared by Miller in Dublin were portraits of Jonathan Swift, King William III, Isaac Newton, and Oliver Cromwell.

One of Miller's pupils was James McArdell, born in Dublin around 1729 and widely regarded as the finest mezzotint engraver of the period. The usual gamut of prominent people undoubtedly formed the staple of his trade, but he made a number of engravings of more ambitious subjects, including a set of six views of Dublin which he issued from the print shop he opened in London in the late 1740s. He had earlier worked on some plates while in Dublin, and some of these appear to have been sold from John Brooks's print shop in Cork Hill. The first of these was probably a portrait of Archbishop Boulter of Armagh, issued in 1742; just four years later both Brooks and McArdell left Dublin to pursue their fortune in London. Such was McArdell's rapid success there that by the end of the 1750s there was scarcely a figure in high society whose portrait he had not engraved, and he also prepared a number of plates from earlier portraits and old masters, notably Van Dyck and Rubens. Death cut short his career at the early age of thirty-seven, though he had never been associated with the kind of hard living and hard drinking in which many of the other London Irish engravers are said to have engaged.

The prices for McArdell's work are nowadays very hard to gauge, as, indeed, it is with much of the work of the eighteenth-century engravers, particularly those in black and white. Sometimes, if a knowledgeable print dealer is at a sale, especially if he has access to a clientele in Britain, prices could be bid up quite highly. After all, McArdell's work is very fine, and if you were to look at auction records from the turn of this century you would notice that his prints and those of all the best eighteenth-century engravers reached, in real terms, prices that are far higher that they would fetch now. You may even find that in money terms the amounts paid were higher than they would be now. To give an example: at a saleroom in Dublin about a year ago, a print by McArdell of Lord Robert Henley after Hudson was sold for £100. Hudson was a portrait artist of some distinction, and during the early 1900s prints by McArdell after his work were fetching between £20 and £400, depending on the condition of the print and the identity of the subject. It's probably true that on the day the McArdell was sold in Dublin there were not many knowledgeable print collectors present; nevertheless it's obvious that there has been a great collapse in the value of black-and-white mezzotints since the early years of this century. For the collector of the moment, prices will generally be found to be pretty unpredictable, with a few items being expensive, depending on who is at the sale on the day, but with many very fine items being knocked down at prices between £50 and £200.

Another Irish mezzotintist whose work is well worth looking out for and which can be bought within the price range mentioned above is James Watson. He appears to have been born in Ireland around 1740. He set up his business in London, however, and engraved a wide range of plates after Reynolds, Gainsborough, and Rubens. At a Dublin saleroom not long ago a portrait of John Hely-Hutchinson by Watson, after Reynolds, was sold for £80. Equally good, and nowadays in the same price band as Watson, or, in Ireland, rather less, was the work of William and James Ward. The best work by William Ward was probably his portraits after Reynolds and his genre scenes after Moreland. Moreland specialised in country scenes of a somewhat idealised nature, featuring pretty farmyards, shire horses, attractive cottages, and so forth. This work has always been extremely popular, and prints after Morland, especially those in colour, fetch around £150. They turn up fairly often at sales, but do beware of relatively modern copies. William Ward's brother James abandoned his career as an engraver in favour of painting and, as a mezzotintist, he is generally agreed to be not so skilled as his brother. He did some nice, rather gentle portraits after the artist Hoppner, and though the best can be expensive, less elaborate ones can be picked up at modest prices, starting at around £50.

One mezzotintist whose works have remained relatively expensive, at least compared with those fetched by his contemporaries in recent years, was Valentine Green. His work appears quite often at sales, especially at country houses, and it's clear that he has a keen band of followers, particularly when coloured versions of his work are found. A rather damaged Duchess of Cumberland made £180 at a recent Dublin house sale; in 1903 a perfect copy fetched £29 8s! Green was enormously popular in his own time as well, becoming, at the age of thirty-four, mezzotint engraver to King George III, as well as to Charles Theodore, the German Elector Palatine. As a businessman he had a shrewd eye to the market, and he engraved a huge number of plates after Reynolds of the most beautiful women of the day; at fifteen shillings each they were a great success when published, and despite the fact that Green also produced fine engravings of other subjects, these glamorous women have remained the prints most in demand with collectors ever since. Over a career spanning forty years, Green engraved more than four hundred plates, so there is no shortage of choice for the collector.

Other engravers whose names denote good-quality work include William Dickinson, Thomas Watson, and Samuel Cousins. Cousins worked during the nineteenth century, and his earliest work is best. His fine portraits are not so easily found, and in good condition may be relatively expensive. His later prints, including some after the artist Edwin Landseer, are, if you can live with their rather large size, really very cheap. I recently acquired one in perfect condition and signed by Cousins, for around £18. Irish engravers to keep an eye out for include Edward Fisher, Richard Purcell, and Charles Spooner.

An Irishwoman who attained to great skill as an engraver was Caroline Watson, the daughter of James. Her best work was done in what is called stipple engraving. This was created by making a network of dots on the copper plate, the ink then being poured into the dots. It was used sometimes in addition to line engraving; used on its own it can, especially if the engraver was not of the first rank, descend into a rather unpleasingly 'twee' appearance. That said, stipple work, even at its most hideously soft and sentimental, as in much of the work of Bartolozzi, ranks high in demand among collectors today. Caroline Watson was certainly one of the best proponents of stipple, being so much admired by Queen Caroline, wife of George III, that she was appointed engraver to the queen in 1785. She did not confine herself to stipple but produced fine plates after work by Reynolds, Hoppner, Cosway and others in mezzotint as well. She is said to have engraved well over a hundred and fifty plates in her lifetime, but for all that they seem rarely to come up for auction, and I have never yet seen one in an Irish saleroom. It would be interesting to see what price one would make should it appear.

Other stipple engravers are regularly seen. Bartolozzi, both in the original and in huge numbers of copies and imitations, many really rather awful, is probably the most often encountered. The most famous series of stipple engravings is undoubtedly Francis Wheatley's 'Cries of London', which is often seen in Ireland, both at house clearances and at salerooms. It is important for collectors who wish to buy a set to know that the complete series consists of thirteen and that they were printed both in brown and in colours. Wheatley was not the engraver of the set but the original artist, the plates being engraved by several people, including Schiavonetti, Vendramini, and Cardon. The purchase of a set of 'Cries' can be something of a minefield for the buyer, for not only are there a number of original sets about, in varying states of preservation, but you will also encounter nineteenth-century engraved copies and twentieth-century photo reproductions. A fine set of originals, in mint condition and preferably not stuck down on cardboard, would be very expensive, but good nineteenth-century and even earlier copies tend to sell at around £1,000 for a full set. If you are uncertain how much to pay for a set, do take some professional advice from a reliable auctioneer or print dealer before you part with large sums of money.

Less expensive than 'Cries' but well worth looking out for are the stipple engravings of P. W. Tomkins, Charles Wilkin, and Thomas Cheesman. Cheesman's work is particularly attractive and appears occasionally at sales. The last lot of Cheesmans I saw sold in Ireland was truly lovely: six stipple engravings of women's heads, in mint condition without frames, and dated 1787. They sold at £340 for the lot, and at just over £50 each I don't know how anyone could deny that that was a bargain.

known artists and engravers, will not be buying pure etchings but will be going for line engravings on metal and wood or choosing from the wide range of reasonably priced mezzotints and lithographs.

Coloured Prints

During the late eighteenth and nineteenth century there was an increasing demand for coloured prints and the development of some new printmaking techniques. The most important of these new methods were aquatint and lithography; and although both could be used for printing in black and white, they have become mainly associated with colour. Aquatint was especially useful in the production of landscape views and topographical prints and was widely used for cartoon and sporting prints. To make the print, the copper plate was covered with a resin dissolved in a spirit of wine known as aquafortis: hence the term 'aquatint'. The method of engraving was highly complicated, involving a process of acid bathing to bite out areas left uncovered by the resin; and, to acquire differing levels of tone and depth, areas of the plate would then be re-covered with resin and bathed again. Finally, a brush soaked in aquafortis was applied to further darken certain parts. Many of the printmakers who are nowadays household names, even to the non-collector, produced their work in aquatint. They include Thomas Malton and his more famous son, James; F. C. Lewis who produced sporting prints after Alken; Charles Hunt, still much in demand for his racing and coaching prints; and the famous firm of Rudolph Ackermann & Sons which opened a print shop in 1796 and only in 1991 finally closed its doors for the last time.

James Malton

For the Irish print collector, the twenty-five views of Dublin in etching and aquatint published by James Malton in 1792-99 probably represent the highlight of print history. Malton came to Ireland with his father, an artist and teacher of art, in 1785, and was employed for a number of years in the office of James Gandon, the architect. He seems to have left Gandon's employment under something of a cloud after three years — for, it is said, breaches of confidence. Some time around 1790 he began the series of drawings for the prints by which he is best known; unusually, he did both the drawings and the engravings himself. They were published in six issues of four views each at twenty-one shillings to those who subscribed in advance and twenty-six shillings to non-subscribing buyers. In the event, the second instalment contained five prints, bringing the total up to twenty-five. Sets were issued in both monochrome and colour, some actually printed in colours and some printed in black and white and later hand-coloured. In 1799, when all the issues had been released, Malton re-published the entire collection in a special bound volume. The collector should note that all original Malton prints were inscribed *James Malton del. et fecit*.

Single original Malton prints turn up fairly regularly for sale, and prices tend to be around £150 or so for examples in good condition. The most interesting singleton I saw lately was an aquatint of 'The West Front of St Patrick's Cathedral', which had been presented to the Chapter of St Patrick's. With an accompanying text, it also included a 'Correct Survey of Dublin

1610' and a 'Correct Survey of Dublin Bay 1795'. The whole collection, with the aquatint in good condition, was good value at £150.

A couple of years ago a set of twenty-five aquatints, hand-coloured, sold at a Co. Kildare house sale for £4,600. They were framed with black and gold glass mounts and were in fine condition. Some time afterwards a similar (it may even have been the same) set was being offered in an antique shop for £8,600. The set I saw sold most recently was also at a Co. Kildare house clearance. The plates were in varying condition, and may even have been made up from the parts of more than one original set. Some were quite badly foxed — that is, marked with small brown stains. They were in black Hogarth frames, and in addition to the usual twenty-five views the set also contained a plan of Dublin Castle, the 'Arms of the City of Dublin', the 'Correct Survey of the Bay of Dublin 1795', and a large plan of Dublin. Despite its defects, the set was fairly enthusiastically bid up to £8,500.

It's important for the collector of original Maltons to know that the plates were originally issued in a 121/4 by 17 inch size, with the actual engraved area being 101/4 by 15 inches. It's also important to realise that Malton's views have frequently been copied and that there are a large number of modern photo reproductions around, including a most attractive set of six issued in calendar form by the National Gallery in 1980. This made an ideal set for framing by the less affluent Malton enthusiast. The trouble is, though, that you don't want such examples sold to you as plates from sets issued between 1792 and 1799 - so beware. Always examine prints out of their frames before you buy, especially if any significant sum of money is involved. Although it can be difficult, even for the experienced collector, to distinguish between original Maltons and later, nineteenth-century engraved copies, the completely smooth surface of the modern photo reproduction should give that particular game away. The nineteenth-century engraved copies, of which there are several versions, are themselves of some value by now, though not as high as originals. Single examples are usually inexpensive and in small sizes shouldn't cost more than £10 or so each. Some were issued in an 8 by 11 inch size in Whitelaw & Walsh's *History of Dublin* in 1818, and several were copied by William Allen in a 6 by 10 inch size. A lithographed copy of the 'Provost's House' was reproduced by W. M. Morrison in a 19 by 29 inch size, entitled 'Dublin 1775'. To avoid paying too much for copies you can protect yourself by being aware of the various sizes of the different issues as well as by examining, as often as you can, the real thing.

Original Maltons

Hunting and Sporting Prints

In Ireland, not surprisingly, hunting prints are perennially popular, and the constant demand in Britain as well means that twentieth-century photo reproductions abound. These can be most attractive buys, but be careful that you don't mistake them for genuine prints and pay too much. In case of doubt ask the auctioneer's advice, and get him to allow you to examine them out of the frame if at all possible. Prices for hunting prints vary a great deal, depending on general quality and condition, whether a full set is present, and whether the artist, engraver and printer had a high reputation. A name to look out for is Henry Alken, a fine painter and watercolourist of 'horsey' scenes, after whose work a variety of high-quality prints was made. Full sets

Henry Alken

Snaffles' 'Andsome is — Wot 'Andsome Does'. Signed.

can be expensive, but singles should be fairly reasonable. Top of the tree would be the set of eight aquatints published by Ackermann in 1835 of the Quorn Hunt. There is, you will discover, a desirability rating for the various hunts, and the Quorn is among the most sought after; a good set of these eight plates in fine condition could make £4,000 to £5,000. However, a pair of coloured prints of Newmarket races, published by James Sheldon after Alken, has made just £200. A set of four prints by Ackermann of Alken's Ipswich, Epsom, Newmarket and Ascot Heath was sold recently for £1,150 and a set of six hand-coloured aquatints by C. Bentley after Alken, of 'Steeplechase Recollections', has fetched £650 in Dublin.

A more modest buy than some of the more expensive Alkens would be the Fores set of twelve coloured lithographs after H. K. Brown (Phiz) of 'Fox Hunting Incidents'. This recently made £520 at a house sale in Co. Dublin, and should really have been worth up to a couple of hundred more. Another fine engraver of sport and hunting scenes was, appropriately enough, Charles Hunt, who worked during the first half of the nineteenth century after a number of important artists, including Herring, Stubbs, and Pollard. His four plates after F. C. Turner, 'A Southerly Wind and Cloudy

Sky', published by Ackermann in 1835, fetched £1,300 at a Co. Meath house clearance in 1988, while in Co. Kildare in the same year a pair of prints by Hunt from the series of 'National Steeplechases' made £260. At the same sale a copy of Hunt's 'Doncaster Great St Leger 1839' after Herring fetched £260 also.

It shouldn't be forgotten that if you find that you just can't afford the best examples in 'hanging' form you can very often satisfy your interest with the purchase of fine illustrated sporting books. The first general edition by one of the finest of all equestrian artists, A. J. Munnings, *Pictures of Horses and English Life* (1927), costs around £200 at auction and contains a number of fine coloured plates. A copy of Snaffles' *More Bandobast* (1936) is equally well illustrated and would be obtainable for £120 to £140, while Nimrod's *Sporting* from 1838 and embellished by twenty-three engraved plates should cost under £200. Slightly more opulent is G. D. Armour's *Humour in the Hunting Field*, a limited edition of 100, containing twenty coloured prints, each signed by the artist; a copy of this made £600 at an auction in 1989. Lional Edwards is another highly sought-after sporting artist; a selection of eighteen coloured prints mounted in an oblong folio, entitled *The Passing Seasons*, recently sold for £320.

Lithography

Lithography is a technique whereby the artist makes his drawing on a special stone with a greasy crayon. The stone is then dampened and it absorbs the water except where grease is present. When a roller filled with ink is passed over this it will be found that the ink only adheres to the parts drawn on, and an almost exact replica of the drawing can be made. This process was developed by Alois Senefelder during the 1790s, and by the early decades of the nineteenth century it was found to be an extremely inexpensive way of producing large print runs. Many early lithographs were coloured by hand, but later a technique by which different stones were used for different colours was developed. Such prints are known as chromolithographs and were much used for fine book illustration from the 1860s. A firm that produced particularly fine chromolithographs was Day & Son, which employed artists as noted as Myles Birkett Foster and R. C. Carrick.

Although some of the best lithographic work is expensive, many good and attractive coloured lithographs and chromolithographs can be bought for just a few pounds. A good many topographical lithographs were produced, and as such items tend always to sell less well outside their native area, if you do not object to views of English and Continental cities and landscapes you can pick up very decorative items at little cost. At recent Dublin sales a rather interesting selection of prints of the city of Coventry was sold for just £10, a folder of forty large engraved and lithographic views of Warwickshire was £20, a collection of French lithographic views was £50, and a fine lithographic street scene of Madrid, framed, was bought for £14. Even Irish views can sometimes be obtained for modest sums: a set of five lithographic views of Ireland after Andrew Nicholl was sold in Dublin lately for £70. Good-quality marine scenes are expensive in any medium, and even in lithograph may be dear. For example, at a recent sale a pair of

Topographical

American

coloured lithographs of boats, after Josiah Taylor, was £400, while a lithograph of the *America* was £220.

The mention of America brings us to the subject of nineteenth-century American lithographs, which can be a source of rich exploration for the collector, and a surprising number can be found in Ireland. The print firm of Currier & Ives in New York published a huge range of lithographs from 1857 to 1906. According to one expert, nearly seven thousand subjects have been identified. This must act as a warning to novice collectors not to pay too highly for such prints, especially if they are dirty or damaged. At a Co. Kildare sale not long ago £200 was paid for a Currier & Ives lithograph of the Lakes of Killarney — rather a high price for an example in very poor condition, with the surface scraped in parts, this being one of the very worst faults in a print. The prices of Currier & Ives prints vary a good deal, depending on subject, rarity, and condition, and careful research is advised to make sure that top prices are paid only for the rarer items.

Buying Prints

You will probably find it quite difficult to purchase fine antique prints through retail outlets, although it should be said that the recent opening of one or two shops by specialist print dealers is beginning to improve matters a little. In general, though, you will probably find yourself doing most of your buying through auction. Here, you will find that the level of expertise in the print field will vary quite amazingly, and in most cases you must be your own guide. To avoid expensive mistakes, you must be prepared to do as much background reading as possible (some of the most useful works on the subject are listed at the end of this book). The primary mistake you will be trying to avoid is paying too much money for a photo reproduction or an inferior engraved copy of a print that, in the original, is highly priced. The bright side is that, because the collection of black-and-white engravings, especially, is not fashionable, there are quite a few bargains to be spotted by the knowledgeable. The best sources of such 'sleepers' are, I think, general saleroom auctions. House clearances are not bad, but beware of buying coloured prints there, for the decorative possibilities of some examples may send bidding by less knowledgeable buyers to more than they are worth. I've noticed that this seems to happen particularly frequently with Snaffles' prints, which often, even where they are recent reproductions, seem to be sold well beyond what one would have thought to be their value.

One of the most satisfactory sources of supply will probably be found to be the specialist book auction. Here the level of expertise offered to the buyer will be rather better than elsewhere, yet prices, for the present at least, are still not too high for many items. At these sales you will generally be confronted with loose prints and sets in folios rather than framed examples. This makes the examination of the prints much easier, and also gives the new collector the chance to actually handle the different kinds of prints and so gradually develop the ability to distinguish between the various print techniques. One of the first things you will discover in fact is that despite your reading having led you to consider different print methods one by one, in practice printmakers very often make use of two or more techniques within a single print!

Unsigned examples of pre-Raphaelite work like this can often be got for just a few hundred pounds.

Damaged Prints

The question arises whether you should buy damaged prints. In general the answer must be no, especially if large sums are being paid and if the print is in a mainstream area of collecting, that is tending to rise in value. As with all antiques, damaged or dirty prints will not appreciate unless they happen to be very rare indeed. Avoid prints that have their white margins trimmed or that are significantly dirty, foxed, or stained with damp, especially on the printed area. Examine the print for tears. Take your time with this: tears on prints are not always immediately obvious, particularly if the print has been framed or mounted in a way designed to conceal the damage. Avoid badly creased prints, too. And finally, do not pay high prices for prints where you see that some of the printed surface has actually been scraped away, leaving behind a nasty whitish patch. Even on a cheap print, I would regard this as an unacceptable flaw and would not buy.

Apart from the last stricture, it may be that these high standards can be relaxed somewhat if the print is very cheap and you only want it for decorative purposes. An interesting mezzotint, for example, may have some of its margin trimmed to fit it onto its mount. There may be a slight crease here or there, a little tear, or some foxing on the margin. If I liked the print and it had some historical interest or was by an engraver I admired, I would not let this stop me buying. But I would not pay more, than, say, £40 or so for such a print. I would not buy if the plate was scraped or if the margin was cropped back to the extent that the name of the print and of the artist and printmaker could not be seen. And, in general, when it comes to the market for black-and-white prints, prices are still sufficiently low for the collector to avoid buying the dirty, the torn, and the stained. It hardly needs saying that any repair or restoration of valuable prints should be left to the expert. With less valuable prints, just leave well alone; don't for heaven's sake go messing about with adhesive tape, glue, and the like. You can only do harm, and if your print ever came into fashion again you would probably have devalued it beyond recall.

Framing

If you are having prints framed, especially expensive ones, go to a reputable firm and request that good-quality acid-free paper be used for the mounts. Acid is a great destroyer of old paper, and if you decide to keep prints in loose folios, it's a good idea to slip a sheet of acid-free tissue between each item. A good picture restorer or art shop should be able to tell you what to buy. Even if you are framing an inexpensive print yourself, do take the trouble to buy some acid-free paper for the work. Cardboard mounts for unframed prints are not the best policy, as cardboard has a tendency to bend and curl, straining the print. Finally, when you frame, do not stick prints to their backing with glue, as this devalues a good print: make sure that mounts fit the print and frame without the need for sticking.

Chapter Ten

CLOCKS

he international market for antique clocks became extremely buoyant two or three years ago, with exceptional prices being reached. Since then, prices for both clocks and watches have slipped a little and at some recent sales, due very largely to over-optimistic estimates, top quality clocks have failed to reach their reserves. In Ireland, the clock market tends to be a fairly quiet affair, for there are few examples of the great English and French clockmakers about. Most of the concern is with late eighteenth and nineteenth century clocks, with carriage clocks and procelain bodied continental clocks being very popular with Irish buyers.

If you intend to spend significant sums of money on an antique clock or clocks, it's essesntial that you do a bit of background reading. The accurate judgement of the quality and originality of a clock's movement is not an easy matter and the serious buyer needs some knowledge of the history of clockmaking and understanding of how the movement of a clock works and how it has been put together. The best book for the beginner in the field is *Britten's Old Clocks and Watches* in its ninth edition edited by Cecil Clutton and others. This was expensive at its time of publication in 1982 but there are some remaindered copies about at a much reduced rate. Lucidly written, it does much to make the complicated comprehensible.

Clocks are driven by weight or by spring; this is what supplies the moving power. However, if the power was not controlled, the hands would fly around the dial at top speed, making time keeping impossible. This control is created firstly by what is called the escapement. The types most frequently met with by the antique collector are the verge and the anchor escapements. The verge is an earlier kind and is a mechanism by which a toothed wheel engages tooth by tooth with two small pallets. This allows the spring or weight to unwind little by little. An anchor escapement is one where the teeth engage with a crescent shaped piece of metal which has a small wedge shaped section at each end. The anchor escapement is considered to be more accurate but, although it was invented in the late seventeenth century, many later table and bracket clocks still featured the verge escapement because the anchor really needed a level surface if it was to work effectively and these clocks were, of course, designed to be portable.

The second element of the clock's control is provided by the pendulum. Before this was invented around 1650, clocks were really quite inaccurate. The pendulum receives impulses from the escapement and controls its accuracy by the regular pace of its swings. Adjustments can be made by

The Pendulum

ABOVE: *Left*; 19th century French gilt metal and alabaster clock retailed by Hackett of Cork. *Right;* Late 18th century French clock surmounted by a bronze figure of the goddess Minerva.
BELOW: *Left*; Late 19th century French marble clock. *Right*; 19th century ebonised and brass inlaid carriage style clock.

drawing it up or down and it can also help to counteract the effect on a clock's mechanism of changes in temperature. The anchor escapement demanded a longer pendulum and it was due to this that longcase clocks became so very fashionable from the late seventeenth century.

Other clock related terms may puzzle the beginner. One you will frequently come across is spandrel: this refers to the triangular corners which are present when a clock face is square but the actual dial section is round. The spandrels are usually decorated with engraving or metal mounts. The hood is the area of casing immediately around the clock face; on the best and earliest longcases this was pulled up in order to wind or examine the clock. Later this was replaced by the more practical front opening door. The chapter ring is the part of the dial which contains the hour numbers and minute divisions and, before the middle of the eighteenth century, it came as a separate piece. It was often silvered or, indeed, actually made from silver. The 'bolt and shutter' was a device which kept a clock going automatically while it was being wound. A repeater is a clock which strikes the hour or portion of the hour by means of the pulling of a cord. A rack striking clock is one in which a form of rack determines the correct number of strikes each hour; it relies on the position of the hour hand. A 'grand sonnerie' clock is one in which the hour and the quarter are struck at each quarter. Such clocks are greatly sought after by collectors. There also exists half-quarter repeaters which indicate by an additional stroke when seven and a half minutes have passed.

Catalogues may also make reference to the arbor and the backplate of a clock. The arbor is simply an axle on which the various wheels and pinions of the clock are mounted. The backplate covers the movement at the rear of the clock and was often very finely engraved.

It may come as a surprise to some novice collectors to learn that clockmakers did not actually make the cases for their clocks, even though it is often the appearance of the case which makes a clock attractive to buyers nowadays. Casemaking was a completely separate trade and, indeed, we don't know nearly as much about these craftsmen as we would like. Even the name of the casemaker working for Thomas Tompion, perhaps the greatest of seventeenth century clock and watchmakers, is unknown. However, we can imagine that the clockmaker would have worked very closely with his casemaker to ensure that the case would perfectly complement the style of the clock face and the arrangement of its movement. It may be that the larger clockmakers actually had a workshop for casemakers on the premises. Cases were also regularly commissioned from cabinet makers and Chippendale, for example, offered a number of designs for both longcase and bracket or table clocks.

The arrival of the pendulum was quickly followed by the spring and fusee driven clock. This eliminated the cumbersome weights in favour of a mechanism whereby the clock was driven by a spring which, after winding, was released at a tightly controlled pace by a grooved, cone-shaped pulley known as a fusee. The disappearance of weights made it possible to enclose the entire movement of the clock into a neat wooden or metal case and so the bracket clock was born. And so was the minute hand! On the earlier open metal work clocks, known as lantern clocks, there was only an hour hand and, even when lantern style clocks were made by late seventeenth and

Terminology

Clock Cases

eighteenth century makers, this practice was continued. It can help the collector recognise genuine examples for, as late as the early twentieth century, copies were made, but these generally had two hands. Lantern clocks dating from the period before 1750 are not often seen on the Irish market and it's probably true to say that they are not all that well liked by collectors. Many, of course, will have undergone alterations to their movements over the years, and despite their relative rarity, they seldom make more than around £1,000, even at top London sales.

Bracket Clocks

Bracket clocks are a very different matter and some of the most beautiful and sought after clocks are of this type. The latter half of the seventeenth century and the first half of the eighteenth were really a golden age of clockmaking in England, especially in London, and all the major makers produced bracket clocks, many to the special order of wealthy clients. The finest makers are generally agreed to be Thomas Tompion, who actually made rather less than 700 clocks, Joseph Knibb, whose clocks are my own favourite, and Daniel Quare. Of the three, Quare's clocks are probably most numerous today, for he had a large export trade, but not all are of the highest quality. It would appear that, as his business expanded, he often contracted the making of movements out to other makers and, although his name appears on these productions, they were not always up to the standard of those made in his own workshop. Another important maker was Christopher Gould. His clocks make relatively high prices today, but are not perhaps quite so fine as the best work of the other three.

Such clocks are unlikely to come within the purview of the ordinary collector. Indeed, I've never personally seen a clock by one of these makers come up at auction in Ireland, though they appear reasonably frequently at the top London salerooms. In March 1992, an ebony cased clock by Tompion, dated 1700, was sold by Phillips' for £70,000 and, in the same month, one by Christopher Gould made £21,000. Although not all fine early bracket clocks fetch this kind of price, it would still be hard to buy any good examples for much less than £5,000.

As the eighteenth century progressed, the great accuracy of the bracket clock led to a huge demand for less expensive examples to suit the middle class home. Many of these clocks were made by provincial makers, who used simpler cases and less opulent decoration than the smart London makers and these are the clocks that can be afforded by the average collector today. From about 1730 till well into the second half of the eighteenth century, the broken arch dial was hugely popular. This featured a half circle segment above the chapter ring, which was usually filled in with fine engraved or wrought metalwork, sometimes fitted with a 'strike-silent' mechanism which could be set in such a way that the clock would not chime. Although originally devised by Tompion and his contemporaries, the inverted bell shaped top with carrying handle also continued into the late 1700s. Bracket clocks were made right through the nineteenth century, with some slender beautifully cased ones being produced by makers such as Vulliamy in the early 1800s. Many were also made in a gothic style, often in oak, and oak continued to be used for many everyday clocks, right up to the end of the century.

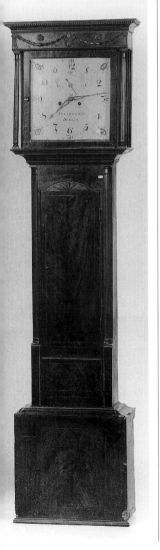

Unusual early Victorian rosewood longcase with painted dial by Ralph Walsh of Dublin. It is inset with a barometer and thermometer.

A fairly ordinary Georgian bracket clock would probably set the collector back by about £1,000, with plenty of choice amongst good provincial and Irish makers between £1,500 and £3,000. A fine Regency bracket clock with repeater, in a domed fruitwood and brass case by Whitehurst of Derby sold recently in London for £3,100. In Ireland, an early eighteenth century bracket clock with broken arch, inverted bell top, brass finials and carrying handles at the sides, sold for £3,400. It was made by John Berry of London. A Regency period table clock in a rosewood case surmounted by a marble bust has sold in Dublin for £1,000. At a house clearance in Co. Meath, a really fine nineteenth century walnut cased repeater, with silvered chapter ring, very rich gilt metal mounts and a broken arch with strike silent dials, was sold about a year ago for £2,300. At another sale, in Co. Kildare, a good Gothic oak bracket clock sold for just £350 and seemed something of a steal and a very plain inlaid bracket clock of the late nineteenth century sold for £300.

Longcase Clocks

'My grandfather's clock was too tall for the shelf / So it stood twenty years in the hall' runs the song written by an American, Henry Clay Work, during the 1870s. That song sold almost a million copies, which probably accounts for the way in which the term grandfather' to describe a longcase clock became so universal in modern times. But, since this term only dates from two hundred years after the longcase clock was invented, I think it's really preferable to keep to the older descriptions.

The first longcase clocks seem to have been made in London around 1660. At first,they retained the verge escapement and short pendulum and were not very tall by later standards — about six feet high. By around 1675, however, the anchor escapement and long pendulum was becoming the norm and the height of the clocks had increased to seven feet. The clock faces were usually flanked by spiral twist columns, later by simple pillars, and the spandrels were decorated with gilded putti (cherubs) or other wrought or engraved work. Cases were at first of plain timbers, such as ebony or walnut, but by the 1690s, there was often a very elaborate marquetry inlay.

Most of the great makers of bracket clocks also produced longcase clocks. Again, Tompion was one of the leaders and in July 1989, Christie's sold one of his earliest longcases for a record £800,000. King William III had a keen interest in all the latest clocks and watches and ordered a good many of them from Tompion and other makers; he very frequently presented foreign dignitaries with gifts of timepieces. In around 1695, the King ordered a Tompion longcase to be made for his bedroom; sad to relate, its ticking was so loud that the King, unable to sleep was forced to have it moved elsewhere. It was a beautiful clock, which only needed winding every three months and had a year long calendar.

Not every early longcase is as expensive as the best Tompions, of course, and, in London, the products of most makers sell at auction for £5,000 upwards for plain cased examples and £10,000 upwards for the marquetry inlaid ones. During the eighteenth century, and for very much of the nineteenth, provincial and Irish makers turned out many such clocks in plain oak and from the early 1800s, mahogany cases. Prices for the best of these

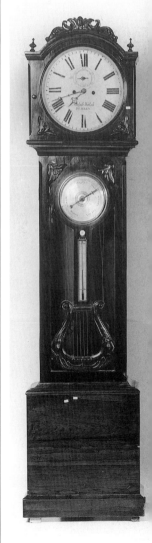

Late Georgian Adams style mahogany longcase signed Delahoyd Dublin.

would not be very much less than those for the minor London makers but there are many very attractive ones which can be got for prices starting at around £800 for later, plain oak examples and about £2,000 upwards for earlier and better ones. Occasionally, clocks were made in lacquered cases with gold chinoiseries (Chinese style pictures and motifs) and these sell in both Ireland and Britain from about £2,500. The collector should also be aware that quite a number of reproduction longcase clocks have been made, a good many having been produced in Britain throughout the 1970s and '80s. It's sensible, if you mean to spend a substantial sum on a clock, that you check it very carefully, both as to case and to movement. It's obviously a bit of a problem to climb up and look properly at the movement of a longcase clock during an auction view. If you can't manage it, inquire if the auctioneer might let you view the clock at a quieter time and discuss it with you. If you are paying top price you will need to be sure that the dial, the case and the movement are all original and belong together. A worn escapement is generally an acceptable fault but check that the rest of the movement has not been the object of extensive or poor repair. Sometimes such repairs will have been carried out by a skilled craftsman and you may decide there is nothing wrong with this but make sure this is reflected in the buying price and remember that it may not hold its value so well as a perfectly untouched clock. If you feel that you are unable to make a full assessment of an antique clock — and for the beginner it is not easy — then you might be better to settle for buying from a reputable dealer. It may cost more but may save you in the long run. Make sure that, along with your receipt, you obtain a written description of the clock, its age and its condition.

Prices

At auction in Ireland, recent prices for longcase clocks include £850 for a very plain late Georgian one, rather heavy in style with a concession to the Adams brothers by way of swag decoration on the hood. It had a square, white painted dial and was signed by Delahoyd of Dublin. At the same sale, a country house clearance, a very unusual, early Victorian longcase in rosewood with a circular painted dial and made by Ralph Walsh of Dublin, sold for £1,900. The arched hood was topped with a delicately carved moulding and two finials and the two bottom spandrels were decorated. The case had a glass door and inside were a barometer and thermometer, while beneath it there was a carved lyre. It was a substantially more desireable clock than the Delahoyd one and well deserved the higher price. At another house sale, an Irish late Georgian longcase in oak with brass dial and its broken arch showing the phases of the moon, took £850. There was some cracking to the plinth. Elsewhere, a good provincial English longcase, a fairly heavy nineteenth century example in mahogany, its broken arch filled with a painted landscape, was sold for £1,000 and probably deserved to make more. I have also seen an Irish George III red lacquered longcase made by William McCabe of Lisburn, the spandrels decorated with scrolls and the dial surmounted with sunburst flanked by scrolls and dolphins. The case featured chinoiseries and the dial was of polished brass. The clock took £2,800 at auction.

In general, collectors prefer to see a polished metal rather than painted dial and are prepared to pay more for it; you'll tend to find that the metal dial appears in clocks which are of better all-round quality in any case. It has to be said that in Ireland, at the moment, longcase clocks can sometimes be a little difficult to sell at auction and occasionally you will notice them being withdrawn unsold. This has probably had the effect of keeping the price of middle range longcases a little depressed and it's my guess that, given the fine craftsmanship that went into many even of the fairly ordinarly examples, at present they are rather undervalued.

Carriage Clocks

In many respects, this is actually the most active section of the clocks market. A very great number were made, especially in France between 1850 and 1910 and although many of them are extremely expensive, there is really something available to suit every pocket. They always sell readily at auction and it may be that in recent times, some of the fairly routine examples have been a trifle overvalued. Not everyone would agree — and if it's true that demand as well as quality creates value, then it has to be admitted that these clocks have always been enormously popular, right from the time that they were made and imported into Ireland and Britain in their thousands.

The first carriage clocks as we know them today seem to have been produced by a French maker named Breguet. They were of extremely fine quality, really quite unlike many of the mass-produced variety so widely made during the following decades. The first maker to manufacture these clocks in large numbers was Paul Garnier, who made many beautifully cased clocks with fine engraving. Another fine maker, and whose pieces quite often come up for sale in Ireland, was the firm of Le Roy of Paris. Some of their carriage clocks are exquisite productions with engraved cases with side panels of coloured enamels and swirling or floral decoration. A clock like this would probably cost around £6,000. However, Le Roy also made a wide range of simpler clocks with plain brass or gilt and glass cases and these can be got at auction in Ireland for between £500 and £800. They tend to fetch a little extra if accompanied by their original travelling case. A simple but attractive carriage clock by Le Roy has sold in Ireland for £650; it had a carrying case but this wasn't judged to be original. Good quality carriage clocks continued to be made until the turn of century and at a recent Dublin sale this a particularly fine early twentieth century one in its original travelling case and key, with a white enamel dial and striking movement, made £500.

French Makers

Fairly ordinary late nineteenth and early twentieth century French carriage clocks now fetch between £300 and £550, even where the maker is unknown and the only signature is that of its English or Irish retailer. This may act as a warning to the beginner; do not, because you see an English or Irish name on the dial of a carriage clock, assume that this is the name of the maker. English carriage clocks were certainly made in some quantity but they are significantly rarer than French examples and generally command a higher price. Important makers include Dent, James Ferguson Cole and William Comyns. A good Dent carriage clock with fine engraving around the dial with a gong strike and a strike silent lever could cost as much as £4,000, with other good English makers fetching around £1,500 and upwards.

English Makers

Other Mantel Clocks

Amongst other mantel clocks, the most commonly seen, and the cheapest, is the black marble variety. Actually, these were generally not made from marble at all but from black Belgian slate which, when polished took on a marbelised appearance. Sometimes sections of real marble are embodied in the slate and occasionally panels of more interesting stones such as malachite or bluejohn. Sometimes there is quite nice brass or ivory inlaid decoration. The movements for these clocks seem to have been mainly continental imports which were then fitted to the English made cases and the names which you may see on the dials are usually those of retailers. Yet many of them are well made and are certainly worth buying at prices which start at around £50. Prices go up according to general quality, attractiveness of the shape and any additional decoration. I recently saw one sold at a house clearance for £250; this was a high price for clocks of this sort but it had very striking malachite panels and was hardly expensive for something which would have looked well on any mantlepiece. The best hunting ground for black clocks is the regular saleroom auction. You will usually find that several have been included and you will be able to buy a good example for between £50 and about £110. Just check before you buy that the movement hasn't been removed; I've seen quite a few for sale that, on inspection, turned out to be quite empty inside!

Continental Gilt

Another kind of mantel clock that regularly appears for auction in Ireland is the continental gilt or porcelain type. Although in rococo style, most of these clocks turn out to date from the second half of the nineteenth century. The majority were made in France with some originating in Germany or Austria. Prices for gilt metal examples range from £180 or so upwards, increasing with quality. The most expensive are those accompanied by matching urns or vases; these are known as garnitures. The best garniture sets can cost up to £4,000 or £5,000 but quite acceptable ones can often be bought for just a few hundred pounds. I recently saw two garniture sets sell for £420 and £320 — the second one was the nicer! For single clocks, a sum between £500 and £800 should bring something of good quality; I have seen a very fine late nineteenth century French gilt mantel clock with porcelain mounts and panels, decorated wtih cupids and flowers, sell for £525 and a not too inferior gilt and porcelain clock, with unusual blue rimmed dial, sell for £320 at a Dublin saleroom.

Oak

During the late nineteenth century, large numbers of oak mantel clocks were made. The cases range from a simple square style with little carving or decoration to quite elaborate Gothic style models. A really fine Gothic style clock could set you back by £800 or so but I have seen quite a number sold at between £200 and £400, including a very good one at a Co. Kildare sale for just £350. For the plainer ones, which are generally very late Victorian or Edwardian, prices start at around £100.

Porcelain

Porcelain clocks, some of which are French and often described as 'Sevres', and others which are German and are dubbed 'Dresden', tend to fall into the same price category as the gilded mantel clocks, with perhaps fewer really inexpensive ones than are available in the gilded style. Nevertheless, I saw quite an attractive small one sell for £90 in a saleroom lately. The French clocks tend to be less florid in style and are really more appealing. For a good quality garniture by Le Roy of Paris, probably with ormolu mounts and with matching candelabra and made in the late nineteenth century, the price would be around £3,000. Sets by less desireable makers can be bought from about £600 - £1,000. The 'Dresden' clock cases are frequently very opulent with masses of encrusted flowers but they are quite popular with buyers and the very best can reach several thousand pounds. However, more modest ones, standing at, perhaps, nine inches or so high, can usually be got for between £500 and £700.

American Shelf and Wall Clocks

It may come as a surprise for the new collector to discover that a good many of the wooden nineteenth century clocks which he sees for sale are American. The shelf clock, which is significantly taller than the British bracket clock, often standing at almost two and a half feet high, began to be made in the years following the American War of Independence in the 1770s. During the Napoleonic Wars in Europe and the maritime war which broke out between Britain and America itself at the same period, there was great difficulty in obtaining metal clock parts and, amazingly, the movements for these clocks were actually wooden. The cases were very attractive and owed much to the Adam style, with slim graceful feet and curved swan neck pediments. In contrast with Europe, it seems that many of the clocks were turned out by makers who manufactured both case and movement themselves. Although a large number of these Connecticut clocks, as they are often known on the antiques market, were made, it was not true mass-production and not many of them come up for sale in Ireland. I did see, a few years ago, an early nineteenth century one with cast brass eight day movement sold for about £250. This was a low price, fetched before the antiques market 'took off' in the late 1980s, and it was particularly so because this clock had the cast brass movement which, at its time, was reserved for the better and more expensive clocks. I would expect it to make considerably more now.

Connecticut
Clocks

Around 1830, a maker named Chauncey Jerome developed a thirty hour clock with a cheaper type of brass movement and mass-production moved into a vastly higher gear. It is from the following decades that most of the American clocks you will see on the market date and indeed, so many were imported into Europe that, for a while European clockmakers were almost overwhelmed by the competition. A very popular style was the pointed Gothic case, with high gabled hood, which had appeared during the early nineteenth century, and later many were square in shape. Most featured a decorated area, perhaps a painted scene, beneath the clock face itself. Production also branched out into wall clocks, many in not dissimilar style to the shelf clocks and some with a round or octagonal front. Timbers used during the latter half of the nineteenth century included rosewood, walnut veneer and oak.

Prices for these late nineteenth century American clocks tend to range from £200 to £400. At a recent sale, I saw a matched pair of walnut 30 hour clocks with painted scenes fetch just £350. This was really quite a low price for two clocks which appeared of good quality and it's probably true to say that in Ireland the market for these pieces is a little underdeveloped and some bargains can be found.

Collectable copper and brass: a set of 7 copper graduating measures and, to the foreground, a rare set of heavy brass barrel-shaped measures.

Two high quality brass fenders.

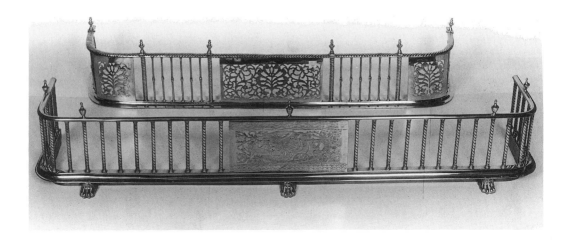

Chapter Eleven

GENERAL COLLECTABLES

Under this heading comes almost everything you can think of! It often seems as though magpie mania is back with a vengeance and that the 1990s person is as dedicated a hoarder as ever the Victorians were. Items that just a few years ago would have been consigned to the dustbin are now being sent to the auction room, and finding eager buyers. Tin seaside buckets with Mickey Mouse on them and dating from the 1950s have been offered for sale for around £25. Now how many of those have the mothers of teenage youngsters tossed on the rubbish heap, lost to posterity? And what about the teddy bear that sold at Sotheby's for £30,000 because a wealthy American, buying a gift for his wife's birthday, had told his agent to buy at any price? Is it the case, as an irritated dealer recently wrote in a trade journal, that we shall soon be hunting down fifty-year-old toilet brushes, calling them toiletiana and selling them for a fortune?

It's unlikely. It's also probable that some of the ephemera and rather useless and unlovely objects that are now fashionable collectors' items will eventually fall out of favour — in all likelihood, of course, to be replaced by other strange objects. It's sensible, therefore, to see the collection of 'fun' items as just that — fun — rather than as something to tie up your life savings in. The only justification for buying an old hat-box or fishing-rod or Victorian egg rack is really that you like it and want it for yourself rather than because you expect it to appreciate in the long term.

In this chapter I shall be concentrating on some collectables that have an established collecting history, are attractive in themselves, throw some interesting light on our social history, and seem likely to be collected into the foreseeable future.

Brass

Brass has long been collected, and of late, with the fashion for old and reproduction fireplaces, brass fenders and fire irons have made a strong comeback. Prices for these objects I have found to be extraordinarily unpredictable, especially for the more modest items that are not keenly sought by the trade but that make very useful additions to the home. A problem is also created by the fact that brass objects are difficult for the non-expert to date, and styles popular during the Georgian era continued to be made during the nineteenth century and even into our own time. In this regard, particular care needs to be taken in the purchase of andirons or fire dogs, formerly used to hold logs in place on the hearth. In England during the eighteenth century coal replaced wood as the primary fuel and andirons

Brass

Late Victorian
brass fire tongs.

went out of fashion. They returned during the first half of the twentieth century, and the styles of the 1700s were regularly reused. In Ireland, logs continued to be somewhat more widely used and some andirons may have been made locally but the chances are that many pairs purporting to be late eighteenth or nineteenth-century were actually made during the last seventy years.

Not until the late nineteenth century was it customary for brassmakers, or braziers, as they used to be called, to stamp their wares with a trade mark. The use of registration numbers indicates a date after 1884, and the words 'trade mark' and 'limited' do not occur before 1862. Words like 'British made' or 'Made in England' mean the item was made during the twentieth century. Before about 1850 much brass ware was finished by hand, and pieces that look smooth and well finished on the base and in other places normally invisible can suggest an early date.

Prices for antique brass fenders depend less on age than on style, weight, and quality, and a well-designed Victorian one will make more than an undistinguished Georgian piece. When buying, you will have to judge the piece on its own merits, deciding what it is worth to you. Some guidelines may help. For a good-quality Georgian fender with D-shaped body and with elaborate pierced design you could pay up to £1,000. If well-wrought pillars, urns or statuettes go with it or are incorporated into the fender, the price may rise. If, with high-quality general design, a Georgian fender is also serpentine in shape, it will probably reach about £2,500, and more if its pierced pattern is particularly fine or incorporates figures. On the other hand, if your Georgian fender is meanly proportioned and its pierced work is fairly basic and repetitive, the price will probably descend to under £200.

It should be noted that very few genuine Georgian fenders have feet; this did not become fashionable till the nineteenth century and can be a useful though not infallible way of dating a fender. You will find that at auctions an extraordinarily large number of brass fenders are described as 'Georgian', to the extent, indeed, that you begin to wonder if anyone ever made them after that. They did, but styles did not change all that dramatically, and many of the fenders offered for sale are Victorian and later. Victorian fenders tend to be rather taller and shorter than Georgian ones and have less in the line of fine pierced work. It is this reduction in scale that dictates the prices rather than the age: a really fine Victorian or Edwardian fender will rival even the good Georgian one in price. Victorian and later fenders of cast iron with brass knobs, or of cast iron with brass wire-work, are relatively cheap and can be found for less than £100.

Victorian grates of the kind that come with brass fittings and are raised on short curved legs are much in demand now, and at auction range in price from £250 to £500. Fire irons tend to come in threes — tongs, shovel, and poker — and for the nice long ones you can expect to pay from £200 upwards. Brass trivets start at around £50 and go up, according to age and quality. The price of coal boxes, especially the carved oak, slanted-front ones with brass fittings, has risen extraordinarily over the last couple of years. They are now regularly fetching £300 to £400 at auction.

Pewter

Pewter is not as eagerly collected as brass, although it does have its followers, and, indeed, not a lot of quality pewter comes up at auction. During Elizabethan times it was the practice to send old, broken or outmoded pewter pieces to England to be melted down for the manufacture of new wares, and no doubt the continuance of this practice is the reason why most of the pewter that is offered for sale here consists of Victorian or early twentieth century dresser pieces. There were some, but not many, pewterers working in Dublin and Cork before the eighteenth century. During the early eighteenth century their numbers expanded somewhat, but during the nineteenth century the craft all but disappeared.

Examples of eighteenth century Irish pewter are very rare indeed, and although some flagons and spirit measures do exist, the ordinary buyer is unlikely to come across them. Good-quality pewter dishes and plates are most desirable, and a set of six plates dating from, say, around 1800 would fetch around £300 on the British market. The Irish market is really so undeveloped that it is difficult to give price guidelines; for example, some time ago I saw a set of six good pewter plates sold for just £24, an unusual two-handled pewter cup for £35, an early pewter salver for £85, and a set of three pewter dishes for £40. This is good news for those interested in buying unusual pieces of pewter, but if you happen to already own some pewter that you suspect is rare or early, you would do well to seek specialist advice before selling. Early twentieth-century dresser pieces, which take the form of quite elegant little milk jugs and sugar bowls, should be around £30 apiece, and nineteenth-century pewter tankards start at around £15 and go up according to quality.

Maps

One area of collecting that is still, I think, rather underpriced is that of antique maps. Many fine and decorative maps can be bought for sums that may be considerably less than those paid for prints and watercolours, and they can often be just as decorative. Odd antique maps may occasionally be picked up at house clearances or other general auctions, and if there is no-one else there with any interest or expertise in old maps you might just get yourself a bargain. However, there are many reproduction maps about too, and if you are serious about collecting maps it is really best to buy at a specialist book auction. There is usually a selection of maps offered at these, and you would generally be able to avail of a higher level of knowledge on the part of the auctioneer than you would find at a general auction. In addition, there are a number of antiquarian bookshops that are able to advise on the purchase and sale of antique maps. You will probably pay more by buying at specialist sales or from dealers, but you are more likely to make a wise purchase from such a source.

Modern maps and facsimiles of older ones can generally be identified without difficulty by means of the publisher's name and date on the border surrounding the map. However, establishing the precise date of an old map can present some problems, not only because the printer may have omitted the date of issue but also because impressions of an original printed map were

Pewter

19th century brass toasting fork.

Maps

often made repeatedly without anyone bothering to change the date. A general period can usually be assigned by reference to the style and colouring of the map and by examination — if you are familiar with them — of the topography and place-names depicted. Some useful bibliographies and booklets have been issued to assist in this area, and I have listed some of these at the end of this book.

For the purposes of most modern collectors, interest in maps begins with the first appearance of printed maps during the sixteenth century. The earliest printed maps appear to have originated in Germany, where as early as 1513 a coloured map was issued. But it was in the Netherlands that the trickle of printed maps became a veritable flood, and by the middle of the century Dutch knowledge of cartography and printing techniques had spread to the main centres of Europe. The greatest of these early Dutch cartographers was 'Mercator', whose real name was Gerhard Kremer. Among his many other achievements, 'Mercator' was the first to accurately determine the length of the Mediterranean Sea. He published his cosmic atlas between 1585 and 1595. He was rivalled in skill by a fellow-countryman, Abraham Ortelius, who published an atlas of seventy maps in 1570.

The first useful manuscript map of Britain and Ireland was issued in 1563 during the reign of Elizabeth I. Drawn by Lawrence Nowell, it was both accurate by the standards of the time and most attractive as well. Ireland was mapped in considerable detail, and in addition the principal Irish families and their territories were included.

Although this manuscript map was found to be of considerable use, Queen Elizabeth's secretary, Lord Burleigh, was not quite satisfied with it and began to toy with the idea of commissioning a full printed map. Interestingly, it was events in Ireland that brought Burleigh finally to the decision to go ahead with this scheme. There had been proposals to colonise or plant the partly pacified province of Ulster, but lack of proper maps of the area was impeding these plans. A young and talented surveyor named Christopher Saxton was employed to carry out work that led to the publication of a new printed atlas in 1579. Ironically, Ireland was not fully mapped in Saxton's atlas, but by the early seventeenth century several printed maps of the Irish provinces had been published in the Netherlands, and in 1610 a series of important maps of Ireland were published by the English cartographer John Speed. His maps, specially engraved by Jodocus Hondius in Holland, were highly decorative, and despite their age they are still reasonable priced. During the seventeenth century a number of important maps of Ireland, including those of William Petty, were issued, and many of these too are quite modestly priced today.

When you are buying maps, the same kind of principles apply as when buying books and prints. Check that there are no pieces missing, no botched repairs, no tears, and no serious staining. If the map is framed, make sure the frame does not mask any damage; and if you have any doubts ask the auctioneer to give you some advice about condition. Copies of John Speed's Irish provincial maps of 1610 usually sell at auction for around £100. The earliest Irish map that I have seen offered for auction is one by Ortelius, 'Hiberniae Britannicae Insulae Nova Descriptio - Irlandt'. It sells for about £160. For Mercator's map of the north of Ireland, 'Ultoniae Orientalis Pars', you could expect to pay around £150, and for a William Petty provincial map from 1650 a little over it.

After 1700 the price drops significantly, but many eighteenth-century maps are attractive and, I think, well worth collecting. Alexander Hogg's 'New and Correct Map of the Province of Connaught', dating from 1790, has been bought at auction for just £35, and copies of Isaak Tirion's Dutch map of Ireland from 1760 would cost about £50. Generally, you will be lucky enough to obtain these maps already framed. With the earlier or more valuable maps the presence or otherwise of a frame will not greatly affect the price; it has more significance in the case of the cheaper, less important maps.

Local manuscript maps dating from the nineteenth century often appear at auction, but as they are not very decorative they are more usefully left to the academic collector or, indeed, the National Library, which frequently buys such things.

Cards

A hobby that has been very quietly growing in popularity is that of card collecting. This actually has a very old history. The Victorians loved to keep letters, love tokens, pressed flowers, colourful scraps and journal cuttings, small prints and watercolours that had been sent to them by relatives and friends. The arrival of commercially produced Christmas and other greeting cards during the 1840s gave a new impetus to this collecting, as these and the other paper collectables were mounted in albums specially made for the purpose. These albums were often richly decorated with velvet or gilt clasps, or, perhaps, bound in fine morocco with a small watercolour or other attractive motif set into the front cover. As the century went on, photographs too received the red carpet treatment, in albums with special cut-out sections for each picture, and fine bindings that were often inset with brass mountings and even glass or semi-precious stones.

After years of being somewhat overlooked by modern collectors, these albums have now begun to be bought, and prices are showing a steady rise. Naturally, the best prices are reached by albums in reasonable condition, containing cards or scraps of a high standard. Good ones have moved from a price of about £40 each just a few years ago to prices of up to £200 now — not a bad return for those who had the foresight and interest to buy early. However, if old cards appeal to you and you don't have much money, there is no need to despair. A good idea is to buy an empty album, which shouldn't cost more than a few pounds, and then gradually build up a collection by acquiring cards singly or in small bundles.

Most of the best albums and cards turn up at book sales. Naturally, this is where knowledgeable collectors turn up to buy, and, as with maps, you will generally find a good selection on offer but with prices relatively high. However, occasional albums do turn up at house clearances or general sales, and here you might have the chance of picking up items for less money. In particular, if it is empty albums that you are after or small bundles of unsorted cards, you are more likely to come across these at general sales. The specialist book sales have higher standards of entry and are not anxious to accept albums in mediocre condition or mixed-up bunches of cards. But such items can be good fun for the beginner and can form the basis of a good collection as

Cards

expertise and funds increase. This is not to recommend that you buy junk, however. As with every other sort of antique, the policy of buying the best you can afford still holds good. Don't buy tattered and filthy albums, and don't pay over the odds for bunches of cards that contain more than their fair share of items that are torn or bent at the corners, or, as often happens with greeting cards that have been cut around the edges to fit into an album. Such cards are best set aside and not displayed with your best items.

When you are building up a collection of cards, it's best to try to impose some kind of coherence on it. That doesn't mean that you have to confine yourself to one kind of scrap or greeting card; but it makes sense to display or mount different kinds of cards separately or, in a small collection, in different parts of the same album. You could decide to gather them chronologically, or by artist, or by theme. One theme much beloved by Victorian ladies was that of flowers. There was what they called the language of flowers. Every different flower embodied a special message, and cards were often chosen on the basis of the flowers depicted in order to send a secret meaning to the receiver. The rose was, of course, the symbol of love; the bluebell represented constancy, the wallflower fidelity. The red poppy was for consolation, and the pansy meant 'Press me to you.' Ivy meant marriage and the sunflower haughtiness, and the narcissus, not surprisingly, stood for egotism.

It's worth being aware of the names of some of the more prominent artists involved in the design of old greeting cards, as many are signed or initialled. A number of these artists were women, and one favourite was a woman called Harriett Bennett. Alice Havers was well known for her beautifully painted religious cards. Y. F. Yeames designed a range of cards featuring beautiful women for the publishers Raphael Tuck & Sons in 1881. You will find the name of this publisher on the back of many Victorian cards. Cards by Kate Greenaway are hotly sought after, and later in the century

BELOW LEFT:
Edwardian Christmas cards.
BELOW RIGHT:
Postcards from the 1914-18 period with war themes.

Louis Wain, whose most popular work was his paintings of cats, is worth looking out for. Dating of cards is generally fairly simple, as the Victorians liked to date their good wishes in their message. Names of artists and publishers act as a further guidance, as can the costumes worn by the figures depicted on the cards.

Postcards

The work of Louis Wain coincided with the arrival of postcards. These were first issued around 1870 and at first seem to have been confined to Christmas and other greeting cards. General postcards followed hot on their heels, and by the last years of the century postcard sending had become a widespread craze. During the First World War the sending of postcards seems to have reached its peak. Many cards of this period feature aspects of the war, and cards were produced as a means of raising funds for war efforts, such as the nursing services. Many were humorous. Louis Wain's Kaiser cats were especially popular, and Bamforth & Sons issued a series featuring the Kaiser's Christmas, as well as humorous aspects of life in the trenches and on the home front. A fine and interesting postcard collection could be made up solely with cards from the 1914-18 period, and fortunately such cards are not too difficult to find. Like old greeting cards, they are often found in albums or collections, for they began to be collected from the time they were issued.

Cards from the 1920s and 1930s are well worth collecting, although they have not yet reached the prices of the finest Victorian ones. Many are beautifully designed in the art deco style, and there were some highly talented comic artists at work. Perhaps the most famous of these was George Studdy, the creator of Bonzo, a dog of rather pig-like appearance. Bonzo cards were published by Valentine & Sons of Dundee, although other firms did issue occasional sets of Bonzo designs. The most valuable of these are the ones in which Bonzo is promoting a named product. Another artist whose work is regularly seen was Mabel Lucie Atwell, whose humorous cards featuring rotund rosy-cheeked children were also issued by Valentine.

Conventional view cards are not greatly favoured by many collectors, although some will always find room for a particularly well-photographed one or for a special example such as those of ships, trains, or cars. The bonus for the beginner is that such cards are usually very cheap to buy, and even at a specialist book auction you could pick up a sizable bundle for £10 or so. Some of the Irish ones can be interesting in showing how familiar places have changed over the years. Cards that are actually photographs are the best buy.

Prices for individual postcards are rather difficult to establish, as they tend to be offered for sale as collections, usually at auction. In Britain prices range from 50p per card for basic examples to about £25 for rarer ones. For good humorous cards from the 1900-1930 period prices are normally between £2 and £4, with really rare ones going higher. Card and photograph dealers do turn up at book fairs in Ireland, so it is worth making enquiries about these. There are a number of specialist dealers in Britain and also a number of postcard clubs for those who wish to buy, sell and exchange cards. Serious collectors would be well advised to contact the British Ephemera Society, 12 Fitzroy Square, London W1P 5HQ for information.

Boxes and Caddies

For those who love old furniture but cannot afford it in the quality they would like or, indeed, haven't enough room in their homes for any more pieces, the collection of boxes and tea caddies can be an enjoyable substitute. With Georgian tea caddies, in particular, you can often admire in miniature the best characteristics of the furniture of the period, although, of course, caddies were made in silver, porcelain, enamel and other materials as well as in wood. There is a wide variety of miscellaneous boxes on the market at present, including dressing-cases and travel cases, writing-boxes, and lap desks, and very attractive boxes for nothing in particular, which are nevertheless useful for mopping up some of the chaos on your dressing-table. Many fine-quality boxes can be bought for under £100, and you can get attractive ones too for less than £50.

Tea Caddies

In general, tea caddies are the most expensive of the boxes that you will see at auction. When tea first arrived on the European market it was extremely expensive, so most early caddies had locks to keep predatory servants at bay. By the second half of the eighteenth century caddies were being made in great numbers with styles reflecting those of furniture design. It would appear that the majority of tea caddies that we see at auction today date from the period 1780 to approximately 1830. The best Georgian caddies will generally be found to comprise two compartments for tea and, between them, one or two circular recesses for glass bowls. It is widely thought that these bowls were used for the blending of tea, but documents from some of the makers of these boxes indicate that they were in fact designed to hold sugar.

Prices for such caddies range from about £150 to £500 depending on quality and the existence and condition of original fittings. More expensive, because believed to be most desirable by many collectors, are tea caddies that come in the shape of a fruit, usually an apple or a pear. These can command up to £1,000 at auction. During the Victorian period the number of high-quality caddies seems to have declined; presumably as tea grew cheaper it was not considered necessary to hold it in a valuable container. Victorian caddies tend to be fairly simple affairs, of mahogany or oak, and frequently consist of just one compartment to hold the tea. During the Edwardian period some tea caddies in the Sheraton revival style were made, and for these, prices would tend to be in the same range as the Georgian examples.

Writing Boxes

In the past, letter writing was as vital as the telephone is to us today, so it comes as no surprise to learn that the writing-box was an indispensable possession. Many of those seen at auction today date from the Regency and William IV period and are often made in rosewood. Although designed for travel, some of these boxes are a little on the long side, and demand for them is not always particularly strong unless they have a good many of their original fittings. These are often of glass and silver mountings. Without such fittings these boxes can often be bought for little more than £100; with them, they can go up as high as £400. Such boxes were often fitted as dressing-cases rather than as writing-boxes, and for these similar prices are paid.

During the Victorian period, writing-boxes became rather more attractive. One popular style was that with a leather-topped slanted lid that lifted up to disclose a compartment for the storage of writing implements.

These are often referred to as a lap desk. Popular with collectors, they can fetch prices in the £200-£400 range. With other boxes, the front side pulled forward to form a straight writing surface. These can often be very small, and prices start at around £75, rising to several hundred, depending on size and quality.

The tantalus or decanter box became a fashionable sideboard piece during the nineteenth century. Many people think these were so called because they locked, thus preventing thirsty servants from taking a quick nip. In fact many of these decanter boxes have no locking mechanism at all. Others have a locking drawer at the base of the box, which was used to store cigars. The decanters — there are usually three — are generally made of cut glass, with glass or silver-plated stoppers. There are a very few Georgian decanter boxes about, but at that period the wine cellaret, which stood on the floor, was where alcoholic beverages were usually stored. The smaller boxes that stood on the sideboard generally date from the second half of the nineteenth century and from the early years of this one. They are very commonly in oak but may also be found in boulle marquetry and occasionally, during the Edwardian period, in the Sheraton revival style. These last fetch the highest prices, and a very fine example was sold during 1989 for just under £1,000. The oak variety make around £300, and good examples in boulle a little bit more.

Tantalus

At almost every auction you will see one or two Victorian boxes without fittings and of no particular rarity but that are attractively made and useful to have about the home. Most fall into the £20-£70 price range, with very plain mahogany ones costing just a few pounds and rising according to size and elaboration. Some kinds of boxes tend to make rather more than this — for example, boxes made from satinwood or carved ivory. Also sought after are Tunbridge ware boxes. Tunbridge was a form of inlay which originated in Tunbridge Wells in England. The inlay was made by gluing together bundles of thin matchsticks of contrasting woods in such a way that when the bundle was viewed end-on a decorative motif was seen. This bundle was then cut into thin slices and laid on the surfaces of boxes and other pieces. The technique reached a high degree of refinement and many examples of Tunbridge ware feature inlaid pictures of human and animal figures or buildings. The picture pieces naturally fetch the highest prices, but simple boxes featuring geometric motifs in regular patterns are still an attractive buy at prices under £100.

Tunbridge Ware

Jewellery

Collecting old jewellery can be fascinating — and not all of it is expensive. I strongly feel that more couples becoming engaged should consider the purchase of an antique ring, as they very often offer better value for money than a new one. For example, I have seen an Edwardian opal cluster ring sold at auction in Dublin for just £160, an antique 18-carat opal and diamond ring for £240, and a very fine Victorian five stone diamond ring for £480. These prices were achieved at a specialist jewellery sale, and although you can expect to pay more at such a sale than if you buy something at a general auction, the prices still compare very favourably with the price of new rings. Bargains in old jewellery can be picked up at house clearances and saleroom auctions, but if you plan to spend a large sum of money on an antique piece you would be better off going to a house that specialises in the sale of jewellery and asking the advice of the auctioneer about any piece you contemplate buying.

Old Costume Jewellery

For the lighter of pocket the collection of old costume jewellery can be just as enjoyable. A word of warning, though. Some time ago a leading London auction house held a sale entirely devoted to old costume jewellery. It was not a resounding success, and many of the items remained unsold. The message was clear, and it was that the knowledgeable buyer was not going to pay high prices for pieces of glass and painted metal no matter how pretty they were or how fashionable. Most costume jewellery of the nineteenth and early twentieth centuries was bought, as such pieces are today, at low prices and was meant for everyday fashion. It had no great value then, and it has little more now. The exceptions are pieces that can be attributed to a known maker or designer and certain early paste set pieces. Some antique shops stock cases of attractive-looking old costume jewellery at decidedly inflated prices. If you have any doubts, don't buy. This isn't true of all antique shops, and I know of several that carry a range of old costume pieces at very keen prices. Don't forget, too, the better swap shops and those dealing in high-quality vintage clothes : many of them carry a cheap and interesting range of old-fashioned jewellery.

One of the most fashionable costume pieces during the Victorian period was the mourning-brooch. These generally consisted of a black glass-fronted enamel case edged in gold or gilt metal, and inside was a lock of the hair of a deceased spouse or other close relative. Those with the hair locket visible at the front are the least-desired by modern collectors, and this is often replaced with a gem of some kind. Others have the hair locket to the back, and some are set in front with pearls or gold or gilt wire decoration. These are more in demand, and prices start at around £50.

Also popular with the Victorians were brooches consisting of a painted miniature of a woman's eye set in a frame of pearls or precious stones. Not to everybody's taste, perhaps, but they can be striking, and prices depend on quality of painting and whether the setting is of gold and precious stones or of gilt and glass or semi-precious stones. Good-quality ones start at around £300.

Drop earrings were very fashionable during the late nineteenth and early twentieth centuries, and costume versions of these in gold and silver-coloured metal can often be bought for just a few pounds. Unfortunately, many of them are fitted with that curious screw catch that always seems to me not quite suited either to the pierced or the unpierced ear. However, they can be worn — at a pinch — for short periods!

Sources

House clearance sales are usually the best source of supply for costume pieces. Auctioneers tend to gather lots of them into cardboard boxes, and you can have a very enjoyable time rummaging through the most unlikely-looking jet and diamanté chains, buckles, necklaces, and other relics of bygone glamour. Keep your eyes open: such lots are often pushed in by unappreciative (male) auctioneers beneath the cases displaying the silver lots.

Arms and Militaria

This field of collecting includes military and sporting guns, pistols and duelling arms, swords, armour, medals, military flags and emblems, and caps, helmets and uniforms of military and police forces. These items have long had a big following in Britain, and in Ireland one or two recent specialist sales in the area have indicated beyond doubt that there is enormous interest here too. Militaria has a very strong appeal for those interested in history, offering, as it does, a link with some of the more exciting and glamorous events of the past as well as allowing us to acquire objects that were actually handled by people of long ago. Definite associations with particular wars arouse the greatest interest and, of course, the highest prices, and some wars are more desirable than others. Anything to do with the Napoleonic Wars is, unsurprisingly, always in demand, as is the American War of Independence. There are lots of First and Second World War memorabilia about, so that although there is widespread interest in this material, prices for a good deal of it are not too high. One exception is Nazi memorabilia, which, despite their unpleasant associations, seem to sell surprisingly well at auction. Irish buyers are as interested in these varied fields as are international collectors, but there are some

particularly Irish areas that are in demand. These include anything to do with the eighteenth-century Irish Volunteers, pre-1922 Irish regiments of the British army, and the Royal Irish Constabulary. Strangely, 1916 Rising items tend to meet with a rather lukewarm response at sales.

Swords come at all prices as they come in widely varying quality. Swords were used, of course, for thousands of years, but important developments in design took place during the sixteenth century. Before that the sword was primarily a slashing weapon, enormously heavy as it had to be in order to make any impression on an armoured opponent, and very often it was held in both hands. The emphasis was then on the blade rather than the point of the sword, with the blade double-edged and sharp and only a slight point at the tip. The work of the swordsman was to swing his weapon in hope of decapitating his opponent or his opponent's horse, or else, by searching out the weak point in his enemy where the helmet met the body armour, by slicing him upwards, as Macbeth did, 'from the nave to th' chops.'

The disappearance of heavy plate or link armour led to the development of finer swords, and the aim of the swordsman was to thrust rather than swing his sword, using the point, now long and slender, to reach

Flintlock pistol with brass mounts and below a Queen Anne style pistol with filigree silver inlay by Barber of London. (Photo courtesy of Adams)

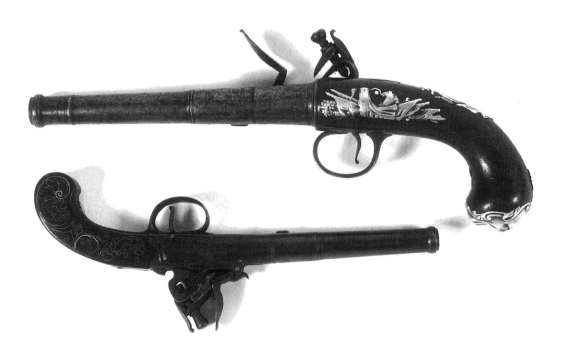

a vital organ within the body. At the same time the practice of duelling and the notion of swordsmanship or fencing as a sport became popular, leading to a demand for very fine swords known as rapiers. These were often used, particularly before the eighteenth century, in conjunction with daggers, which defended the swordsman against the rapier of his opponent while he attacked with his own. During the eighteenth century the wearing of what were called small swords became an article of fashion; also known as 'walking swords', these were broader than the rapier, and had a two-edged blade and often a highly decorated hilt. Also popular at this period were hangers, rather modest swords with only one edge and often a rather insubstantial hilt, which afforded little protection to the user's hand.

For the soldier, guns had all but completely replaced swords by the eighteenth century, although officers continued to wear dress swords. Cavalry regiments, however, retained their battle swords, for, of course, the carrying and loading of firearms was a largely impractical proposition for the horseman. The cavalry sword was generally straight and rather heavy, broader than the small sword and with a double edge. It was usually called a broadsword, and was mainly used by heavy cavalry regiments. For light cavalry, such as the hussars and light dragoons, the sabre tended to be the preferred weapon, its slightly curved blade and fast slashing action being ideal for use in a rapid charge.

At auction, prices for swords start at around £60, although at general sales they can often be bought very cheaply indeed. Unless the item is very rare or very fine, you will want to buy a sword that still has its scabbard. Deciding whether that scabbard is the original one is not always easy. Check that the decoration and apparent age are generally similar to the sword. Slide the sword in and out of the scabbard; if it fits properly the weapon should move fairly easily. Make sure, of course, that this is not because the scabbard is too wide. Check that the scabbard comes comfortably up to the base of the hilt and, at the other end, that the tip of the sword is not suspiciously far up, indicating that the scabbard is too long. As the decoration on a scabbard does not normally match exactly the decoration on the hilt of its sword, absolute certainty whether the two began life together will not always be possible; often a general appearance of harmony must suffice. Of course if the piece is very expensive, this may not be enough; if you are unhappy, don't hesitate to ask the help of the auctioneer, bearing in mind that such assistance is more readily available at a specialist arms sale — one of the reasons why the house or general sale, despite its original bargains in this area, is really a less satisfactory place to buy.

An English officer's broadsword of high quality, with elaborately worked steel guard of semi-basket form and well-moulded grip and made by Runkel of Solingen, would, with matching scabbard, cost about £400. A more modest one would probably set you back around £200. A French heavy cavalry sword would probably come a bit cheaper. Without scabbards, the price of such swords will generally dip below £100, but these may be acceptable for interior decoration purposes. Late nineteenth-century officers' swords are even less expensive and can be very attractive; in a leather scabbard and with single edge you could expect to pay about £70 for one.

Two crossed sabres can make a very striking display mounted on a wall; for a late eighteenth-century light cavalry sabre in its original scabbard you would pay between £100 and £150.

Swords with Irish connections will be more expensive. At a recent specialist sale in Dublin a fine Volunteer sabre made by John Read of College Green, Dublin, with semi-basket guard, richly decorated in brass foliage, with a curved single-edged blade inlaid in gold with figures of Justice and Hibernia and a patterned leather and brass-mounted scabbard, was offered at an estimate of around £1,000 and it quickly shot up to £1,700. At the same sale an Irish Revenue Police sword, with brass hilt and pierced guard, sold for £120.

Guns are an equally important area for the collector of antique arms. Although rifles and shotguns tend to make the highest prices, the study of old hand-guns is especially interesting. One of the most popular kind with collectors is the Queen Anne pistol. These were not, in fact, necessarily made during the reign of Queen Anne (1702-1714), for they continued in production right through the eighteenth century. They usually have a brass cannon barrel, with a wooden butt, often ebonised, which is inlaid with silver wire twisted into scrolls. They vary in quality, but for a reasonably good one, in average condition, the price would be around £300; one by Barber of London sold recently in Dublin for £320. Nervous ladies in the eighteenth and early nineteenth century occasionally took small pistols with them on their journeys. Called muff pistols, these are interesting, decorative pieces, and nice ones make around £100. The gentlemen often carried small pistols in their greatcoats; more ordinary examples tend to fetch less than the muff pistols and start at approximately £50. Pairs of pistols are much more expensive, especially if they come in their original fitted case. A pair of percussion muff pistols by Butler of Dublin, with chequered grips and in their original case which also contained a copper powder-flask, was sold at a Dublin sale for £400; a Continental pair of similar type would probably cost about £100 less. Good pairs of flintlock duelling pistols are even more expensive, with prices starting at around £600 and fine cased examples fetching a good deal more. All eighteenth century pistols were operated by flintlock ignition, with one position for firing and one for safety. Invented by a French gunsmith, Martin le Bourgeoys, in the early seventeenth century, it was used for most firearms until the 1830s. Although duelling pistols often had a hair trigger worked by means of an extra spring in the lock, the main problem with flintlock weapons remained the fact that there was an appreciable delay between the act of pressing the trigger and the gun actually firing. The problem was finally solved, possibly by the London gunsmith Durs Egg, by the production of the copper percussion cap, which contained the detonating powder. This was set upon a steel nipple, which, when struck by the hammer of the pistol, resulted in an instantaneous firing. The percussion cap was highly reliable even in damp weather and from the 1830s replaced the flintlock system. Because it was easy to manufacture, it quickly led to the mass production of hand-guns in Britain and America, where in 1851 Samuel Colt produced the famous six-shooter revolver beloved of cowboy fans. The Colt revolver was a reliable and accurate weapon; if you see one at a sale viewing today you will be struck by its solid weight, its simple mechanism, and its perfectly balanced feel in the hand.

For Colt revolvers, prices start at about £200, rising to about £400. A similar price would be paid for a reasonable-quality early English percussion pistol; one made by Durs Egg himself made £180 in Dublin recently. One thing to note, though, if you are interested in buying high-quality nineteenth-century pistols is that during that period many English provincial gunsmiths who were buying gun parts for assembly or who were making cheap pistols appear to have sometimes engraved the names of top gunsmiths on their own, inferior products. The names of Durs Egg and H. Nock are known to have been used. Always examine a gun carefully to assess its quality and, as in other areas of collecting, keep a weather eye out for composite pieces, which may combine the butt of one with the barrel of another gun, as well as for botched repairs or restoration.

Most gun collectors advise that it is also best to avoid weapons that appear overcleaned or show signs of having been stripped down.

General militaria include an almost mind-boggling variety of items. Even uniforms and part uniforms are sought after. A full infantry officer's dress uniform in its original cardboard box from Callaghan's of Dame Street was recently sold for £600. A nineteenth-century British naval officer's cocked hat made by Philips of Dame Street, Dublin, was sold for £200, and a nineteenth-century Bavarian officer's helmet was knocked down for a mere £550. Because, presumably, they are easier for the private collector to display, the headdress items tend to fetch proportionately higher prices. Peninsular War objects make very high prices and parts of the uniform of a Connaught Ranger who served there were sold some time ago for £5,000.

Medals come at all prices, and even very young people can put together an interesting collection at modest cost. The most expensive are those associated with famous military engagements such as Waterloo or the Charge of the Light Brigade. A Waterloo medal could cost as much as £500, and one associated with the defence of Lucknow during the 'Indian Mutiny' could fetch as much. But more common medals can be obtained for as little as £10, a sum that would probably buy you a Second World War service medal, third class, or perhaps a German Imperial service medal for the nineteenth century. During the First World War over 150,000 medals and crosses were awarded,

Top: Flintlock brass barrel blunderbuss by Rigby of Dublin.
Bottom: Brass barrel blunderbuss by Hutchinson of Dublin converted from flintlock to percussion. (Adams)

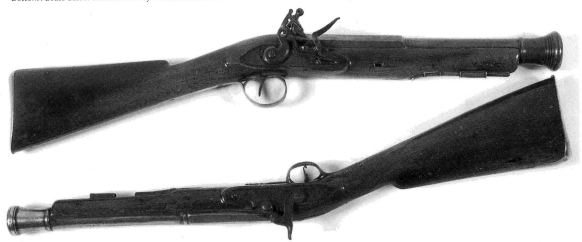

and prices range from about £50 to £200. Second World War medals are probably rarer — after all, many of the recipients are still alive — but they are no more expensive. In fact they are generally a bit cheaper: possibly the market is aware that in the short to medium term they can only become more common and therefore won't really appreciate in value for some time. A German First World War Iron Cross, first class, would cost about £50; with oak leaves and black-and-white ribbon, a bit more. A British First World War Military Cross would be around £40, and a 1914-15 Mons Star would fetch up to £20 more. A German Second World War Iron Cross with ribbon should make about £35, with brass and white metal service medals around £10 to £15. British service medals make roughly the same amount.

Black and Tan War medals are occasionally found and they sell for about £20; 1916 Rising medals fetch up to £10 each and Irish service medals about £15.

It is a strange reflection on human interests that Nazi memorabilia are so sought after. For example, Nazi side-arms tend to make about double the price fetched by similar objects not so related. Wehrmacht dress bayonets in original sheaths can make £5,000 or more; officers' dirks make about £300, and good naval officers' swords around £600. German officers' caps fetch £70 to £90, and police shakos around £100. Nazi car flags cost about £100, pairs of SS epaulettes about £25, and Nazi toy soldier sets make several hundred pounds.

Top to bottom: British half-basket hilt sword with double-edged broad blade, mid 18th century; 19th century officer's sword; officer's broadsword, its semi-basket guard filled with scrollwork; late 18th century cavalry sword with fluted oval pommel and wire bound fishskin grip in a steel mounted scabbard. (Photo courtesy of Adams)

Coins

I have often suspected that, although it gets little attention in the fine arts columns of the newspapers and in the collectors' magazines, coin collecting is one of the areas that most interests the public. Most people, of course, have a few old coins tucked away somewhere and hope they will turn out to be of value. Unfortunately, they usually don't, because most of these hoards are found to contain fairly common coins from the nineteenth and early twentieth century. Just the same, it seems to please many people to own some small thing that was personally handled by those living long ago, even if it is nowadays not worth very much money.

Elizabeth I crown

Apart from those who are merely interested in valuing or finding out something about coins that they already own, there does seem to be a rapidly growing band of active coin collectors. I attended a major coin sale in Dublin some time ago, and while such events are rare enough to be sure of bringing out the enthusiasts whenever one is held, I was surprised to find great difficulty in obtaining a seat, while many buyers had to content themselves with craning their necks round a crowded doorway to hear the proceedings! For the new collector, the best guide, as with all areas of collecting, is to buy what gives you pleasure in the best condition you can afford. Do not hope for a big financial killing. Although there are certainly investment collectors about, operating at the top end of the market, and lots of modest buyers as well, coins, with their rather firm grading structure, vaguely academic overtones, lack of furnishing appeal and links with the bullion markets are less likely to see the rapid rises in price that we've seen in recent years with paintings and furniture. Coins, with a few exceptions, seem to chart a steadier course, showing a fairly modest though generally consistent rise from year to year. They're more likely to provide a 'safe house' for your money (though this cannot, of course, be guaranteed) than hopes of a big coup.

Price Guides

You should provide yourself with a reliable and up-to-date price guide, and you will probably find that in this area of collecting the best guides will tend to give a firmer indication of what you are likely to have to pay for the coin you want than is the case with guides to prices in other fields. This is partly because of the clearly defined categories of condition that operate in the coin market. Condition is considered to be of the utmost importance in coin collecting, and there is an internationally recognised grading structure. Prices from grade to grade can vary by a factor of ten and more. Therefore, before you ever venture forth to buy an old coin, you must know what these grades are and what they mean. Here they are:

Terminology

Proof: Struck not for circulation but for collection and presentation. They often come in their own special case. Special clean and polished dies are used in their manufacture.

Uncirculated: In perfect condition, without wear or scratches and with a fine lustre (sheen).

Extremely fine (EF): Almost perfect, with some sheen, but the high points of the design show some slight wear. Still, all fine details should be clear.

Very fine (VF): Definite signs of circulation, with a certain flatness appearing in the design. The highest parts of the design will show wear, but every detail and letter outline should still be clear.

Fine: High points and fine detail will show considerable wear, but the main feature should still be clear.

James I crown, fine.

Very good (VG): Rather a misleading term for the novice, as coins in this state look anything but good in the normal sense! A very worn coin but one that should be free from actual gouges or bending. A condition of very little interest to the collector unless the coin is exceedingly rare. Any coin in a lesser condition than this — that is, good, fair, or poor — would have to be rare indeed to inspire any interest among collectors.

The serious collector will be aiming to buy most of his coins in the uncirculated or extremely fine state, though age and rarity may from time to time force down the standards to very fine. Certainly the modest or novice collector or, perhaps, those who collect for fun or out of purely historical interest can find much to enjoy in the very fine state. You could hope to acquire many interesting eighteenth, nineteenth and twentieth-century coins for just a few pounds or, if buying in job lots at auction, for even less. But you mustn't expect such coins to rise in value significantly. What such purchases will do is give you lots of experience in handling coins and learning how to distinguish the various conditions from one another; for the young collector it can provide fascinating ways of increasing his feel for the past.

Some of the terms used in coin catalogues may puzzle you when first you go to buy coins. All of these will be explained in any of the useful books on coin collecting mentioned at the end of this book, but here are some of the most common. The 'obverse' of a coin is the front, the side where the most important part of the design, such as the head of the monarch, is stamped. The back, or less important side, is the 'reverse'. 'Clipping' was a method of cutting small pieces from the edge of a coin in order to use them for their metal value. It was illegal, but often practised during the middle ages and beyond where coins of suitable small denominations were unavailable. A 'dump' is a small thick coin. The 'field' is the part of a coin not occupied by inscriptions. The 'mint mark' is a letter or some other mark that indicates where the coin was minted. A 'commemorative' is a coin struck specially to mark some special event; they often come in a presentation case and were not really intended for circulation, although a commemorative coin is usually legal tender; this is not the case with a commemorative 'medallion', which is intended for decorative purposes. Finally, collectors of Victorian coins (and there are many) need to know the various catalogue terms used to describe the changing portraits of the queen as she passed from youth to old age. 'Young head' appeared between her accession in 1837 and 1860; the 'bun head' was used from 1860 until its replacement by the 'jubilee head' in 1887 and the 'veiled head' appeared from 1893 till her death in 1901.

Hammered and Milled Coinage

The first coins seem to have been minted around 700 BC, possibly at Lydia, in Greece, the kingdom of the famous Croeseus. From that time until the middle of the seventeenth century virtually all coins were 'hammered'. This was a method of manufacture whereby a 'flan', a thin, blank piece of metal, was held between two engraved blocks, known as dies, with a tongs. The whole was then struck a blow from a heavy mallet and the design impressed upon the sandwiched metal. These coins are generally thinner and more irregular in shape than later machine-made ones.

Charles I crown.

Collecting hammered coins is not always as expensive as the novice buyer may think, because many, if not most, collectors are most interested in the more modern, minted variety. The first coins minted in England appeared on an experimental basis during the reign of Queen Elizabeth I. The 1560s saw an issue of minted sixpences, shillings, groats, and other small coins. There were other such experiments during the early seventeenth century; but it wasn't till 1662, during the reign of King Charles II, that the minted coin finally triumphed. The machine-made coin can be distinguished from the hammered one by its more uniform shape, its frequently greater thickness, and its grained or lettered edge. The new coins made greater refinement of design possible, which is why so many collectors prefer them, but many of the older, hammered coins carry designs of great charm and are more attractive to historically minded collectors. They also include some of the most fascinating areas of international collecting, of which the most important is the coinage of ancient Greece and Rome.

James I crown, very fine.

Collecting Irish Coins

Naturally, many Irish coin collectors are most interested in the Irish issues. For most of the last eight hundred years many of the coins circulating in Ireland were of English mintage, but there are some very interesting specifically Irish issues, especially among hammered coins. The Norse seem to have introduced coinage into Ireland, and at first they contented themselves with the circulation of Anglo-Saxon silver coins obtained through English trade and pillage. It seems to have been the famous Sitric Silkbeard who struck the first coins in Dublin, around the year 1000. At first these appear to have been virtual copies of English coins. Some even carry the name of King Ethelred the Unready as well as the names of English mints, and the conclusion must be that a number of dies were imported from England for the manufacture of Irish coinage. However, a good number of these early coins were clearly made from fresh dies and carry the legend *Sihtric Rex Dyflin*: Sitric, King of Dublin. In the beginning these Hiberno-Norse coins, as they are called, were of very good quality, but by the end of the eleventh century they had greatly deteriorated, many incorporating base metal instead of silver, and by around 1150 they had become quite crude indeed.

Many Hiberno-Norse coins are nevertheless rare and sought after, even in far from perfect condition, and this is not a cheap area of collecting. As far as collectors are concerned, Norse coins are divided into six phases. Phase I coins, dating from about 1000 to 1015, command high prices and would not generally be seen in much more than very fine condition and often worse. In the very fine state, an Ethelred 'short cross' silver penny could make well over £2,500; the pennies known as 'long cross' are commoner and might fetch only a tenth of that. At a recent coin sale in Dublin a phase II silver penny fetched £240, a phase VI (shortly before 1150) silver halfpenny made £280, and a phase VI penny made £80. None of these coins was in much better than fine condition, so the prices must be judged to have been fairly high on that occasion. By phase VI the weight of the Irish penny was hardly half that of the English, and often inscriptions were virtually unreadable, so

Elizabeth I milled shilling.

Edward VI crown.

the poor condition in which many of them are now found is scarcely surprising.

The first coinage issued by the Normans appears to be that of King John, under whom there were actually three coinages. The first, dating from about 1185, when John was Lord of Ireland, had a head in profile, the second, a full face with rather rounded features, and the third, which consisted of pennies and farthings as well as the halfpennies that had formed the total of the first two coinages, showed a rather elegant full face of the king, whose hand is also seen holding a sword aloft. Of this issue the pennies are the most common and would probably make £70 to £80 or so, with halfpennies making significantly more and the farthings perhaps three times as much when seen in very fine condition.

An especially interesting and, nowadays, expensive period for Irish coinage was the reign of Edward IV, who ruled from 1461-1483. The groat, which was a fourpenny coin, is very rare, though there were mintings of the coin at Dublin, Limerick, and Drogheda, and prices can go as high as £2,500 to £3,000 for such coins in the very fine state. Edward IV pennies are much cheaper, and even very fine ones don't go much higher than £100.

A coinage that many collectors love to see is the James II gun money. During his campaign against William of Orange, King James found himself critically short of funds with which to pay troops and furnish supplies. The historian Macaulay amusingly described James's solution to his problems: 'He could, he conceived, at once extricate himself from his financial difficulties by the simple process of calling a farthing a shilling ... Pots, pans, knockers of doors, pieces of ordnance, which had long been past use, were carried to the Mint. In a short time, lumps of base metal, nominally worth a million sterling, intrinsically worth about a sixtieth of that sum, were in circulation. A mortgage of £1000 was cleared by a bag of counters made out of old kettles.' Shopkeepers who refused to accept the coins were threatened with hanging in front of their own doors. After William's victory the coins, not unexpectedly, were redeemed at their resale metal value; clearly, a crushing financial loss to those tradesmen who had been forced to accept them. At auction, most denominations of gun money fall into the £50 to £100 price range, with the crowns, which are really quite attractive coins, featuring King James on horseback, fetching about £400 in very fine to extremely fine condition.

Wood's Halfpence

The most notorious Irish issue during the Georgian period was that of Wood's Halfpence. There was a constant problem of keeping up the supply of small-denomination coinage, and in 1721 William Wood was granted a patent for the minting of Irish halfpennies to be manufactured at his Bristol works. Condemned as a base and fraudulent issue by Jonathan Swift in his *Drapier's Letters*, they were not a success, and in the end, it seems, many of the coins were sent out to America. Auction prices for the various kinds of Wood's Halfpence range from about £10 for the commonest in fine condition to over £300 for the rarest in extremely fine state.

Modern Irish Coinage

During the rest of the Georgian period only small-denomination coins were issued for Ireland, and under Victoria there were none. The real story of modern Irish coinage begins with the Irish Free State issue of 1928, and the new collector will be pleased to discover that proof sets for this year are not all that expensive, being around £100 at auction. The most coveted item in modern Irish coin collecting is the 1943 florin. It is not recorded how many of these were minted, but it was a very small number, and examples in extremely fine state have made £3,500, with around £6,000 being paid for uncirculated ones. This is followed by the 1937 half-crown, which makes from £500 upwards, the 1943 half-crown at £300 upwards and the 1937 florin at around £200. These would all be coins in an extremely fine or at least very fine condition and you could expect prices to drop along with quality. A full set of Irish coinage from 1928 to 1968 in very fine condition, including the more valuable florins and half-crowns, recently made £4,400. With all coins in an extremely fine state it would undoubtedly have made considerably more. Other Irish coins worth looking out for (but highly unlikely to be found) in an extremely fine or uncirculated condition are the 1939 threepence, which can make over £150 if uncirculated; the 1937 shilling, which has fetched £200 for the best states, and the 1933 shilling, which can make around £100 for the best. The 1940 halfpenny has also topped the £100 mark when found in uncirculated state. Be warned, though. These prices only apply to coins in superb condition. Coins that have been through the hurly-burly of commercial life will not fetch these sums, so don't hold your breath if you find a very ordinary example in an old jam-jar at home. A 1940 halfpenny in only very fine state, for instance, would not make £5.

Philip and Mary shilling.

Collecting Other Coins

As the field of coin collecting is so enormous, all collectors tend to confine themselves to just a few specialist areas. Interesting collections could be made at relatively modest cost from a wide range of Victorian coinage (the collection of crowns is extremely popular), of Georgian small denominations, of commemorative coins, or of the eighteenth-century token coins that were issued by private companies at periods when there was not enough small-denomination coinage to go round. Medallions from the nineteenth century are often very inexpensive, yet a very high standard of craftsmanship went into the making of many of them. At a sale in Dublin recently a fine bronze Victorian jubilee medal was sold at the knock-down price of £3, and three lovely Trinity College medals with portraits of Queen Elizabeth I as Gloriana were only £45. It could be that the collection of high-quality medallions might prove to be a profitable hobby for the future, but even if it isn't, at such low prices they are an enjoyable buy anyway.

Charles I half crown.

Continental and American coins offer wide fields of interest to the collector. A collection of proof sets, say, from different countries, could be a very rewarding hobby for the younger collector in particular, and many sets can be got for well under £20, even in uncirculated states and original cases. For the more affluent buyer the collection of gold coins is an interesting possiblity, but do be careful what you pay, and always keep a weather eye on the prices in international markets. At the moment extremely fine George V gold sovereigns are making from £65 to £80, most Edward VII sovereigns are around £70 to £80, Victorian sovereigns in very fine state cost about £60 at auction, and are often seen in lots of about half a dozen, and very fine George III guineas are around £140 to £240, depending on the rarity of the coin.

Victorian 'Gothic Crown' 1847.

Care of Coins

The storage and display of coins requires some thought if you are to avoid the possibility of corrosive damage. When you buy coins at auction you will probably find that they are sold to you in small plastic holders; indeed this is often also the case when you buy from a coin dealer. When you get home, take your coins out of these containers at once. When you do you will probably find that already the plastic has caused a sticky deposit to form on the surface of the coins, and this causes great damage, especially to bronze and copper. Wipe the coins carefully with a piece of soft cloth to remove the stickiness, but on no account engage in any sort of cleaning operation, and never, never use any sort of metal polish on old coins. If you do you will almost certainly seriously devalue them.

For storage, ordinary manila envelopes will be found to be quite safe, as are the useful little coin holders made of paper with a clear cellophane centre that can be got from your friendly coin dealer. Make sure you don't leave your coin collection where it may be affected by damp. Of course the nicest way to display your collection is in a special coin cabinet, which has round fitted compartments for the coins and pull-out sections for easy examination. Unfortunately these can be very expensive, but sometimes at a specialist coin auction you might be lucky enough to pick up an old cabinet or case that may fill the bill nicely at a reasonable price. One trick can be to look out for a lot that comprises some rather uninspiring collection of coins in a useful-looking case. The chances are that the dealers and the experienced collectors will have no interest in it, and you can buy it for the case at relatively little cost.

Pine Furniture

The fashion for natural woods in kitchen furnishings which has grown over the last couple of decades has led to an increased interest in antique pine pieces. Inevitably, this has meant a very high level of export trade in old Irish pine and until very recently one often saw advertisements in British trade papers offering Irish pine for sale by the truckload. This appears to have levelled off of late partly, no doubt, because of the diminishing supply but also, one hopes, because of increased appreciation for these pieces on the Irish market. Nevertheless, much old pine furniture can still be bought at very reasonable prices, although for very high quality pieces demand can be very strong. Eighteenth century pine bookcases, for example, are very sought after and prices can rise to several thousand pounds for the best. Good dressers, too, can be expensive, but they are large for the modern kitchen and it is still perfectly possible, if you have the space for it, to buy a well made dresser for under £1,000 at auction.

Most old Irish pine furniture seen today dates from the second half of the nineteenth century and the early years of the twentieth; the poverty of most Irish homes in the pre-Famine era precluded the ownership of any furniture of quality and before that time most pine pieces which were made would have been large cupboards and dressers for the kitchens of the wealthy. One kind of piece which was owned by some of the more comfortably off peasantry was the storage chest, which seems often to have come into a family

Anglo Saxon penny struck by Offa of Mercia around 787 at the Canterbury mint in honour of his wife Cynethryth. This is the only instance of a Saxon coin being issued in the name of a consort. This coin made £7000 at a sale in London in 1991. (Photos of coins courtesy of Glendings, London)

as a bridal dowry, probably with its drawers filled with linen and lace. These chests often came in two sections with one or more drawers below and a blanket box above. Sometimes the lid was slightly slanted to allow for its use as a writing surface and one can imagine that the chest was used to store all the family valuables, including documents — a very useful piece of furniture when you were trying to bring up a large family in a confined space!

Both the rarity and the fine quality of many eighteenth and early nineteenth century Irish pine pieces means that prices can be high and, indeed, it would appear that in Britain and America, at least until recession bit, customers have been prepared to pay more than Irish buyers for the best pieces. In Ireland, at a very recent sale, a very fine Irish cupboard with dentil moulding and unusual octagonally carved panels was sold for £1,200 and a fairly simple late Georgian bookcase and cupboard has made £1,600. A plain eighteenth century panelled food cupboard would probably set you back about £800. Dressers were rarely, if ever, made before the early 1800s and it's difficult to find one which can confidently be dated to before 1840. Good ones from around this period can be bought from about £800 for simple ones with higher prices being paid for those with special features such as plate racks. Particularly interesting are those known as fiddle front dressers which generally have a base with two drawers and, beneath, an open cupboard divided by a fiddle shaped slat. Many of these seem to be quite early in date and a good number appear to have been made in Ulster though the design was certainly copied in virtually all parts of the country. They were often darkly stained to resemble oak or mahogany and the most desirable still retain their old paint. Depending on age and quality, prices for these would start about £1,500 and upwards.

Pine wardrobe, possibly Dutch.

After the Famine and even more quickly after the various land acts gave the Irish small farmer gretater security and better hope of prosperity, the quantity of domestic pine, both native and imported, increased. It is from the period 1860-1930 that most of the pine pieces we see at auction and antique shops will date. The most expensive are the large cupboards and dresssers but you will find that there is a wide range of furniture, including chests of drawers, coffers, tables, hanging shelves, candle boxes, dressing tables and washstands where prices can start from less than £100. Nice solidly made chests of drawers can regularly be got both at auction and at antique shops for around £250. Edwardian period dressing tables, which can often be found in ash as well as pine, can be bought from £150-350, hanging shelves tend to come between £100 and £200 and washstands, frequently seen with attractive tiled backs, can be easily found from about £80 upwards. Coffers or blanket boxes can be got from about £100 with £400 or more being paid for the better ones and settles can be bought from £300 rising according to quality. Pieces which are not usually found in pine are those which fetch the highest prices. A good sideboard with curved or moulded back would cost at leaset £400-500 now and bookcases fall into the same price range. Desks and bureaux are not all that often seen either and you would expect to pay around £250 for small and simple ones rising to about £800 for larger, better made examples.

Many houses and saleroom auctions will include a quantity of small, miscellaneous pine articles which, though not especially valuable or well made, can look decorative in the modern kitchen. Roughly made pine platters and troughs can be bought for between £10 and £50, with small hanging cupboards and plain towel rails starting at £70-100. Good candle boxes can sometimes be surprisingly expensive with a price range of about £50-130. Objects such as pine meat tenderisers, rolling pins, cheeseboards, draining spoons, condiment boxes and so on will often be found at house sales for just a few pounds.

The fashion nowadays is, of course, for stripped pine but in fact most nineteenth century pine furniture was actually painted. Blue and green were especially popular colours, closely followed by dark red, brown, white and, occasionally, black. Some pieces even had floral decoration painted on. During the last few decades the paint has been stripped from many nineteenth century pieces by dealers, buyers and those who own pieces which have long stood in a family farmhouse. However, you may occasionally get the chance to buy at auction a piece which has not been thus treated and I would be inclined, if the paint were reasonably well laid on and not flaking away, to leave such a piece alone. If the surface were scumbled, that is, where the pine has been lightly stained and, while still wet, scraped with a graining comb or stick, or when a floral or other painted decoration has been applied, I would on no account strip the piece.

There are many, many more areas of collectables than it has been possible to consider here. Of these among the more important at present are toys, photographs, garden furniture, clocks, scientific instruments, and fine art deco sculpture. Astonishing sums are now being paid for some pop and 1960s emphemera, and the ever-soaring prices for the ceramics of Clarice Cliff seem to be increasingly at variance with the large quantity of her wares that have appeared on the market in Britain. How long this upward surge in prices for objects that ten years ago no-one would have thought of paying substantial sums for will last is anybody's guess. The Americans, the Japanese, the Arabs — every day we hear of new players in the game, and always we are told that since the supply of antique items must inexorably become less and less the prices must inexorably rise more and more. But could there be an antique market crash? The next few years are bound to be interesting!

Collection of inexpensive old pine pieces.

Chapter Twelve

LIVING WITH ANTIQUES

Room Conditions

he great enemy of many antiques is not time but the changes in the environment in which they live. Glass and porcelain, on the face of it the most fragile of objects, are, providing careless handling does not lead to smashing or cracking, the most resilient to damage from damp, infestation, and unsuitable temperature and light conditions.

It is home heating that probably poses the greatest hazard to furniture. The trouble is that wood is highly water-absorbent. If an old piece has been sitting relatively happily in a cool, slightly damp room and is suddenly subjected to a rapid warming-up from central heating or a coal fire, it will lose moisture and contract. If it is exposed to such temperature changes over a long period the timber will eventually begin to show cracks. The problem is greatest with broad timber surfaces such as tables and sideboards, and it is compounded where timber veneers are involved, resulting in differing rates of expansion and contraction across the two glued surfaces. The inevitable result is a cracked and lifting veneer. With table legs and with chairs the differing rates of expansion will cause stress at the joints, and this, combined with the effect of temperature and humidity changes on old glues, can result in a chair beginning to come apart.

Avoiding extremes of heat and cold is the answer. Don't place valuable pieces close to localised sources of heat such as radiators. When you first switch on central heating, bring it up to the desired temperature slowly, and try not to let the room become very cold when it is not in use. Use a humidifier with central heating. This is all, of course, much easier said than done in the modern home. You may find that you simply can't afford to keep a reasonable level of heat in an unused room all day long during the winter months. A particular problem may arise where a coal fire is used that may only be lit in the evenings. This may result in a very sharp difference between the evening temperature and that during the day, particularly if the room is a small one. Bearing in mind that old furniture will be fairly happy in a cold room providing that it stays cold, it might be a good idea, if you can't provide a constant temperature in your sitting room for the winter months, to move the most valuable pieces to a room where they won't be subjected to regular fluctuations in heat. This would be particularly advisable with regard to veneered pieces.

Although a certain amount of coolness will be tolerated by furniture, very damp conditions will not be. In such circumstances furniture can fall victim to dry rot and warping. In the modern home, condensation can be a particular risk, so always make sure there is plenty of ventilation; and if you have valuable furniture in rooms that are rarely used, be sure to open windows from time to time, especially on sunny or breezy days.

Remember that light, too, can damage the surface of your furniture, so don't place good pieces under windows where they will get a lot of direct sunlight. This will eventually result in the bleaching of the wood and possible cracking. If bleaching does occur, surfaces can be revived with a little teak oil rubbed into the grain.

Woodworm

The question of woodworm is often a moot one among collectors. Some refuse to give house room to even a slightly infested piece, others don't seem to worry about it at all. The sensible answer is to avoid buying such pieces if you can, but if you like something, a small amount of worm that does not deface the piece may be acceptable. In most cases it can be successfully treated at home using a proprietary product. As some questions regarding the health risks of such products have been raised recently, it is wise to be very careful when using them.

If at all possible, take infested pieces outside for treatment. If you can't do this, open every window and door in the room. Use rubber gloves, and tie a large handkerchief over your mouth and nose. If you are doing a lot of de-worming, change this mask frequently during the work. If there is only a small amount of worm a small bottle with a dropper will do the trick. Pour plenty of the fluid into each bore-hole, making sure that the piece is standing or lying in such a way that the insecticide doesn't just run out onto the ground. Afterwards, don't sit in the room with treated pieces for a week or two or until the smell of the insecticide has disappeared. After a few weeks, check that the piece is not showing any signs of life. You can detect living woodworm by the presence of little piles of dust around the bore-holes. If you are in doubt, repeat the treatment, taking the same care as before. Each spring you should check all your furniture for signs of infestation.

Cleaning

Minor damage to the surfaces of solid timber furniture can usually be treated at home. Many old pieces, especially those bought at auction, may have accumulated an unpleasant layer of wax and dirt on the surface. Do not tackle this with a scour pad and detergent and water. This can lead to rotting and warping of the wood, and on a veneered piece, if water seeped beneath thin cracks in the surface you could have a real disaster on your hands. Instead, in a bottle make up a mixture of equal parts of linseed oil and turpentine and add about two-thirds of a part of vinegar. Shake it and apply it with a soft cloth, using another, dry cloth to wipe off. Change the cloth regularly to avoid working dirt back into the surface. If the piece is veneered the highest degree of care is needed, as the penetration of solvent beneath the veneer could result in its lifting. If a veneered surface is so dirty that you feel cleaning cannot be avoided, be careful to squeeze your cleansing cloth very thoroughly before application, so as not to flood the surface of the piece with fluid.

It may be that your cleaning operation exposes certain defects, such as scratches or black and white marks on a table top or sideboard. White marks, usually made by wet glasses or by heat, are relatively easy to remove. Shake up in a bottle equal parts of turpentine and linseed oil, and dribble it over the mark until it's completely covered. Next day wipe away with a soft cloth slightly moistened with vinegar. If the mark has not completely disappeared, repeat the treatment. Black marks, sometimes caused by water penetrating the finish, sometimes by burns, are extremely difficult to remove. If the black area is small, the best solution might be to simply place an ornament strategically over it and forget it! If the mark is large and the piece is in any way valuable, consult a professional restorer. If the piece has little value — and you are very, very sure it has not — you could try abrading the mark with the finest sandpaper. However, it must be said that this is unlikely to work, because such marks have a tendency to penetrate the wood very deeply. On no account tackle burn marks with heavy sandpaper or scrapers. You can only do more harm than good. If you do succeed in shifting a shallow burn mark with light abrasion, you should work a little teak oil into the area and later polish it gently.

Many scratches can nowadays be treated using one of the new scratch creams. Be sure to follow the instructions on all such proprietary products to the letter. For very shallow scratches it is often a good trick to lightly rub them with the tip of a child's brown marker. Sometimes when the surface of a piece shows a number of scratches or dents, people feel tempted to strip off the whole thing and repolish. Don't. Not only is part of the charm of an old piece the fact that it shows some of the signs of many years of use but, it also bears a patina, that lovely mellowed appearance that is only the result of time and years of tender polishing. Without it an antique piece becomes a shadow of itself and, to many knowledgeable collectors, little better than a reproduction. It takes so long to build up a fine patina, so little time to destroy it completely. So if you are faced with a cabinet or table that seems scattered with stains and dents, clean it thoroughly, treat the flaws by the conservative methods I have suggested above, and then buff up with a beeswax polish — a good proprietary one such as Antiquax will do fine. I think you will find that the surface is considerably improved, and you will have done your bit to enhance the patina the years have conferred on your piece, rather than defacing it.

Restoration

This naturally brings us to the vexed question of restoration. I say vexed, because the truth is that many collectors would rather have an unrestored, albeit flawed, piece than one that shows obvious signs of restoration. Ill-advised restoration will reduce rather than increase the value of an antique piece — and this is becoming more and more the case as knowledge of antiques spreads among private buyers. People who come to have an interest in antiques through the home restoration class with the idea of buying pieces with rather tired-looking surfaces and stripping and repolishing them in order to sell them at an increased price are making a great mistake. Almost certainly the piece that appears at auction with a hard, glossy new coat of french polish will fetch less than it would have if it had been left with its original matte surface, even if that surface had been marred by a scattering of blotches and scratches. Moreover, french polishing was not introduced until after 1800, so that to subject any piece made before this to the french polish treatment is inappropriate, and looks it. Even with Victorian pieces, on which french polish was the original surface, it will, over the years, have softened and mellowed and will in no way resemble the harsh glitter of the recently applied coat.

The only good reason for stripping down an old surface and repolishing it is that there is absolutely no alternative. If a piece has been defaced over a great expanse of its surface, if it has become white through the removal, by years of damp, of its original wax or polish so that it has become exceedingly ugly or unusable, then there is no choice but to strip and repolish. If the piece is in any way valuable or has the potential for value once the work is done, then the job should be handed over to a professional. The same care should be taken over leather desk-tops, damaged chair legs, broken pieces of carving, or old handles. If what is on the piece can be saved at all, it should be. Only pieces of minor value should be tackled at home — and have the piece valued before you begin.

Sometimes you will come across old oak or mahogany pieces that have been painted in some lurid coat of blue or white. Occasionally a good piece can lurk beneath. In such a circumstance, of course, stripping will be necessary and can be embarked upon, as it were, without fear. However, there do exist pieces that were painted at the time of making and of which the paint carries a great deal of the value. An example would be the green paint on an eighteenth-century Windsor chair. In fact, be very slow to strip paint of any colour off a Windsor chair or any other old pine piece without taking professional advice first.

General Care: Books

Leather and paper, like wood, are water-absorbent, meaning that books tend to require the same kind of care as furniture does in matters like heat, light, and damp. Heat makes leather bindings brittle and can cause spines to crack. Damp, as well as imparting to pages an unpleasing wavy appearance, will eventually cause spotting, foxing (brown dots), and mould. Light will fade binding rapidly. When you are considering a bookcase, make sure it is against an inside wall and is not positioned opposite a window. Open shelves are probably best, as they allow the free circulation of air, but in a room where dust or soot is likely to be about, a glass-fronted bookcase is most suitable. Pack your books so that they stand upright but not too tightly wedged together. Try to avoid having them tilt to one side as this can put strain on the bindings.

It comes as bad news to book owners that the same little fellows who like to eat furniture are equally partial to a meal of fine books. Keep your books dusted and your eye alert for signs of infestation. If you find bore-holes or the creamy granular dust that tells of eggs being hatched on a book that is valuable, it is best to take it to a good book restorer. On the other hand, if your book is not so highly prized or if the infestation is fairly slight, you could have a go at de-worming it yourself. First, using the blunt end of a needle, gently ease away as much debris as you can. Next, find yourself a tin box — the one left over from the Christmas biscuits is ideal — and place the book inside. Surround the book with small wads of cotton wool that have been soaked in woodworm killer or some other suitable insecticide — but don't let the pads touch the book. Close the tin, which should be as airtight as possible, and leave it for a week or so. Then repeat the procedure. This should deal with mature insects and grubs, but keep a weather eye out for signs of continued life, and if necessary repeat the fumigation procedure. Always check bookcases for woodworm as well, because it can spread from the timber into your books.

As with furniture, when it comes to the restoration of books be very, very slow to discard old bindings. Only when the book can no longer be read with anything approaching comfort, or when a disintegrating binding is posing a threat to the book itself, should a rebind be considered. If only the hinges have given way it may be possible to re-back the book and even lay the old spine on top, if it has survived reasonably intact. However, it may be that the original binding is truly a lost cause. In this case bring your book to a good antiquarian binder, of whom there are several, and order the best binding you can afford.

Your binding should be as appropriate in style for the age of the book as your pocket will allow. For nineteenth and twentieth-century books, fine cloth may be adequate, but for older and more precious books some form of leather binding is advisable. It is possible to order a half — or quarter — calf binding if funds do not run to full calf, and with suitably coloured boards the result can be just as attractive. Home bookbinding is not a good idea unless you have proper training and the right tools. Botched repairs can devalue a book even more comprehensively than bad restoration can devalue furniture. And never, never be tempted to run up a quick repair using adhesive tape, either on the binding or to secure loose pages.

Leather bindings should really need no more routine care than dusting with a soft cloth. Remember, too, that the natural oils from your hands are an excellent conditioner for your leather-bound books — so read them often! Very brittle bindings can occasionally be dosed with castor oil. Moisten a soft cloth lightly with the oil and rub it in gently. With very brittle bindings, the application can be repeated every couple of days until the book begins to look like itself again. On no account let the leather become saturated with oil. As soon as there is the slightest indication of this happening, end the treatment.

Silverware

In the days of housemaids, even up to thirty years ago, the sight of a sideboard groaning under the weight of a glittering display of highly polished silver and plate was an essential feature of the drawing-room of the good housewife and the successful man. Now that housewives have found more interesting things to do than stay at home and polish silver, many people have become reluctant to buy it because of the extra work they imagine it will bring in its wake. Indeed, it's generally supposed that this is one of the reasons that the price of wrought silver has risen more slowly than the price of other antiques and valuables during the last decade or so.

The irony, and the good news for modern buyers, is that all this polishing was a bit of a mistake anyway! Silver is a very soft metal, and every time it is vigorously polished the thin top layer of the metal is rubbed away so that there is a little less silver left in your hand. This is especially true of plated wares, where the chief cause of the copper base appearing through the plate is years of overenthusiastic polishing. The truth is that the best way to clean silver is in a basin of warm soapy water, rubbing with a soft cloth. Don't use scour pads, steel wool or any abrasive material to clean silver. It will result in a network of hideous scratches, impossible to remove. Don't wash it in a dishwasher either, where pieces may clank together or harsh detergent may damage the surface. If a piece is seriously tarnished you will probably have to resign yourself to using a proprietary cleaner, but don't use it often. It is best to keep silver clean by using it as often as possible and by storing it in a dry, dust-free place. If you find you do have to use a cleaning agent, be sure to rinse the piece afterwards under warm running water to remove any cleanser that may still lurk in the crevices. If possible, leave teapots open when not in use to discourage unpleasant metallic odours.

Take care when storing silver and plated cutlery. Don't leave pieces loose in drawers and boxes where they are bumped together and scratch one another. Do not, however, store them in small bundles tied round with rubber bands. The rubber may react with the silver and cause severe and permanent discoloration. The best way to keep cutlery is in fitted drawers or canteens. These often pop up at auction and may be bought for just a few pounds, though very attractive ones may be a little more.

Try to wash up silver and plated cutlery as quickly as possible after meals to ensure that food does not set on the pieces and become difficult to remove without scouring. Remember, too, that certain substances spell danger to silver. These include tomatoes, vinegar, mayonnaise and salad cream, egg, and salt. On no account leave silver-plated spoons sitting in mayonnaise; it can strip the plate from a piece in a matter of hours. Be careful too, with silver and plated ladles and tablespoons. Avoid using them to serve dishes with sauces such as tomato and curry spices. And don't immerse knives fully in water, especially if they have ivory or bone handles. Not only will the hot water dislodge the glue on the handle and cause it eventually to part company with the blade but in hard water areas particularly a grey, grimy coat will appear on the handle that is very difficult to shift. If it does happen you could try cleaning the handle with a little white spirit. Use it with a soft cloth, and try it out on a small invisible area first. Leave more valuable pieces to a professional.

Glass and Ceramics

If you can manage not to drop them, glass and ceramics are very easy to live with. Gentle washing, without heavy scouring, in water that is not too hot, and all is well. Don't put pieces of fine old porcelain or glass into the dishwasher. Dry them with a soft cloth and, with glass, make sure it doesn't leave a lot of fluffy bits behind. Dry glass as thoroughly as possible, as leaving it damp may cause discoloration and dullness. Getting a deep jug or decanter clean can be a bit of a challenge, but I have a secret way of dealing with this! The answer is an ordinary hairdrier directed towards the opening for a few moments. With delicate glass, though, make sure it doesn't get too hot or a crack may ensue. For stubborn stains, particularly in the bottoms of decanters and jugs, a solution of vinegar left sitting in the vessel for a few hours may be the answer. For dull-looking drinking-glasses, some vinegar added to the rinsing water can restore the sparkle.

Be careful how you pick up old glass and ceramics. Hold glasses by the bowl rather than the stem, with a supporting hand under the foot. With old porcelain cups and jugs be careful not to pick them up by the handle when you examine them at viewing. These have been known to come away suddenly, with disastrous consequences! The same applies when looking at vases or urns. Get a good grip on them somewhere around the middle — and look out for unexpected lids.

The mending of glass and ceramics is really a job for the professional, and all too often broken pieces prove to be beyond repair. However, with less valuable items for which the alternative to repair would be the dustbin, there is nothing wrong with having a go yourself. If the piece has just broken in half, clean the raw edges and gently bring them together with the glue of your choice. The modern epoxy resin glues are good, but remember that many modern glues won't give you a second chance if you should happen to align the piece incorrectly. So be sure to have a couple of trial fittings before applying the glue. When the piece is stuck lay some strips of adhesive tape around it so that the broken edges cannot slide out of place. Leave it for twenty-fours hours. If there is more than one break, it is more satisfactory to tackle these one at a time in separate operations.

Pictures

The care and display of watercolours and prints may be guided by the same principles that apply to books. Like them, they are subject to spotting and mould and can quickly fade if hung opposite a window. It is a very bad idea to hang good paintings or prints over a fireplace that is used. The effects of heat and of soot and dust can be very damaging.

Framing should in general be left to a professional. Acid-free mounts should be used, and on no account should the surround of a fine print ever be cut to fit a frame. It can devalue it immeasurably. The cleaning and restoring of paintings and fine prints should not be carried out at home. If you have bought an oil painting that is dirty, or perhaps a watercolour that has staining at its edges, and you can't afford to have it done, then leave it there until you can. Even a somewhat damaged picture can still be enjoyed, and it is far better to leave it in its shabby state than to risk damaging it for ever.

When you hang a picture, allow it to tilt forward slightly at the top in order to discourage the dust a little. Everyday care should involve no more than a gentle dusting occasionally and closing the blinds or curtains if a room containing valuable pictures is getting too much sun. Every spring take down your picture, dust the back, and check for signs of woodworm. If you find one or two bore-holes, you can treat it yourself. Make very, very sure that no fluid reaches the painting.

Antiques are meant to be used, displayed, and enjoyed. It's a great pity when buyers collect antiques and works of art purely as an investment, which they then protect by locking them away from all human eyes. I remember once standing with a young employee of a well-known Dublin auction house, admiring a particularly fine Regency settee. This young man longed to possess a piece like it, and he told me that if ever he could afford to buy one he would place it carefully in his best room, where it would stand, unused, like a shrine. Now I do not agree with this at all, and he was rather shocked when I confided that I use my antique furniture in much the same way as I use my more ordinary pieces. He was horror-struck to learn that the family dog regularly took his nap on a mahogany Edwardian armchair. I know that many people would jib at this, but after all, upholstery is easily replaced as families grow older, and the truth is that old solid furniture can take a lot more abuse than cheaper modern pieces. Of course it is necessary to take care of more fragile pieces, particularly those that have been veneered. These are best left in less-used rooms away from the untender mercies of children and pets. But there is no reason why, with a little care, old glass, porcelain and silver can't be placed on the table when your friends come to visit. I suppose you have to resign yourself to keeping particularly precious items out of reach, but most old pieces should be used whenever practical.

Although it's desirable to keep valuables at home rather than to hide them away in a safety box at the bank, unfortunately living with antiques can result in the threat of burglary. It is a good idea to consult your insurance company for advice. Some companies require an inventory to be made of valuable items, and in any case it's a good idea to draw one up for your own use. Antiques should be carefully photographed and the photographs, with a good written description of each piece, kept in a safe place. When renewing insurance, be sure to update the value of your antiques when necessary.

Your security and alarm systems should also be chosen with due regard to the value of the objects in your home. Insurance companies can often advise on this too, and indeed many companies will not accept new customers without a reasonable system of home security, particularly in cities. If your living-room has a number of valuable pieces, be sure to draw the blinds or curtains when leaving the house empty, so that prospective burglars can't look in the window to see what might be up for grabs. It's a good idea, too, if you live in a rural area where your house is set back a little from the road, to padlock your gate while you are out. No thief will feel inclined to carry valuables down a drive and then shin over a gate with them and he may be deterred from parking his van visibly at the side of the road while he fiddles with your locks.

Finally, do beware of what the trade calls 'knockers'. These are dealers who travel around, especially in the countryside, calling at houses to inquire if there are antiques for sale. Often they are perfectly honest individuals but sometimes they can 'fast talk' people, particularly elderly people who may not appreciate the current value of what they own, into parting with antiques at a good deal less than they are worth. A few of them employ a technique of purporting to offer a huge sum for an unwieldy piece such as an old wardrobe while offering something very small for a more valuable but portable piece. The deal is clinched on the small item and the knocker walks away with it; he can't take the wardrobe away just now, because he didn't bring his pick-up, but tomorrow he will be back to collect it, bringing with him the hundreds or thousands of pounds which he has promised to pay for it. Only tomorrow never comes...

The lesson is that you must never allow strangers into your house to examine your possessions. If you wish to sell an antique piece, the best way is to ask someone from a reputable auctioneering firm to come and have a look at the object and advise you. If you are satisfied with his valuation you can then decide to put it in a sale. Your auctioneer will be able to help you to set a suitable reserve, if you so wish. With small items which you wish to sell, there is nothing wrong with simply taking the piece into a good antique shop and asking the owner to make you an offer. As with buying, it's sensible to get several offers before you part with your goods.

Remember, if you decide to sell something at auction that, just as is the case with buyers, there are charges and conditions which involve the seller as well. To begin with there is the seller's commission, typically 10% of the hammer price, together with the prevailing rate of VAT. The seller may also be asked for a contribution towards the auctioneer's insurance, probably at a rate of 1% of the hammer price. Note, too, that if your piece does not reach the reserve, the auctioneer will have to 'buy it in' and a commission will be charged. Often you will find that there is a minimum commission payable; about £25 would be usual. In general, the auctioneer will not allow you to place a reserve on anything deemed likely to fetch less than £100. If your piece sells, you should be able to expect payment within two to four weeks.

Places to View Antiques

Where to View Antiques

The keen collector should try to visit as many museums and great houses as possible, in order to see antiques in their natural surroundings.. Here is list of houses which are particularly attractive:

Republic of Ireland

Ormonde Castle, Carrick on Suir, Co Tipperary: Not really a castle at all buy an Elizabethan mansion where a fine collection of oak furnishings can be seen. Under the care of the OPW and open during summer only.

Dunguarire Castle, Kinvara, Co Galway: A tower house which has been sympathetically renovated. Attend the medieval banquet if you can!

Castletown House, Celbridge, Co Kikdare: Here the Irish Georgian Soociety have spent many years restoring the Connolly mansion to its 18th century splendour.

Strokestown House, Strokestown, Co Roscommon: Recently restored and one of the nicest great country houses open to the public.

Russborough House, Blessington, Co Wicklow: Beautiful house and setting, and, of course, one of Ireland's most important art and furniture collections.

Rothe House, Kilkenny City: Late Tudor townhouse with some fine old oak in view.

Muckross House, Muckross (near Killarney), Co Kerry: Not just a house bur an exhibition of traditional crafts as well, such as bookbinding and saddlery.

Malahide Castle, Malahide, Co Dublin: Not too far from Malahide, this houses a particularly interesting collection.

Lissadel House, Drumcliffe, Co. Sligo: Late Georgian house with lots of furniture and plenty of literary and historical connections. It was the home of Countess Markievicz and her sister Eva Gore Booth and W.B. Yeats visited often. Open June to September.

Bantry House, Bantry, Co. Cork: Good early nineteenth century furniture and fine art objects. Good opening hours all year round with opening until 8pm during the summer months.

Fota House, Cobh, Co. Cork: Lovely house with early nineteenth century furnishing and serene atmosphere. The park, including the wildlife park, is open all year round but the house is open daily only during the summer. From November till March it is open on Sunday afternoons.

Dunkathel House, Glanmire, Co. Cork: Only open four afternoons a week in summer, but Saturdays and Sundays are included. There is a good collection of antiques.

Derrynane House, Caherdaniel, Co. Kerry: Once home to Daniel O'Connell and now a museum with antique furniture and articles linked with the great man himself. The house is open for most of the day from June to September; more restricted hours are in force during the winter, so check in advance during this time.

Johnstown Castle, Murntown, Co. Wexford: The crafts of the past, country furniture and some interesting old agricultural exhibits are on show. Good opening hours all year round.

Westport House, Westport, Co. Mayo: Georgian house with lots of old Waterford glass and Irish silver. Open mid-May to mid-September.

Cratloe Woods House, Bunratty, Co. Clare: A seventeenth century longhouse, still inhabited by descendants of the O'Briens of Thomond. There are displays of antiques, fine arts and old farm machinery. It's open from 2-6 on summer afternoons, with the exception of Sundays but other times can be arranged by special appointment.

Castle Matrix, Rathkeale, Co. Limerick: Built in 1440 by the seventh earl of Desmond, the house contains furnishings, fine art objects and documents. Open from mid-May to mid-September, from Friday to Tuesday, 1-5 p.m.

Glin Castle, Glin, Co. Limerick: Recently opened to the public, this seat of the Knight of Glin has a fine collection of eighteenth century furniture and Adam style interior.

Carriglass Manor, Longford: Tudor style house with costume and lace displays. Open June to September, Friday, Tuesday and Sunday afternoons.

Northern Ireland

Castle Coole, Enniskillen, Co. Fermanagh: One of Ireland's very finest Palladian mansions. Open from April to August.

Florence Court, Enniskillen, Co. Fermanagh: Important demesne and house but house open for very limited period. Check before travelling.

Mount Stewart, near Newtownards, Co. Down: Irish home of the Londonderry family. Splendid gardens around the house. House open throughout most of the summer but check the rather variable opening times.

Castle Ward, Strangford, Co. Down: A most unusual house with some Gothic features and you can also see a fifteenth century tower house, formal gardens and a Greek style temple. The grounds are open all year round, the house from April. However it's not open every day, so, once again, check before travelling.

Springhill House, Moneymore, Co. Derry: Attractive manor house with furniture - and a ghost! There is also a costume museum.

Ardress House, Annaghmore, Co. Armagh: Interesting seventeenth century farmhouse, with agricultural museum. Open in the afternoons for most of the summer, but in June and September only at weekends. Check in advance.

The Ulster Folk Museum is just a few miles from Belfast and is accessible by bus. A wide variety of old everyday objects and furnishings can be seen. The folk park nearby has streets reconstructed in a bygone style with displays of crafts and trades. There is also a transport museum. It is open every day.

Also in Belfast is the city museum and art gallery on Stranmillis Road. It houses a good collection of Irish artists including Jack B. Yeats and Colin Middleton. The Tom Caldwell Gallery is a good place to see works by contemporary artists; it's at Bradbury Place. Worth seeing, too, is the Bell Gallery at Adelaide Park which has a collection of old furniture and rare books.

The Ulster American Folk Park, Camphill, Co. Tyrone (near Omagh): Fascinating exhibits linked with the Irish emigration to America, and the house from which Thomas Mellon, ancestor of a banking family in the U.S., left Ireland may be visited. There are reconstructions of old buildings and trades as well as a farm museum. Open virtually all year round but closed on Saturdays and Sundays during the winter months.

The District Historical Centre, Larne, Co. Antrim: Open all year, this features turn of the century kitchen and other domestic appliances.

For those interested in **ceramics and glass**, several factories offer guided tours which will give you an insight into how such things are and were made. The *Belleek factory* in Co. Fermanagh has guided tours for most of the summer, except for the first two weeks in August when it closes .

The *Tara pottery* in Galway has displays as does the *Waterford crystal* factory, the latter offering a tour which shows glassmaking at virtually every stage. It's open all year round except for some weeks in August. Very many studio potteries are open to visitors and workers are usually more than happy to talk to you about the intricacies of their craft.

Antiquarian books can be seen in the Long Room at Trinity College, Marsh's Library and the Bishop Bolton Library at Cashel, Co. Tipperary. The Cashel Library also houses a fine collection of maps. Newspapers and print history objects may be seen at the Irish Print Museum, Gardiner Street, Dublin and a wonderful collection of antique toys is on display at the Museum of Childhood, Palmerstown Park, Rathmines, Dublin, which is open on Sunday afternoons all year and also Wednesdays in July and August. Anyone interested in oriental artefacts should visit the Chester Beatty Library at Shrewsbury Road, Dublin, which conducts tours on Wednesday and Saturday afternoons.

There are a number of other interesting houses in view to the public but some, like Dunsany, in Co. Meath, may only be open for very limited periods. Always telephone to check opening times before travelling.

A recent form of tourist development which gives the visitor an opportunity to learn about the homes and the lives of ordinary people of the past is the folk park or museum. The Bunratty Folk Park is one of the best of these and the Ulster Folk Museum is also excellent. More of these, albeit sometimes on a more modest scale, are coming onstream and local tourist offices and Bord Failte will give you plenty of up-to-date information.

It's also possible to stay at a statley home or fine country house! Some of them have opened to the paying guest, offering bed, breakfast and dinner as well as more extended holidays. Some, of course, are very expensive but by no means all. A list of such houses is available through Bord Failte.

If you are in London, take the opportunity to visit the Victoria and Albert Museum in Kensington. A mind-boggling array of antiques and fine furniture is on display; it will teach you a great deal. Not too far away from it is the Linley sambourne house in Stafford Terrace. This was built and furnished in 1870 and, a few years ago, was sold by the mother of Lord Snowden to the city of London. Everything in the house is still very much as her grandparents arranged it over a hundred years ago, and no lover of Victorian should neglect a chance to visit it should it ever arise.

Antiques fairs are a perfect way of viewing small collectables withour feeling under any obligation to buy. In Dublin, the Collectors' Club runs regular fairs t the Mansion House, Dawson Street and at the Royal Hospital, Kilmainham. Similar events are held fairly frequently at hotels and other locations round the country. The local press generally has advance details. For book lovers, there is the regular Book Barrow Fair at Dublin's Mansion House. It's usually held on the first Monday of each month but dates vary so check first. They're often held to coincide with Bank Holidays or Christmas Week. The Mansion House itself can usually give you the latest information.

Also held at the Masion House during the first week in August is the prestigious Irish Antiques Dealers' Fair. The displays are generally organised to resemble room settings and there is an enormous selection of furniture, paintings, jewellery, silver and bric a brac. Prices tend to be rather high but there is the compensation that items have been vetted for quality and authenticity so there is less risk of making mistakes. There is no pressure to buy, standholders tend to be informative and helpful and as things are sold they are at once replaced so that even if you visit on more than one day there is always something new to see. All exhibitors are members of the Irish Antique Dealers' Association so there is the comfort of knowing that someone will take an interest in your problem in the unlikely event of anything going wrong.

Auction sales are held throughout Ireland all the year round, with a slight slackening off in the weeks after Christmas. There are few interesting house sales that are not now advertised in the national press bur keep an eye in local papers for smaller events. The *Irish Independent*, this *Irish Times* and the *Farmers' Journal* carry regular auction reports. The newspapers usually feature these on Saturdays, towards the back pages, and include advertisements for the sales that will be held in the week or two ahead.

Bibliography

General

Cumming, R (ed.): *Christie's Guide to Collecting* (1984)
Klein, R (ed.): *Encyclopedia of Antiques* (1989)

Ceramics

Dunlevy, Mairéad: *Ceramics in Ireland* (Dublin 1988)
Godden, G A.: *British Porcelain: an Illustrated Guide* (1974); *Concise Guide to British Pottery and Porcelain* (1989)
Sandon, John: *English Porcelain of the 18th and 19th Centuries* (London 1989)

Silver

Bennett, Douglas: *Irish Georgian Silver* (London 1972)
Blair, Claude (ed.): *The History of Silver* (New York 1987)
Culme, J.: *Nineteenth-Century Silver* (London 1977)
Feild, Rachel: *Buying Antique Silver and Sheffield Plate* (1988)
Jackson, R.W.: *Irish Silver* (Dublin 1972)
Oman, Charles: *English Domestic Silver* (various editions)

Glass

Barrington Haynes, E: *Glass Through the Ages* (1966)
Gros-Galliner, Gabriella: *Glass: a Guide for Collectors* (1970)
Honey, W. B.: *English Glass* (London 1946)
McCawley, J: *Antique Glass Paperweights from France* (1968)
MacKay, James: *Glass Paperweights* (London 1981)
Westropp, M. S. Dudley: *Irish Glass* (Dublin 1920; 1978)

Furniture

Beard, G: *The National Trust Book of English Furniture* (1985)
Butler, R: *The Arthur Negus Guide to English Furniture* (1970)
Hayward, Charles: *Antique or Fake?* (London 1970)
Pearsall, R: *Antique Furniture for Pleasure and Profit* (1990)
Robertson, Alan: *The Insider's Guide to English Furniture* (London 1988)

Clocks

Clutton, C. (Ed): *Britten's Old Clock and Watches* (various eds)

Pictures

Crookshank, A. and the Knight of Glin: *The Painters of Ireland* (1978)
Ford, P and Fisher, J: *The Picture Buyer's Handbook* (1988)
Gascoigne, Bamber: *How to Identify Prints* (London 1986)
Hayden, Arthur: *Chats on Old Prints* (London 1956)
Mallalieu, Huon: *How to Buy Pictures* (London 1984)
Slater, J.V.: *Engravings and their Values* (repr. London 1978)

Bibliographies

This list includes only bibliographies relating to Irish works and is far from exhaustive:
Best, R. I.: *Bibliography of Irish Philology and Printed Irish Literature* (Dublin 1913)
Carty, James: *Bibliogrpahy of Irish History 1870 — 1911* (Dublin 1940)
Carty, James: *Bibliography of Irish History 1912—21* (Dublin 1936)

Dix, E. R. McClintock: *Printing in Dublin Prior to 1601* (Dublin 1932)
Dix, E. R. McClintock: *Books, Tracts, etc. Printed in Dublin in the 17th Century* (Dublin 1898-99)
Dudley Edwards, R. W. and O'Dowd, Mary: *Sources for Early Modern Irish History* (Cambridge 1985)
Gilcher, E.: *Bibliography of George Moore* (1970)
Harmon, M.: *Irish Studies Handbook for Anglo -Irish Literature* and it's *Backgrounds* (Dublin 1977)
Jeffares, Norman: *Yeats — Man and Poet* (London 1949)
Levitt, P.: *J. M. Synge: A Bibliography of Published Criticism* (Dublin 1974)
Mason, Stuart: *Bibliography of Oscar Wilde* (London 1914)
Mikhail, E. H.: *A Bibliography of Modern Irish Drama 1899 — 1970*
Munter, R. L.: *A Handlist of Irish Newspapers 1685 — 1750* (London 1960)
Sheehy, M.: *Studies on Frank O'Connor with a Bibliography* (London 1965)
Simms, S.: *A Select Bibliography of the United Irishmen 1791-8* (Irish Historical Studies, Vol 1, p. 158-80)

Books

Cargill Cole, R: *Irish Booksellers and English Writers* (1986)
Carter, John: *ABC for Book Collectors* (various eds)
Connelly, Joseph: *Modern First Editions* (London 1984)
Harrod, L. M.: *The Librarian's Glossary and Reference Book* (London 1971, 1977)
Thomas, A.: *Great Books and Book Collectors* (London 1975)
Ward, Robert (ed.): *Prince of Dublin Printers : Letters of George Faulkener* (Kentucky 1972)

Cards

Blair, Arthur: *Christmas Cards for the Collector* (London 1986)
Willoughby, Martin: *Postcards* (London 1989)

Coins

Dowle, Anthony, and Finn, Patrick: *Coins for Pleasure and Investment* (London 1969)
Dowle, Anthony, and Finn, Patrick: *The Guide Book to the Coinage of Ireland* (London 1969)
Hobson, Burton: *Coin Collecting as a Hobby* (New York 1982)
Link House (pub.): *Coins : Market Values* (annually)

Militaria

Blackmore, H. L.: *Arms and Armour* (London 1965)
Wilkinson, F: *Antique Arms and Armour* (London 1972)

Maps

Andrews, J.: *Ireland in Maps* (Dublin 1961)
Hayes McCoy, G. A.: *Ulster and Other Maps* (Dublin 1964)
Hodgekiss, A. G.: *Discovering Antique Maps* (Aylesbury 1981)
Tyacke, S., and Huddy, J.: *Christopher Saxton and Tudor Map Making* (London 1980)
Wiford, John Noble: *The Mapmakers* (London 1981)

Glossary

Acanthus: decoration featuring leaves.

Air twist: glass stem decorated by means of drawn-out air bubbles.

Anthemion: decoration based on honeysuckle.

Antique binding: modern bookbinding in antique style.

Armorial ware: porcelain, usually Chinese, that was made to order and bearing a family coat of arms.

Artist's proof: of a print; special early copies that are 'pulled' for the artist.

Assaying: testing of metals to ensure that they are made from legally permitted proportions of precious and base metals.

Association copy: owned by the author of a book or the person with whom the book is concerned.

Ball and claw: on furniture, a foot representing an eagle's claw, clasped round a ball.

Balloon back: very round chair back, fashionable during the middle of the nineteenth century.

Baluster stem: glass stem shaped like a slender urn or glass.

Baywood: mahogany from Honduras.

Biedermeier: furniture style associated with nineteenth century Germany, incorporating rather heavy, unbroken wooden fronts.

Bird's eye: a dot-like pattern in maple or walnut.

Bite: the 'cut' made by acid into a metal plate, as in etching.

Blind tooling: stamped pattern on a bookbinding that does not employ gold or any colour.

Bonheur du jour: elegant, long-legged desk for a woman, generally small with neat drawer or cabinet superstructure.

Bookplate: special label to indicate ownership of a book, usually mounted on front endpaper.

Boulle (Buhl): marquetry composed of tortoiseshell and brass. Invented by André-Charles Boulle during the seventeenth century, but most of what is now seen in Ireland dates from the nineteenth century.

Bracket foot: wedge-shaped foot on much furniture of the George III period.

Breaker: tattered book, fit only to be broken up for the illustrations.

Buckram: heavy cloth filled with size, used sometimes for bookbinding.

Bulkhead: portrait of George III on half-crowns during 1816-17.

Bun foot: round foot on furniture; found below a short stem on late seventeenth and early eighteenth-century pieces, revived without stem during nineteenth century.

Burr: fuzzy appearance around a freshly engraved line on a metal plate.

Butler's tray: drinks tray with foldaway stand.

Cabriole leg: curved leg, first used on late seventeenth-century furniture but fashionable many times since. May end in a pad, a scroll, or a claw and ball foot.

Caddy spoon: used for distributing tea; usually features a short handle and proportionately large bowl.

Canterbury: low slatted music stand, usually with drawer and turned legs.

Cartwheel: large pennies and twopences of 1797.

Carver: dining-chair with arms.

Casting: the shaping of metal by pouring it when molten into a mould.

Chasing: decoration of silver by punching and pushing the metal into shape.

Cheval glass: tall mirror in timber frame that pivots on its supports.

Chiffonier: low sideboard with cupboard; often shelved or with carved frieze at the back.

Commode: low, decorative chest of drawers, especially French.

Console table: large, heavy, often gilded table that leans against a wall and has legs at the front only.

Credenza: low side cabinet in three glass-fronted sections; usually Victorian; often in boulle or walnut veneer.

Cross-banding: section of veneer whose grain run crossways in relation to other sections.

Crown: coin first introduced in the sixteenth century and worth five shillings. The term now generally applies to large silver coins such as the German *thaler* or British commemorative coins.

Cut glass: glass decorated by passing it over a cutting-wheel.

Decanter: flask with matching stopper, used for holding wine or spirits.

Delft: tin-glazed earthenware; also called majolica or faience. Much made in England during the seventeenth century.

Demi-lune: of table, semi-circular shape.

Double flask: flat oval flask, with twisted double opening; sometimes old Waterford.

Drypoint: working on a bare metal plate with an etching needle.

Dumb waiter: serving table with two or three movable circular tiers.

Duty mark: the mark on silver of the monarch's head, indicating that duty has been paid.

Earthenware: a porous, baked clay ceramic, made liquid-proof by glazing.

Embossing: the decoration of silver by punching from the back.

Endpapers: blank or decorated leaves at each end of a book.

Engraved title: title page of a book, sometimes with patterned device that has been printed from an engraved plate.

Engraving: the making of designs by cutting into a surface.

Escritoire: cabinet on chest with drop-down writing section.

Escutcheon: the metal plate around a keyhole.

Facsimile copy: an exact copy of a document, print, or book.

Flint glass: glass made using silica.

Footring: ring projecting from the base of a cup, glass, or bowl.

Frontispiece: an illustration opposite the title page of a book.

Fruitwood: wood from pear, apple or other fruit tree. Often found in French provincial furniture.

Gallery: railing running round the top of a piece of furniture.

Gothic(k): furniture in pseudo-mediaeval or ecclesiastical style, made during the late eighteenth or nineteenth centuries; Gothic revival.

Grain: the direction of the marks and lines on a piece of timber.

Graining: the serrations at the edge of a coin.

Groat: silver four-pence coin introduced during the thirteenth century.

Gutta percha: rather nasty rubber-based glue used to hold together the pages of a book. Used in many nineteenth century gift books, the substance tended to disintegrate, leaving the book to fall apart.

Half-calf: in bookbinding, the corners and spine are of calf leather when the rest of the cover is cloth or, more usually, marbled board.

Hallmark: a mark impressed on metal by an assay office, indicating that it has been tested and found to meet all legal standards.

Harewood: wood stained green, or grey-green. Usually sycamore.

Hunt-table: long narrow table, with deeply oval drop-leaves. Often Irish and eighteenth-century.

Inscribed copy: a book signed by its author.

Knop: knob or ball-shaped decoration, usually on the stem of a glass.

Lalticino: a white thread or lace-like decoration beneath the surface of glass.

Lead glass: heavy, crystalline glass containing lead oxide.

Limited edition: edition limited to a set number of copies.

Loo table: oval Victorian centre table, supposedly used for the playing of a card game, loo, in which forfeits are paid into a pool.

Loving cup: two-handled cup, principally made between 1760 and 1860, often in earthenware.

Majolica: see *delft*.

Marbled paper: paper coloured in rich, swirling patterns.

Maundy money: silver coins distributed by the English monarch at a special Holy Thursday service.

Milk Glass: dense white glass, almost porcelain-like in appearance; popular during late nineteenth century.

Miniature: small portrait painted on metal, vellum, ivory, or porcelain.

Mint mark: often an initial, indicating where a coin has been made.

Morocco: goatskin binding or cover.

Mottled calf: leather binding with uneven mottled effect: usually eighteenth-century.

Mule chest: coffer with drawers in the base; often found in nineteenth-century Irish pine.

Murano glass: Venetian glass; the Venetian glass industry was established at Murano during the middle ages.

Navette: term often used to describe boat-shaped cut-glass bowl on pedestal foot.

Oyster veneer: fancy veneer, displaying circular growth rings in the timber.

Panel: piece of wood on which an oil painting may be made.

Papier mâché: a material used for making occasional furniture and other small objects during the nineteenth century. Made primarily of paper and gluey substances that are dried and painted, usually in black lacquer. Floral and mother of pearl decoration was then applied.

Parian ware: white, unglazed porcelain material, much used for figures and busts.

Partners' desk: large pedestal desk, designed so that one person can sit at each side.

Pastel: a picture created by using powdered pigments made up into a stick.

Pattern: a coin struck to illustrate a new design. Not intended to be legal tender.

Pier glass: narrow mirror designed to hang between windows.

Piercing: decoration by a pattern of holes.

Pistole: seventeenth-century gold coin; some were issued for Ireland by Charles I.

Plates: of a book, illustrations on different paper from the text.

Porcelain: ceramic made from white clay (kaolin) and its stone (feldspar).

Potash glass: glass made with potash extracted from wood ash. Typically, a German glass.

Presentation copy: of a book, one presented by author.

Pressed glass: glass made in a mould rather than by blowing.

Prism cutting: the use of V-shaped cuts on glass, usually on a stem, to give a jagged pattern.

Provenance: identification of the place an item comes from.

Quarter calf: in bookbinding, when the spine only is covered in leather.

Queen's ware: type of cream earthenware made by the Wedgwood factory.

Rebacked: in bookbinding, when a book has been given a new spine.

Reeding: decoration by means of narrow convex sections; the use of concave sections is called fluting.

Repoussé: decoration of silver by hammering from behind. May be used with front chasing.

Rubbed: a term indicating that the spine and corners of a book may need some repair.

Rummer (roemer): thick-stemmed drinking-glass.

Saltglaze: stoneware glazed by throwing salt into the kiln, giving the glaze an 'orange peel' effect.

School: the assigning of an anonymous painting to a place or to a follower of a named artist, e.g. school of Titian, Flemish school.

Secretaire: bookcase or cabinet that embodies a writing compartment.

Secretaire à abbatent: drop-front writing-cabinet over drawers or cupboard; often associated with Biedermeir styles.

Serpentine: S-shaped front, often found in the very best eighteenth-century chests.

Ship's decanter: decanter with very wide base and deeply slanted sides.

Slip-case: a fitted box used to protect a book.

Slipware: earthenware decorated with a liquid clay, white or coloured, known as 'slip'.

Soda glass: glass containing sodium carbonate, which acts as a 'flux', reducing the melting-point of other materials in the glass. Used for much everyday glass.

Staffordshire figures: mass-produced earthenware figures made from the eighteenth century; often made by small factories employing children. Many represented political and literary figures. They are usually unmarked and painted in strong, unsubtle colours.

Stile: slim, vertical section of timber forming the uprights of a chair back or the corner portions of case furniture.

Stoneware: clay body fired at very high temperatures. Liquid-proof even when unglazed. Much made by the Doulton factory at Lambeth.

Striations: faint wavy marks to be seen in glass.

Stringing: thin line of inlaid wood or brass.

Sutherland table: very small drop-leaf table with narrow centre section; usually late nineteenth century.

Swags: pattern formed by garlands of flowers or fruit.

Tantalus: container, usually wooden, for decanters; sometimes with matching glasses.

Teapoy: a wooden tea container on legs or tripod base.

Tipped in: of book illustrations, when a picture or other sheet is inserted in a book by means of a light application of glue.

Transfer printing: decoration of pottery and porcelain with printed pattern transferred by paper from metal plates.

Uncut: of a book, with leaves that have never been trimmed, lending it a rough, almost tattered appearance. Nevertheless, a desirable state.

Vellum: untanned leather often used for bookbinding; usually cream in colour and made from calf or goatskin. Lasts well but very inclined to retain dirt and fingermarks.

Vernis martin: method of painting on furniture invented by the Martin brothers, eighteenth-century French furniture makers. Often used to describe painted scenes on late nineteenth-century furniture, especially vitrines.

Vitrine: decorative display cabinet with extensively glazed front.

Volunteer glass: Irish glass engraved with motifs relating to the eighteenth-century Irish Volunteers.

Volute: decorative spiral or scroll.

Windsor chair: country-made kitchen chair with turned or cabriole legs and hoop or comb back. Found in pine, ash, yew, and elmwood. Older examples now highly priced.

Wrappers: of a book, paper covers as in a paperback.

Special Catalogue Terms and Abbreviations

Books Catalogues

D.J. dust jacket / L.P. large paper / Fol. folio /n.d. no date / D.N.D. Dublin, no date / L.N.D. London, no date / mor. morocco binding / hf. half / hd.cold. hand-coloured / w.a.f. with all faults: indicates a book in imperfect condition / S.N.S.R. Sold, not subject to return (indicates imperfect or incomplete copy, or a mixed or made-up set) / Plts. plates / t.p. title page / ex. lib. ex libris (from a library / t.e.g. top edges [of pages] gilt / as issued original condition / reading copy poor condition, probably with binding loose and dirty, and text scribbled on fold / folded usually refers to maps or other illustrations / imperfect damage to text / defective damage to binding / joints cracked spine torn at the sides / hinges cracked book pulling away from its binding / only (as in '10 only') suggests volumes missing from a set or plates from a book. May be followed by, say, 'ex 12', revealing the number of a complete set. / sound copy not in the very best state, but reasonable / disbound a book that has lost its binding

Art Catalogues

These generally include an explanatory note on the terms used. The following are some of the most frequently met and that may not always be understood.

conversation piece: informal group portrait.

genre: painting or print of a domestic scene or incident

gesso: plaster-based material on which a painting may be made

gouache: a painting in which gum has been used to enrich watercolour

interior: painting of an indoor scene, often Dutch or in the Dutch manner

state: of a print, refers to the varying appearance of prints from a run in which the artist made modifications to the plate as he went along. The earliest prints are known as the 'first state'

topographical: of print or painting, broad, light landscape, often viewed from a height. It is generally very detailed, often includes buildings or ruins, and generally shows the countryside in its 'civilised' mode

Where the surname and first name (or initials) of an artist are printed over the name of a painting, the buyer can take it that this is the artist who painted the picture. Other terms indicate various degrees of uncertainty about the artist, and the following are some of these:

attributed to: probably the work of the artist.

manner of: in the artist's style but of later date

signed: probably signed by the artist

bears signature: the signature may not have been made by the artist himself. Also 'with signature'.

after: a copy of the work of the artist

studio of: probably painted by a pupil or employee of the artist, possibly under his supervision.

INDEX